Don't Take My Word For It, Read It Yourself!
A DEVOTIONAL

To my wife, Jill….

At this point it has been 46 years. I told you that I don't believe in love at first sight, but the second glance grabbed me! You have been a source of energy and inspiration!

I love you!

———————————

To Jennifer, Jason and Jamie…

I love you so much! You all work so hard and you will leave a substantial mark, wherever you go and whatever you do!

There is a fourth whose name we do not know. If I am to believe in what the Holy Bible tells me, we will have a glorious reunion some day. You are not forgotten!

———————————

To Tammi, Brytni and Brooklyn…

Pops is so proud of you. You have so much to offer and give. I'm inspired by the line from the song Father & Son by Cat Stevens, "Take your time and think a lot. Think of everything you've got!"

Dream big, ladies!

———————————

To Harley and Aspen and Freddy…

Take care of your owners and they will love you forever!

Don't Take My Word For It, Read It Yourself!
A DEVOTIONAL

Unless otherwise indicated, all Scripture quotations are taken from the Holy Bible, New Living Translation, copyright © 1996, 2004, 2015 by Tyndale House Foundation. Used by permission of Tyndale House Publishers, Carol Stream, Illinois 60188. All rights reserved. The text of the New King James Version (NKJV) may be quoted or reprinted without prior written permission with the following qualifications: (1) up to and including 1,000 verses may be quoted in printed form as long as the verses quoted amount to less than 50% of a complete book of the Bible and make up less than 50% of the total work in which they are quoted; (2) all NKJV quotations must conform accurately to the NKJV text. Any use of the NKJV text must include a proper acknowledgment as follows: Scripture taken from the New King James Version. Copyright 1979, 1980, 1982 by Thomas Nelson, Inc. Other text of the Holy Bible included in this book are provided Scripture quotations marked (NIV) are taken from the Holy Bible, New International Version®, NIV®. Copyright © 1973, 1978, 1984, 2011 by Biblica, Inc.™ Used by permission of Zondervan. All rights reserved worldwide. www.zondervan.comThe "NIV" and "New International Version" are trademarks registered in the United States Patent and Trademark Office by Biblica, Inc.™

Photo from cover is self taken and is from the BearTooth Mountains, Red Lodge, Montana

Table of Contents

Don't take my word for it, Read it Yourself!   3

Credits and Endorsements   5

Introduction   15

Devotion Book Scripture List   18

The Journey Begins   28

3 Generations and a Linebacker   51

The Storm of all Storms   134

Yes, They Really do Have an Airshow in Dayton!   243

The Boxer and the Prison   350

About the Author   467

Credits and Endorsements

I thought about this for quite a while, and while it would be nice to have a nationally known Minister or Pastor lend an endorsement, it seems like a great chance to tell you about some individuals whose lives have been changed by reading the Bible; after all, that is what we are doing as we read through the Bible together.

Randy S.

I met Jeff over thirty years ago by chance through the friendship of our daughters at First Baptist Church in Indianapolis, IN. Little did I know this was also the beginning of my personal Faith-walk. The memories of our mutual activities now stand out as a major factor in how I think, react and

Worship today. Our friendship developed through a series of bible studies, men's groups and mission trips. I was unaware what effect these activities were having on my personal Faith at the time. Our early Monday meetings were called "Jump Start". The group began as a way for businessmen like ourselves to start each week with prayer and study on early Monday mornings to be better able to face Corporate World stresses. I believe this lead to an increase in enthusiasm in many of the attendees lives and activities within the group. One book we studied was "A Purpose Driven Life" which inspired our group to serve and participate in many Church centered activities including "Heavenly Hammers", mission trips to the Crow Indian Reservation, weekly coffee Bible study, and working the Church Food Pantry. We had a Mutual friend who was Jewish and through Jeff's early contact with him, Greg became a believer. Greg joined our church on our yearly trips to Lodge Grass Montana to work with the Crow. Watching others growing in faith helped me to to realize I did not have to be a victim of a less than ideal childhood which I had struggled with. I learned to let go of the past and focus on today and tomorrow. Jeff taught me to forgive those in my past in order to bless my future. It worked! My life changed overnight. I have had the pleasure of watching Jeff's Faith grow by leaps and bounds. Jeff and Jill were willing to give up all and trust God to take care of their future. Jeff and his family have been blessed many times over by the Grace of God. I have personally witnessed Jeff and his wife Jill change their lives by embracing their Faith and actually living it each day through their actions. Jeff will tell you it is all in the Bible. Don't take his word for it, read it for yourself! Joshua 1:9

David H.

I love these words Jeff Mathews wrote in his intro…
"Engage in what I now understand to be the life changing word of God."

When I was baptized in the summer of 2007 along with my oldest son, by my good friend pastor Steve O'Dell, I shared with those present, why I decided to be baptized. Remembering what Peter the disciple of Christ had said to the 3,000 in Acts 2, those who said we believed Jesus is who he says he is, they asked, *"what must we do?"* Peter said, *"repent and be baptized,"* meaning change your old way of thinking, turn from your sinful ways and turn to God. Peter said, *"be baptized, and you **will** receive the gift of the Holy Spirit."* To receive the gift of the Holy Spirit was the reason I choose to be baptized in the living waters of a small lake in Michigan. You see I had just read Romans 8 days before I was baptized, to know the Holy Spirit better, and His mission within me and us as believers, and followers of Christ Jesus. What I shared with those who came to witness the baptism of my son Jonathan and I, was this, I wanted to see how the Holy Spirit would change my life – excited to see where He would take in life, contemplating the full scope of being Spirit-led as Paul has shared with us in Romans 8. For me, in that moment, "life changing."

In March of 2020 I was one of people my good friend Jeff Mathews reached out to and asked, to join the others, good friends and family, in an Email daily devotional titled "Read every word of the Bible" and so I did. Even now I still read Jeff's Email message first thing in the morning. Jeff has mastered the craft, surely a gift of the Holy Spirit, to pick the right verses to focus on for the day, and his commentary and insight of the verse or verses he has chosen, remarkable resonate with the times and the people the message is served up to. "Life changing" most of the time; at least it is for me!

I leave you with this; we live in a fallen world, a broken world. It is because our rebellious nature, for most of us it is hard to let go of a worldly mindset that we must be self-sufficient, independent, and in control of our own destiny, rather than putting our trust, our hope by faith in God; instead we chose to forage away from our own life experiences, a belief which forms opinions of our own making, which we rely on to guide and protect us and our loved ones in this broken world. It is no wonder why so many fail when they live by opinions formed in the culture of a fallen world view. As you read this devotional put together by my good friend Jeff Mathews, it is my confident hope that you will learn that God, our Creator is the One who created us to live in harmony with Him and each other. It is my prayer that each of you, come to understand that we were created to live a life to the full as Christ Jesus promised in the presence of our God, just as Jesus did over 2,000 years ago, and still does; I pray that each of you through God's word shall come to know that the kingdom of God is our natural environment.

Jesus is not done yet, many other things to do, many lives yet to be saved, still work to be done in us and in you. I pray you enjoy the journey, living a Kingdom Life, this devotional will help. In Jesus' name I pray.

At the end of the book of John you will find these words, *"Jesus did many other things as well. If every one of them were written down, I suppose that even the whole world would not have room for the books that would be written."*

Lord Jesus has a work in you yet to be completed, another book to be written. Read your bible, study every word, and share your journey with others. The dream of Jesus realized.

David J Hall
Prayer Warrior

AL F.

In the West African bush at the border between rural Liberia and rural Guinea, one doesn't need an alarm clock. The cock crows at dawn, awakening a symphony of birdsong unlike any other, never forgotten once heard. This celestial chorus rouses the dogs, followed by the sweet voices of infants and toddlers, and the voices of women as they take charge of daily life: cooking, cleaning, and tending to the farm. The sound of fresh water being pumped from a rich aquifer and bagged in a factory built in response to the Ebola crisis of 2014 fills the air. The aroma of parboiled rice, plants, peppers, spices, and fresh cabbage, combined with cassava, creates a sensory experience of pure delight. In this impoverished country, every morsel of food is cherished.

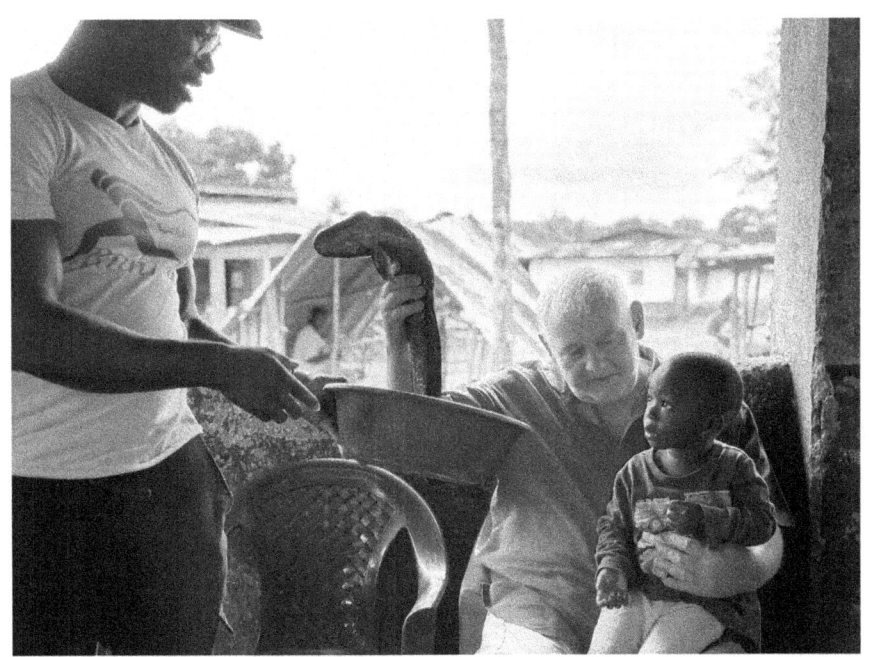

Omnipresent in every aspect of life, God's presence is evident in the daily routines. Morning and evening devotions, prayers of thanksgiving before meals, and prayers before and after management meetings are integral to the fabric of life. Of course, there are the hours spent at Gamu, Liberia, the headquarters of our foundation, which has grown from adopting orphans of the Civil War to extending God's kingdom to a region of 250,000 people. Six months ago, I was baptized in the St. John's River connecting Liberia and Guinea, bringing immense joy to my sainted mother.

My upbringing was a blend of Catholic and Baptist influences, leaving me with a touch of both traditions. I never had a religious home, but my mother's advice before she passed away was profound. She told me that while my father was engrossed in his medical studies at Ohio State Marriott House, she took my ankles and dipped them in the toilet bowl.

So, I embarked on a journey to college, pursued family, careers in government, business, and enjoyed reasonable success. I lived the illusion of being a happy man doing good things the right way. But then, the Holy Spirit revealed a shocking truth: those first 72 years of my life were a practice round for my new role in God.

He reminded me that He had meticulously crafted this plan for me during this season of Reclamation and Redemption in Africa. Every experience I had, from sports to politics to government, to business and philanthropy, was an opportunity to apply my skills and help these people lead meaningful lives and instill hope in their children.

We take for granted basic necessities like food, water, education, and jobs. I can relate to the Apostle Paul's encounter on the Damascus Road, where Christ interrupted his life. My mission now is to bring wealth and resources from the material world to the spiritual realm and establish God's Kingdom in the poorest communities globally.

It's all so new, and sometimes, I feel torn between human and divine forces. I used to avoid your daily messages (Read Every Word of the Bible) driven by shame, ignorance, or insecurity. I was consumed by power, wealth, and notoriety.

In hindsight, I realize that I believed I was messianic, convinced that I could change the world. I was a fool and a sinner, yet I convinced myself of my own grandeur. Now, I eagerly await the daily messages and insights from other brothers in Christ. Each day brings a fresh perspective, brighter colors, sweeter sounds, and more hopeful feelings.

I've found myself in the business of addressing global mental health and food insecurity in Africa.

In Genesis, God placed the Garden of Eden at the center of four major rivers, two of which are the Tigris and Euphrates River valleys. The Fertile Crescent became the cradle of civilization and modern science and archaeology has confirmed the existence of Noah's Ark on Mt. Ararat in Turkey. The agriculture revolution took place in the early days of Sumeria, which is mentioned in the Bible.

God has a plan to create a new Fertile Crescent in the half-million fertile and undeveloped lands in West Africa. This land can accommodate 2 million members of the ancient KPelle tribe, who were separated by the St. John and St. Paul's rivers (similar to the Tigris and Euphrates rivers). The land lies atop one of Africa's most significant aquifers, making it the most resource-rich continent on the planet. Over the next ten years, the population of this region is expected to surpass that of China, with one out of every two people on the planet residing there.

This is a complex situation.

Food security poses a threat to over a billion subsistence farmers globally. This is not God's plan. These people have been deceived and exploited for thousands of years, making them particularly vulnerable to overpopulation and climate change.

I am being urged to commit everything I have - NOW.

What a blessing!

Greg S.
11/6/1957 - 2/21/2010

I wish Greg were alive to be able to tell us his story. It is quite remarkable. We spent a good part of our youth together. In fact, we fist met in the 5th grade. After High School we moved on in our lives, little did we know what the future would have in store for us. Greg became a Christian later in his life and we reconnected upon our move back to Indianapolis in 1999. Greg is a Messianic Jew. This one we read about in the book of Revelation, the material of Peter, Paul, John, Luke, James and many of the original Apostles. Greg's faith was very important to him and he would frequently tell me of stories of being basically cast out of his family because of his faith in Jesus. We had the pleasure of traveling together out to the Crow Reservation in Montana where we laughed. lived and loved. It was when he became ill that I learned to appreciate my friend so much. He had a background in sales and he would often call me and say "come pick me up and we can have a donut". I knew what that meant, he wanted to talk about my sales role and some of my prospects. We then would strategize how to sell those accounts. He really helped me, looking back, I realize that the exercise was as much for him as it was for me. It was as if he was working his passion of selling through me. We would also pray. Lot's pf prayers! For our families, for his illness, our wives and his reconciliation with his parents. It became that we did not have any secrets between us. Greg passed away in 2010 from colon cancer. Greg's wife, Micki called me when they were transporting him to hospice and I met them there. She would later tell me the story of one night in that facility. There were 2 figurines, Moses and Elijah over his bed and one night the room seemed to illuminate and those two figurines on the wall appeared to be conversing. It was as if they were making plans on escorting Greg to heaven. On Greg's grave marker reads these words: "But as for me and my family, we will serve the LORD." (Joshua 24:15)

Jeff and Greg trying on a buffalo skin

Miss you buddy!

Bobby H.

I was about 8 years old when my mom and dad realized that I had a little singing ability. And they took me to Chicago and we did a show called Ted Mack's Amateur Hour. It was a national television show, like the Milton Berle show. I actually started early, a legend in my own mind, even by the age of 10. Truly, I was addicted to applause and people pleasing and accolades. It just felt good for people to clap for me. And usually when you're that young and you have that much attention, later on down the line it catches up with you. And I'll explain that as we go along.

When I was a youngster, my mom and dad wanted me to be like a little Frank Sinatra. And they dressed me up in a black tuxedo. And then rock and roll came around in the mid 60s. And the Beatles were on the Ed Sullivan show. And I told my mom and dad, that's what I want to do. And they didn't really like that so they pulled me out of show business. I first went to a Catholic high school in Evansville, Indiana. That didn't work out so well with me because I wanted the attention and I was the class clown. So they sent me to a public high school in Evansville. And that's where I started planting all the wrong seeds in my young life with marijuana and alcohol. And that would come to harvest later on, which really didn't turn out well either.

With the show business taken out of my life, There was an emptiness inside that I tried to fill up with a lot of wrong things. I ran away from home around 16. I had the opportunity to play and tour with some rock bands around the country. Eventually around 1979 or 1980 I landed in Hollywood for the first time.

By worldly standards my career was going well. I had the world on a string, but I still had this empty feeling inside. And because of the marijuana use, which continued throughout the 80s, I

actually graduated to cocaine. I moved in with some guys that played with some bigger bands, Ozzy Osbourne and a few others.. I started living the life of being a so-called rock star. My five minutes of fame landed me with a cocaine addiction. I even had a video on MTV. The party really started for me in the 80s. For lack of a better term, the sex, drugs, and rock and roll took me to a very, very dark place. The deeper I got, The more it became about self. It was about standing on stage and being accepted by people and my peers. And it's just a self absorbed way of life. It's almost as though you stand on stage and people worship you. And for me, it got twisted.

The alcohol and cocaine addiction got worse and worse. And by the 90s, I was a mess. And by the late 90s, I was falling off stage. I was impaired and I wanted to get a good night's sleep because the cocaine is an upper and it had my nervous system in quite a wreck. So I began to use heroin and started injecting the drugs in the late 90s and by the year 2000, I found myself homeless with a heroin addiction, living in a cardboard box in Los Angeles skid row, standing on the side of the road with a sign that said, I will work for food, only I was working for the drugs. And this went on for eight dark years. I started injecting drugs in the late 90s, I thought I could handle it at first. And I kept saying, tomorrow I'll stop, tomorrow I'll stop. Well tomorrow never comes in the life of addiction. It just gets worse and worse. So eventually I became a completely different person, a recluse. A guy that pulled a shopping cart with tin cans in it. I didn't take a bath for a year at a time. Needle marks all up and down my arms to the point I couldn't use them anymore. Then I started injecting in my neck. I had to start on both legs and would just shoot the drug through the blue jeans. This is a life of destruction. And when you're in it that deep, there's no way out. And then to live in a cardboard box and sleep on the ground, it's just total humiliation. After a while. it gets to the point where you just quit caring. And there was absolutely no way in sight of me recovering from this addiction. And it went on for 8 years.

I was laying in my cardboard box one day, A man came up to my cardboard box and said, Bobby, you're dying. And I said, yeah, I wish I could get this life over with. I came from a life of MTV all the way to this dark, dark place of being an addict living in a cardboard box, and he said Bobby you need to pray in the name of Jesus. And I looked at him, and I really didn't want to hear anything about Jesus or God and and I said hey I'm not really interested. I know who God is I was raised Catholic.

He looked me dead in the eye, and he said well, "How's that working out for you?" A little light went on in my head and I said, well, it's not working out for me at all!. And he said, well, let me show you something. And he pulled out a book, **which was the Bible,** and he turned to the **Book of John**. It said, "I am the way, the truth, and the life. No one goes to the Father except through the Son". And I said, you mean Jesus? And he said, yeah. So at that very moment I realized that Jesus was a mediator and that there was power in the name of Jesus.

A couple of days went by and I found myself injecting heroin in a dumpster in Skid Row on the streets of Los Angeles. You understand, the dumpster is a safe place to be. You can't see in because you're down so low. I'm talking about a big dumpster. So I injected the drugs and I was hungry. There was some pizza laying there in the dumpster with ants on it. And I took a bite of the pizza and the ants bit me on the inside of my neck as I swallowed. And at that very moment, I had had enough. I hit rock bottom. And out of complete desperation, with nowhere to turn, I remembered that man told me to pray in the name of Jesus. And I raised my hand and I said, **Father God, in the name of Jesus, send me some kind of hope.**

Two days later, a man knocked on my cardboard box by the name of Mr. Esperanza. And he said, Bobby, a family called me on the phone yesterday. They know who you are and that you're homeless and they want me to put you on a bus to Phoenix, Arizona to rehab. I said, who are you? He said, my name is Mr. Esperanza. I didn't know it then, Esperanza in Spanish means hope. So not only did he send me hope, the fellow's name was Mr. Hope. So for some reason, I got on that bus to Phoenix, Arizona, and I turned on Christian television, and I started finding out about this guy named Jesus.

Well, I quit smoking, I quit drinking, I got off all the medication for this addiction and then my sister who lived in Carmel, Indiana called me in Arizona and said, we want you to come back to Carmel. So I came back eight years ago to Carmel, Indiana and a pastor came up to me one day and said, we'd like for you to come to our church and play the guitar. And I'm a rock and roll guitar player. And I said, you mean hymns? And he said, yeah. And I said, sure, I'll come. So I went to church, sat in the first row. I hadn't been to church for 30 years. And there was a fellow in the church playing guitar. So I hung around after the church service was over, and I said, yes, sir, Mr. Jones, I said, you're quite the guitar player. I said, could you maybe give me guitar lessons and maybe I can rekindle my career. And he said, I'll do better than that, Bobby. I'm gonna have you come to my recording studio here in Indianapolis. I'm a record producer, we're gonna cut you a new record and rekindle your career. And I said, praise the Lord, Jesus. I knew there was something to all this! So I said, well, give me your address, I'll be down Monday. Now, my cardboard box in Los Angeles was at the corner of 31st and Broadway in downtown Los Angeles. You know where his studio was? 31st and Broadway, downtown Indianapolis, Indiana.

Man, I knew there had to be something to this praying in the name of Jesus. Much more than hope, this was real, this was tangible, it was available. I found out who my daddy was. My Daddy is Father God. He hangs planets and stars up on nothing. You understand? So I started praying to God like He was my daddy. I said, Father God, in the name of Jesus, give me a purpose in life.

When I look back over the past several years, God's hand is still directing me. It has not stopped!

Bobby Hayden lives in The Nashville TN area and continues to travel all over sharing how God saved him.

Abbie R is Bobby Hayden's sister. As amazing as Bobby's story is, adding Abbie's story makes the whole event even more incredible, and it continues to unfold!

Abbie R.

My brother Bobby is 10 years older than me. I remember loving him and missing him, but I also knew there was much strife that was kept from me as a youngster.

We had just recently moved into a new home, and I found a little framed photo of him in a moving box. No one had heard from him in over 8 years. I decided to put the photo on the windowsill of my kitchen sink, and determined I would throw up a quick prayer of protection and transformation when I found myself doing dishes or passing through the kitchen. One year later, the phone rang. It was him.
Shortly thereafter, I was in church with my husband, Scott, and after a sermon on the glory of God when we care for the marginalized, he turned to me and said, "It's time to bring Bobby home." We had no idea what that would look like. Or the impact it would have on future generations, even now as I write, 16 years later.

Although my immediate family struggled with our decision at first, they were faithful in respecting that it simply was something we could not ignore. It was a directive from the Lord. We had three young children, and three of our 4 parents were beginning to require lots of help. We weren't looking to put more on our plate. My family came alongside slowly and surely. As did our neighbors, our church family, old friends, new friends, acquaintances, even strangers who heard our story. As my brother has grown into his relationship with Jesus, faithfully seeking Him and following Him to minister to addicts just like him, so has our family leaned into all our ministries.

Because your ministry is before you everyday. Your purpose is laid out in front of you everyday when you get out of bed in the morning. It's no doubt that all the people who came alongside us were supposed to be part of this story. They said yes to the journey.

Finally, and what does the Bible say about itself? Why should we read and believe it? So I give to you some top reasons why, because even today we can embrace what the Bible says about itself....

John 1:1-2
In the beginning was the Word, and the Word was with God, and the Word was God. He was in the beginning with God.

Hebrews 4:12
For the word of God is living and powerful, and sharper than any two-edged sword, piercing even to the division of soul and spirit, and of joints and marrow, and is a discerner of the thoughts and intents of the heart.

Proverbs 30:5
Every word of God is pure;
He is a shield to those who put their trust in Him.

Psalm 18:30
As for God, His way is perfect;
The word of the LORD is proven;
He is a shield to all who trust in Him.

2 Timothy 3:16
All Scripture is given by inspiration of God, and is profitable for doctrine, for reproof, for correction, for instruction in righteousness, that the man of God may be complete, thoroughly equipped for every good work.

Psalm 119:105
Your word is a lamp to my feet
And a light to my path.

1 Thessalonians 2:13
For this reason we also thank God without ceasing, because when you received the word of God which you heard from us, you welcomed it not as the word of men, but as it is in truth, the word of God, which also effectively works in you who believe.

Isaiah 40:8
The grass withers, the flower fades,
But the word of our God stands forever."

Matthew 19:4
"Haven't you read the Scriptures?"

To be sure, there are many, many more and you will read those as you venture through this devotional. Just remember, Don't take my word for it.... Read it yourself! (Scripture references are provided by The NKJV)

Introduction

Why another devotion book?
That's a great question, and I would say that one secret in our lives is that we really do desire and have a deep longing to know God. This book hopefully will help! I don't pretend to have some deep philosophical knowledge or education; I don't. My experience is simply that I needed to be reading the Bible more. There is a great line in Don Henley's song " New York Minute" (The End of Innocence, Geffen Records) that mentions "The wolf is always at the door." And it's true; our enemy is on the 168-hour program. He is watching and waiting to destroy you. He would kill you if he could; we see that early in the Book of Job, but he will be just as satisfied to ruin you and your testimony as we have seen so many times before. If we think going to church for an hour or two once per week is enough to counter our enemy, we are kidding ourselves. We need a flood of God to come upon us so that we are in constant thought of our heavenly Father. This is not badmouthing of the Church; it is just a way for you to get more of God's story in your heart. And that really is what the Bible is— God's story. As you continue to read, you also may become aware of something else: it's your story as well. Let's just clear one thing up though: who is this wolf I mention? Well, certainly it involves the devil, but remember, he is not God. He is not around you at every turn, waiting to trip you up. The damage he has done, however, will. I am talking just as much about the world and the junk you and I digest with our eyes, ears, and minds. It's an onslaught of corruption that is presented as something exciting and seductive, and we are being bombarded continuously. Worse part, we may not even realize it.

This book, *Don't Take My Word For It, Read It Yourself, A DEVOTIONAL* has been a process. I realized a few years ago that I needed more of God's word in my life, my head, and my heart. This did not come easily; I spent most of my adult life ignoring the very word I needed. Then one day, I woke up. I simply stated, I can't live this way anymore. Something very important was missing, and I needed to find it. This isn't the typical "I need to find myself" thought process; No, I was looking for something different, something beyond me. I knew where to look; I just needed to start. Perhaps you know what I am talking about; I had attempted to read the Bible several times, and I would get to Numbers or Leviticus and lose interest. For me, to just sit down and start reading was not the answer. What I found was reading a chapter of the Bible a day. Maybe even more than that was the commitment to take 3 years and roughly a month to engage in what I now understand to be the life-changing Word of God. Here is the thing I have found: there is life in these words. There is meaning in these words. Now, as I am into round four of reading a chapter a day, these words continue to strike me in new and different ways. So this devotion book takes us into some scriptures you may not be familiar with. My hope is that as a reader of God's word, you will join me on an adventure. A place where there is comfort and, at the same time, a place of unease. You see, this is God's story, and as you read, you may very well see yourself as well! That is how we know this thing we call the Bible is the real deal; it reveals the good, the bad and everything in between. It contains mystery, murder, all kinds of violence, and the heroes do not always win in the end. There is a victor, however, and we see this flow throughout the entire text of the Bible. Ultimately, there is good news for each of us, reading God's story - You can KNOW God! Not only is that our objective, it is God's desire for you as well.

I mentioned earlier that I was on round four of reading the Bible a chapter a day. After I finished the first time, I began the second. I invited 25 folks to join me, and together we walked through the experience of reading The Bible a chapter a day. We kicked off July 1, 2016, and finished August 2, 2019. I began to read through again starting on August 3; this time solo, not realizing, of course, that in March of 2020, we all would face a pandemic and not really knowing what might happen. On March 18th, 2020, God impressed upon me while I was reading The Bible and discovering - we can share in His promises. The 25 who joined me on Reading the Bible a chapter a day jumped in, as did many others, and we began to fight the effects of the pandemic with the promises of God. Those promises continue to this day, and after several members of the group suggested I write a devotion book, I decided it was worth looking into it.

If you are reading Don't Take My Word For It, Read It Yourself, *A DEVOTIONAL*, I have some suggestions:

> Equip yourself with a Bible (for the most part, I use the New Living Translation, The New King James Version, New International Version, and there are a few from The Message), a highlighter, a pencil or pen, a notebook, and this book. This is not to say you can't use your phone or tablet; I have just found holding the Bible in my hand to be more meaningful.

> Commit and make a daily appointment with the Lord. Be intentional and ask Him to join you as you read His Word. On numerous occasions in the Bible, Jesus went out of His way for an encounter with someone. Check out John 4 and read the woman at the well. He is always with you; treat this as a very special time between the two of you!

Find yourself a nice, quiet place to read and write.

> As silly as it may sound, try to read out loud as you read. The Book of Revelation states in Chapter 1:2-3: *who testifies to everything he saw—that is, the* **Word of God and the testimony of Jesus Christ. Blessed** *is the one who* **reads aloud** *the words of this prophecy, and blessed are those who* **hear** *it and take to heart what is written in it, because the time is near*. We increase our attention span when we listen and not just read. See if it works for you.

> There are 365 devotions for you in this book. There are also scripture references for you to dig deeper. There are many more; you will enjoy your excavation of God's Word. What does the Bible say? Seek the Lord while He may be found.

> If you are interested, I have also included: Read the Bible a chapter a day with each page. You may notice that I began with the book of John. I found that some of the questions of early Genesis are more understandable when you have already read John.

> There is a note section after each 7 devotions in the book. Since this book may take several forms, writing on the notes page may prove to be more difficult on the digital version. It may be easier writing in a notebook or journal— your choice! I am hopeful you will fill it and your Bible with so many notes you will never be able to bear losing either book.

Finally, you will notice that each page includes the phrase: "Don't take my word for it, read it yourself." I am not trying to be flippant or sarcastic; I really don't want you to take my word for it. No, God has intended His word to impact each of us in a unique way, and the best way is for you to read each passage on your own. I really do believe that we can truly know God on a personal level, and that will mean getting your hands dirty as you dig into His word. He will honor your time and commitment— It's really a command! Dig, there are more cross-references in the Bible than you can probably comprehend. I am not even sure how many, but the chart below is an excellent reminder of the ability of God's word to authenticate itself. If you will look right at the center of the chart (below), you will see Psalm 119, very close to the center of the Bible. Psalm 119 has several interesting facts about it. It is the largest chapter in the Bible, and every verse has a quotation about the promises of the actual word of God in it. Don't take my word for it; read it yourself!

I hope that you find this book inspiring and helpful on your spiritual journey. Thank you for trusting me as you go through it.

-Jeff Mathews

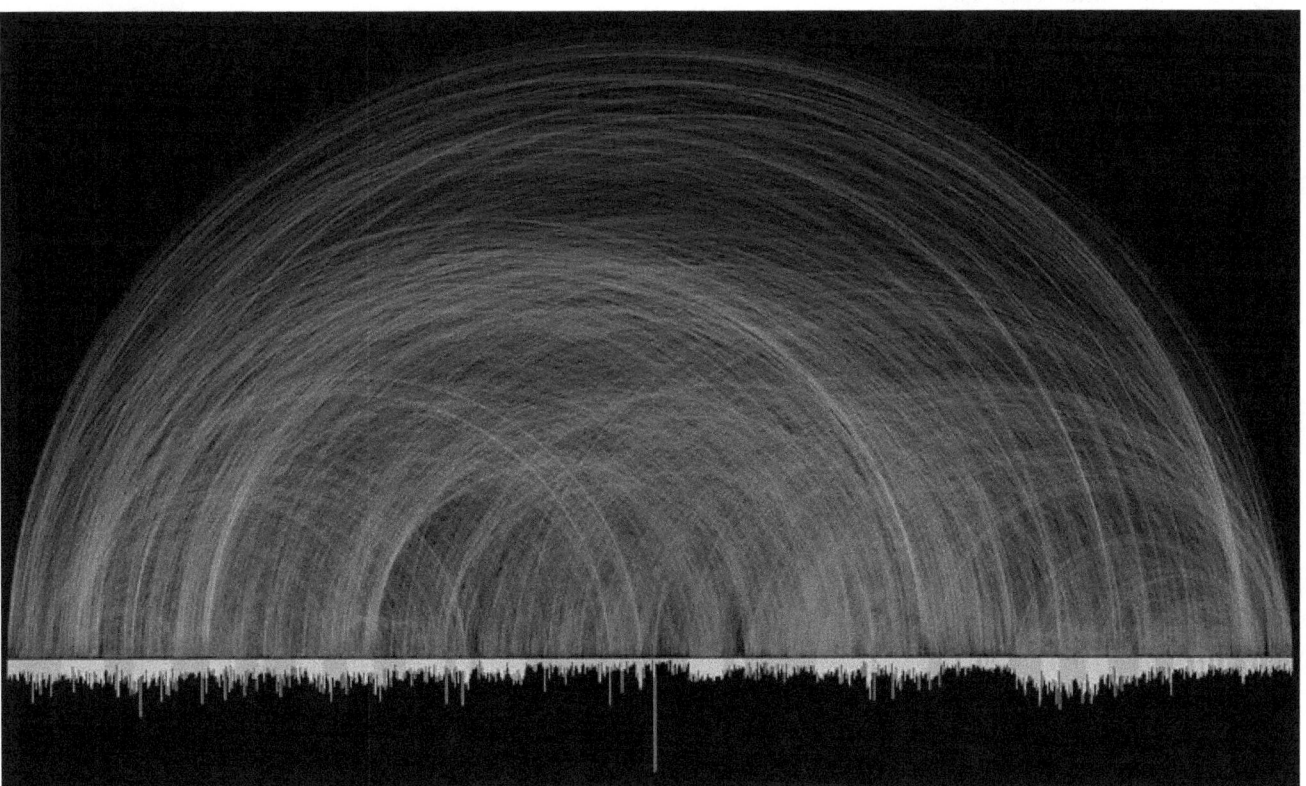

Chart provided by Chris Harrison

Devotion Book Scripture List

Day 1 - 1 Samuel 3:21
Day 2 - Isaiah 54:5
Day 3 - Galatians 6:15-16
Day 4 - Deuteronomy 9:1-3
Day 5 - Proverbs 30:5-6
Day 6 - Acts 17:16-31
Day 7 - John 3:3
Day 8 - James 1:22
Day 9 - Luke 5:12-13
Day 10 - Psalm 46:10
Day 11 - Isaiah 49:15-16
Day 12 - 2 Corinthians 1:8-11
Day 13 - Galatians 1:15-16
Day 14 - John 14:6-7
Day 15 - Joel 2:32
Day 16 - Proverbs 18:21
Day 17 - 2 Chronicles 7:14
Day 18 - Numbers 6:24-27
Day 19 - Matthew 2:16-18
Day 20 - Hosea 14:1-4
Three Generations and a Linebacker
Day 21 - Romans 12:2
Day 22 - Deuteronomy 30:19-20
Day 23 - Genesis 1:1
Day 24 - Jonah 2:7-10
Day 25 - Genesis 19:26
Day 26 - Luke 10:41-42
Day 27 - Psalm 19:1-6
Day 28 - 2 Samuel 22:31-33
Day 29 - Romans 8:14-17
Day 30 - 2 Corinthians 5:17
Day 31 - Acts 3:19
Day 32 - Deuteronomy 34:5-12
Day 33 - Acts 2:36
Day 34 - Hebrews 6:13-20
Day 35 - 2 Kings 22: 8-13

Day 36 - 1 Samuel 17:48
Day 37 - Proverbs 3:7-8
Day 38 - Obadiah 15
Day 39 - Joshua 1:1-9
Day 40 - Acts 10:34-36
Day 41 - 1 John 5:13-15
Day 42 - Job 19:25-27
Day 43 - Isaiah 43:18-19
Day 44 - Matthew 6:5-6
Day 45 - Psalm 5:3
Day 46 - Acts 13:38-41
Day 47 - Proverbs 13:11
Day 48 - Isaiah 26: 2-4
Day 49 - Acts 17:11
Day 50 - Mark 7:6-8
Day 51 - Acts 8:1
Day 52 - Zechariah 8:16-17
Day 53 - Genesis 32:24-30
Day 54 - Esther 3:5-6
Day 55 - Esther 4:14
Day 56 - Habakkuk 2:3
Day 57 - 1 Thessalonians 5:19-24
Day 58 - Psalm 1
Day 59 - James 2:21-24
Day 60 - Ephesians 3:20-21
Day 61 - Acts 17:24-29
Day 62 - 1 Timothy 1:15-17
Day 63 - 2 Timothy 3:16-17
Day 64 - Hebrews 4:12-13
Day 65 - James 1:12-15
Day 66 - John 3:16
Day 68 - Psalm 37:23-24
Day 69 - Matthew 27:50-51
Day 70 - Matthew 28:20
Day 71 - Genesis 50:19-20
Day 72 - Amos 5:4
Day 73 - Psalm 3
Day 74 - Genesis 15:1-6

Day 75 - Joshua 5:13-15
Day 76 - 1 Peter 1:23-25
Day 77 - Isaiah 44:24
Day 78 - Matthew 8:2-3
Day 79 - Matthew 19:19-26
Day 80 - Ecclesiastes 12:13-14
Day 81 - Joshua 21:43-45
Day 82 - 1 Corinthians 6:18-20
Day 83 - Hosea 6:6
Day 84 - Ephesians 2:8-10
Day 85 - Acts 27:21-26
Day 86 - Deuteronomy 31:6
Day 87 - Judges 17:6
Day 88 - John 18:37-38
Day 89 - John 1:1-5
Day 90 - Malachi 3:6
Day 91 - Matthew 21:28-32
The storms of all storms
Day 92 - Luke 24:13-32
Day 93 - Matthew 16:13-15
Day 94 - Daniel 3:16-25
Day 95 - 2 Kings 4:1-7
Day 96 - 2 Peter 1:12-21
Day 97 - Matthew 17:1-5
Day 98 - John 4:4
Day 99 - Matthew 14:34-36
Day 100 - 1 Chronicles 28:9-10
Day 101 - Joshua 24:14-15
Day 102 - Hebrews 11:1-3
Day 103 - Psalm 33:4
Day 104 - Ezra 8:21-23
Day 105 - John 6:26-29
Day 106 - Isaiah 55:8-9
Day 107 - Psalm 139:17-18
Day 108 - Zephaniah 3:17
Day 109 - Daniel 4:35
Day 110 - Ecclesiastes 7:10
Day 111 - 2 Timothy 3:1-5

Day 112 - Jeremiah 1:4-12
Day 113 - Psalm 37:3-5
Day 114 - Hebrews 13:1-9
Day 115 - Psalm 148
Day 116 - Deuteronomy 7:9
Day 117 - Joshua 8:34-35
Day 118 - Matthew 6:33
Day 119 - Matthew 6:33-35
Day 120 - Matthew 10:28-34
Day 121 - Luke 21:13-19
Day 122 - Psalm 78:56
Day 123 - Joshua 3:9-10
Day 124 - Joel 2:12-14
Day 125 - Luke 5:27-28
Day 126 - Daniel 1:8-9
Day 127 - Joshua 10:7-15
Day 128 - Psalm 23
Day 129 - Luke 22:31-34
Day 130 - Romans 8:11
Day 131 - 1 John 4:2-3
Day 132 - Luke 12:54-56
Day 133 - James 1:5-8
Day 134 - Psalm 119:73
Day 135 - Micah 6:5-8
Day 136 - 1 Corinthians 3:6-9
Day 137 - 1 Timothy 4:4-5
Day 138 - Romans 10:9-15
Day 139 - Proverbs 3:5-6
Day 140 - Revelation 1:1-8
Day 141 - 2 Corinthians 3:16-18
Day 142 - Isaiah 40:28-31
Day 143 - Revelation 22:12-15
Day 144 - Genesis 1:26-27
Day 145 - Galatians 1:11-12
Day 146 - Psalm 81:10-11
Day 147 - John 20:24-29
Day 148 - Jeremiah 17:7-9
Day 149 - Philippians 4:4-7

Day 150 - John 3:18-21
Day 151 - 1 Samuel 8:6-9
Day 152 - 2 Corinthians 1:18-22
Day 153 - Joshua 23:14-16
Day 154 - Romans 1:1-7
Day 155 - Exodus 7:10-13
Day 156 - John 20:30-31
Day 157 - Ecclesiastes 7:29
Day 158 - Romans 3:20-22
Day 159 - Romans 4:20-25
Day 160 - 1 Kings 19:9-18
Day 161 - Jeremiah 29:11
Day 162 - Romans 7:21-25
Day 163 - Psalm 139:13-16
Day 164 - Psalm 85:8-9
Day 165 - Romans 11:33-36
Day 166 - Psalm 114
Day 167 - Isaiah 48:12-13
Day 168 - John 17:3
Day 169 - Jeremiah 30:18-22
Day 170 - Malachi 4:4
Day 171 - Ephesians 6:17
Day 172 - Proverbs 1:33
Day 173 - Deuteronomy 6:4-9
Day 174 - Genesis 3:15
Day 175 - Isaiah 35:4
Day 176 - Mark 7:14-23
Day 177 - Judges 2:1-5
Day 178 - Hebrews 3:4
Day 179 - Jonah 2:1-2
Day 180 - 1 Samuel 17:37
Day 181 - Judges 6:16-24
Day 182 - Mark 9:17-24
Yes, they really do have an airshow in Dayton
Day 183 - Judges 10:6-16
Day 184 - Hosea 4:1-3
Day 185 - John 15:5-8
Day 186 - Malachi 1

Day 187 - Revelation 1:17-18
Day 188 - 2 Kings 6:1-7
Day 189 - Psalm 110:4
Day 190 - Matthew 28:17
Day 191 - Isaiah 55:10-11
Day 192 - Judges 16:18-20
Day 193 - Acts 9:10-19
Day 194 - 2 Kings 6:15-17
Day 195 - Psalm 100
Day 196 - Isaiah 41:8-10
Day 197 - Provers 30:8-9
Day 198 - 1 Thessalonians 2:13
Day 199 - James 4:1-8
Day 200 - Psalm 9:9-10
Day 201 - Galatians 6:7-10
Day 202 - 1 John 4:18
Day 203 - Revelation 3:14-22
Day 204 - Psalm 33:6
Day 205 - 2 Corinthians 4:16-17
Day 206 - Psalm 2
Day 207 - John 5:25-30
Day 208 - 1 Peter 2:9-16
Day 209 - Luke 1:1-4
Day 210 - Hebrews 12:1-4
Day 211 - 1 Corinthians 1:18-25
Day 212 - Psalm 73:21-28
Day 213 - Revelation 19:9-11
Day 214 - 1 Corinthians 2:13
Day 215 - John 1:12-13
Day 216 - Colossians 3:1-5
Day 217 - Isaiah 29:14
Day 218 - Psalm 139:23-24
Day 219 - Hebrews 9:22
Day 220 - Exodus 33:11-17
Day 221 - Psalm 130
Day 222 - Jeremiah 33:1-3
Day 223 - John 5:17-18
Day 224 - Hosea 14:9

Day 225 - Daniel 2:47
Day 226 - Daniel 6:35
Day 227 - Ezekiel 36:27
Day 228 - Luke 11:28
Day 229 - 1 Corinthians 8:3
Day 230 - Job 1:9-12
Day 231 - John 14:25-26
Day 232 - 1 Corinthians 10:13
Day 233 - Proverbs 1:7
Day 234 - Luke 17:12-19
Day 235 - Psalm 67
Day 236 - 2 Samuel 6:6-7
Day 237 - John 21:24-25
Day 238 - Proverbs 28:26
Day 239 - Ecclesiastes 12:6-7
Day 240 - Acts 1:9-11
Day 241 - 1 Corinthians 13:4-8
Day 242 - Psalm 80:3
Day 243 - Exodus 16:35-36
Day 244 - Amos 1:1
Day 245 - Genesis 12:1-3
Day 246 - Matthew 14:27
Day 247 - 1 Corinthians 15:3-9
Day 248 - Ephesians 5:18-20
Day 249 - 1 Samuel 5:1-4
Day 250 - 2 Corinthians 5:1-5
Day 251 - Psalm 140
Day 252 - Ruth 4:13-22
Day 253 - 1 Corinthians 16:13-14
Day 254 - Psalm 32:2-5
Day 255 - John 14:8-10
Day 256 - 2 Thessalonians 1
Day 257 - Exodus 3:13-14
Day 258 - Matthew 15:16-20
Day 259 - Haggai 2:4-5
Day 260 - Mark 16:6-7
Day 261 - Genesis 5:21-24
Day 262 - James 5:17-18

Day 263 - Mark 6:37-38
Day 264 - Amos 5:8
Day 265 - Ezekiel 1:18
Day 266 - Jeremiah 6:16
Day 267 - Acts 2:24
Day 268 - Deuteronomy 1:29-31
Day 269 - Psalm 8
Day 270 - 2 Chronicles 32:7-8
Day 271 - Isaiah 45:1-7
Day 272 - John 19:30
The Boxer and The Prison
Day 273 - Ecclesiastes 3:11
Day 274 - Revelation 11:8
Day 275 - Ephesians 1:16-17
Day 276 - Colossians 2:8-10
Day 277 - Psalm 121
Day 278 - John 10:9
Day 279 - Genesis 17:1-8
Day 280 - Jeremiah 39:17-18
Day 281 - Psalm 145:13
Day 282 - Psalm 91:4
Day 283 - Joshua 18:3
Day 284 - Matthew 10:34-39
Day 285 - Isaiah 43:1-3
Day 286 - Matthew 16:33
Day 287 - Exodus 20:1-6
Day 288 - Luke 12:22-26
Day 289 - Psalm 117
Day 290 - Jude 24-25
Day 291 - Daniel 7:13-14
Day 292 - 2 Thessalonians 2:13
Day 293 - Psalm 18:30
Day 294 - James 1:16-18
Day 295 - Genesis 6:8-9
Day 296 - 2 Corinthians 6:14-18
Day 297 - Ezekiel 37:5-6
Day 298 - 1 Samuel 10:6-7
Day 299 - Joshua 1:2

Day 300 - Psalm 50:7
Day 301 - Acts 1:23-26
Day 302 - Romans 1:18-32
Day 303 - 2 Corinthians 6:14-7:1
Day 304 - Job 38:1-7
Day 305 - Psalm 138:1-3
Day 306 - 1 Samuel 16:7
Day 307 - Proverbs 20:22
Day 308 - Proverbs 20:27
Day 309 - John 16:26-28
Day 310 - Nehemiah 9:3-8
Day 311 - Malachi 3:1
Day 312 - 1 Samuel 2:1-10
Day 313 - Matthew 13:44-45
Day 314 - 2 Corinthians 9:6-15
Day 315 - Isaiah 25:1
Day 316 - Acts 9:5
Day 317 - Ecclesiastes 11:5
Day 318 - Acts 2:21
Day 319 - Revelation 4:8-11
Day 320 - Exodus 15:22-26
Day 321 - Leviticus 20:7-8
Day 322 - Isaiah 46:4-5
Day 323 - 2 Peter 1:3-13
Day 324 - Acts 1:4
Day 325 - 3 John 11
Day 326 - Proverbs 21:30
Day 327 - Deuteronomy 32:39
Day 328 - Matthew 19:4-6
Day 329 - 2 Timothy 1:8-14
Day 330 - Genesis 18:14
Day 331 - Job 28:20
Day 332 - Acts 4:18-20
Day 333 Luke 18:1-8
Day 334 - Jeremiah 32:17
Day 335 - Isaiah 41:4
Day 336 - 1 Samuel 1:19
Day 337 - Psalm 103:13-17

Day 338 - Genesis 1:31
Day 339 - Psalm 12:6
Day 340 - John 6:51
Day 341 - 1 Thessalonians 4:16-18
Day 342 - Isaiah 57:1-2
Day 343 - Matthew 22:23-33
Day 344 - Nahum 1:7
Day 345 - Ezra 6:22
Day 346 - Titus 1:1-3
Day 347 - Psalm 40:6-8
Day 348 - John 14:15-17
Day 349 - Zechariah 1:3-4
Day 350 - 1 Thessalonians 3:11-13
Day 351 - Colossians 1:15-20
Day 352 - Job 1:20-22
Day 353 - Habakkuk 1:1-5
Day 354 - James 3:13-18
Day 355 - Luke 2:19-20
Day 356 - Proverbs 6:16-19
Day 357 - Matthew 5:13
Day 358 - Acts 8:31
Day 359 - Isaiah 26:9
Day 360 - Matthew 12:38-41
Day 361 - Mark 13:19
Day 362 - Philippians 4:19
Day 363 - 1 John 4:10
Day 364 - Numbers 23:19
Day 365 - Revelation 22:20-21

The Journey Begins

Day 1

1 Samuel 3:21

The LORD continued to appear at Shiloh, and there he revealed himself to Samuel through his word.

Here is a promise for you: God has certain mysteries we can never fathom. It's not so much that he hides them, they are simply too amazing for us to fully understand. He wants us to know him! The Bible tells us that God reveals himself through His word. We can have a deeper understanding, knowledge and friendship with God by dusting off that Bible and cracking it open. This is one of the scriptures that got me thinking: He showed up for Samuel, maybe He will will show up for me as well - And He Did!

And the journey begins!

Supporting Scripture:
Numbers 12:6
2 Corinthians 12:2-4

Read through the Bible a Chapter a day

John 1

Day 2

Isaiah 54:5

*For your Maker **is** your husband,*
*the LORD Almighty **is** his name;*
*the Holy One of Israel **is** your Redeemer;*
*He **is** called the God of all the earth.*

Every word of these glorious scriptures has meaning. From smallest to largest, from what appears to be the least significant to most complex - Every word of scripture is true!

You can KNOW God!

Supporting scripture:
2 Timothy 3:16
Psalm 95:6

Read through the Bible a Chapter a day

John 2

Day 3

Galatians 6:15-16

It doesn't matter whether we have been circumcised or not. **What counts is whether we have been transformed into a new creation.** *May God's peace and mercy be upon all who live by this principle; they are the new people of God.*

Genesis contains wonderful information about the creation of the universe. My friends, God is still in the creating business! It's you and I! Every Christian, transformed by Jesus Christ, is an entirely new creation! 2 Corinthians 5:17 tells us this: *Therefore, if anyone is in Christ, the new creation has come: The old has gone, the new is here!* Let's rid ourselves of old and worn out philosophies this tainted world brings and shine like the new creation we are! By the way, this only happens through Jesus Christ. We cannot magically morph ourselves into this new creation on our own.

Supporting Scripture
2 Corinthians 5:17
John 1:12-13

Read through the Bible a Chapter a day

John 3

Day 4

Deuteronomy 9:1-3

"Listen, O Israel! Today you are about to cross the Jordan River to take over the land belonging to nations much greater and more powerful than you. They live in cities with walls that reach to the sky! The people are strong and tall—descendants of the famous Anakite giants. You've heard the saying, 'Who can stand up to the Anakites?' **But recognize today that the LORD your God is the one who will cross over ahead of you like a devouring fire to destroy them.** *He will subdue them so that you will quickly conquer them and drive them out,* **just as the LORD has promised**.

We have all seen these giants in our lives. There are too many to list here, today. Yours are unique to you, yet the Bible tells us that we have not been given a burden that is unheard of, others have encountered them as well (1 Peter 5:9). Here is where we encounter the victorious Jesus: He has already gone ahead to destroy the very stumbling block you fear! God has promised that you can and will conquer them. I don't know about you, I cannot even fathom walking on a path that does not include God, yet that has not been a simple lesson.

Supporting Scripture:
1 Peter 5:9

Read through the Bible a Chapter a day

John 4

Day 5

Proverbs 30:5-6

Every word of God proves true.
He is a shield to all who come to him for protection.
Do not add to his words,
or he may rebuke you and expose you as a liar.

We can be sure what the Bible tells us is from God. There are so many references to the truth of the Bible. In it we read about the accounts of so many people, their strengths and weaknesses. Their highs and lows. There is crime and murder, adultery and stealing. Incest and lewd behavior. It's all there. Good or bad, the Bible tells the truth of humanity and how God still carried out His plan to save us. And God has told us this story - all of it. Now it is really up to you and I to read it. Ask God to reveal his wisdom and His heart to you while you read it. When you do, expect the unexpected - Nothing is impossible for God!

Supporting Scripture:
Psalm 119:89
Daniel 1:17
Luke 1:37

Read through the Bible a Chapter a day

John 5

Day 6

Acts 17:16-31

Now while Paul waited for them at Athens, his spirit was provoked within him when he saw that the city was given over to idols. Therefore he reasoned in the synagogue with the Jews and with the Gentile worshipers, and in the marketplace daily with those who happened to be there. Then certain Epicurean and Stoic philosophers encountered him. And some said, "What does this babbler want to say?"
Others said, "He seems to be a proclaimer of foreign gods," because he preached to them Jesus and the resurrection.
And they took him and brought him to the Areopagus, saying, "May we know what this new doctrine is of which you speak? For you are bringing some strange things to our ears. Therefore we want to know what these things mean." For all the Athenians and the foreigners who were there spent their time in nothing else but either to tell or to hear some new thing.
Then Paul stood in the midst of the Areopagus and said, **"Men of Athens, I perceive that in all things you are very religious; for as I was passing through and considering the objects of your worship, I even found an altar with this inscription: TO THE UNKNOWN GOD.**
Therefore, **the One whom you worship without knowing, Him I proclaim to you: God, who made the world and everything in it, since He is Lord of heaven and earth, does not dwell in temples made with hands. Nor is He worshiped with men's hands, as though He needed anything, since He gives to all life, breath, and all things.** *And He has made from one blood every nation of men to dwell on all the face of the earth, and has* **determined their pre-appointed times and the boundaries of their dwellings,** *so that they should seek the Lord, in the hope that they might grope for Him and find Him, though He is not far from each one of us; for in Him we live and move and have our being, as also some of your own poets have said,* **'For we are also His offspring.'**
Therefore, **since we are the offspring of God, we ought not to think that the Divine Nature is like gold or silver or stone, something shaped by art and man's devising.**
Truly, these times of ignorance God overlooked, but **now commands all men everywhere to repent,** *because* **He has appointed a day on which He will judge the world in righteousness by the Man whom He has ordained. He has given assurance of this to all by raising Him from the dead."**

You might be thinking, enough of this idol worship stuff! I wish I could, but it is everywhere, and it creeps up on us until we are knee deep in it...we need to focus our attention. This scripture describes Paul in Athens as he spoke to the Areopagus. Note what he says about them being very religious. He then presents to them that s"religious" entails all sorts of things, not necessarily a personal relationship with God. He even tells them that an altar he had seen with the inscription: "To the unknown God" They were worshipping a God they did not even know! Paul told them that **that** God was the one he was telling them about! We see this today don't we? There are zealots of many religions today. People worshipping all sorts of things, but not necessarily a personal relationship with God. Be it science, lifestyles, earth, government, sexual identity, jobs, kids, spouses, money, hobbies, homes, cars - the list goes on and on - if we put any of these items in front of God - we are guilty of idol worship. And since Paul spells out that God created us and everything and every place in our lives we need to identify ourselves as God's children. The personal relationship begins (or is renewed) by repenting. See, he has already given us evidence of this with Christ resurrection.

Read through the Bible a Chapter a day

John 6

Day 7

John 3:3

*Jesus replied, "**I tell you the truth,** unless you are **born again,** you cannot see the kingdom of God."*

You must be born again!
Many today do not understand, or they choose to not accept Jesus's words here. **Born again!** The term has been pirated, emptied of meaning and dragged through the gutter and then given back to us minus the power it represents. Some say, "I am a Christian, but I am not one of those 'born again.'" Listen to the words of Jesus, There is no such thing as a Christian who is not born again. We have covered several different scriptures that describe this regeneration Jesus gives us. Galatians 6:15-16, 2 Corinthians 5:17 and Romans 8:9-11 are among some of the promises that describe this transformation.

We need spiritual rebirth because, according to Jesus, unless we are born again, we cannot see the Kingdom of God.

Supporting Scripture:
Galatians 6:15-16
2 Corinthians 5:17
Romans 8:9-11

Read through the Bible a Chapter a day

John 7

Notes

Day 8

James 1:22

*But don't just listen to God's word. You must **do** what it says.*

Can you hear the voice of God calling you? Do what he tells you to do, respond with "Here I am" or "Speak, your servant is listening". I contend that God uses a number of ways to speak to you:
    1. Through the Bible (remember B.I.B.L.E. - **B**asic **I**nstruction **B**efore **L**eaving **E**arth)
    2. That silent voice you receive in your spirit.
    3. Your experiences may help guide (you need wisdom for this one)
    4. God can pick any number of ways to reach you.
Knowing that God can speak to you, How receptive are you? How willing are you to hear his voice? When you do hear it - and you will... why not respond with: Here I am - then Do what He tells you to do.

Supporting Scripture:
John 2:1-10
1 Samuel 3:10
Exodus 3:14

Read through the Bible a Chapter a day

John 8

Day 9

Luke 5:12-13

*In one of the villages, Jesus met a man with an advanced case of leprosy. When the man saw Jesus, he bowed with his face to the ground, begging to be healed. "Lord," he said, "if you are **willing**, you **can** heal me and **make** me clean."*
*Jesus reached out and **touched** him. **"I am willing,"** he said. **"Be healed!"** And instantly the leprosy disappeared.*

Jesus in the trenches.
A dreaded Leper, a person condemned to isolation for what would amount to be the rest of his life met Jesus. That would have to mean Jesus went to him. Similar to the woman by the well (John 4), Jesus sought this man out. The meeting is no accident, there was an appointment, the man with leprosy just did not know it was a planned event. The man knew Jesus could heal him if only he was willing to do so. The man wanted to be rid of his illness and literally be cleansed. This is not something Jesus feared and actually touched him and said "I am willing"! We see this over and over in the gospels. Jesus in the trenches - These stories remind us that God seeks us out and finds us despite our hiding from him. He is still willing; now, he not only touches us, he lives in our hearts!
Don't be afraid to get in the trenches, that's where the real need is found!

Supporting Scripture:
Genesis 3:8-9
John 4:1-42

Read through the Bible a Chapter a day

John 9

Day 10

Psalm 46:10

*"Be still, and **know** that I am God!*
*I **will** be honored by every nation.*
*I **will** be honored throughout the world."*

Recently, I had a moment. I love the simple scripture of Psalm 46:10 - Be still and know that I am God. I think often about this Psalm, or maybe I should say God reminds me often about it. He challenged me. When I think about all the areas of my life, there is not one not covered by this. I simply can't do it. You see, when I think about my concerns, my worries, my life, no matter what it is: I am left with a simple thought - Do I trust God? Because if I don't - then this has no meaning. Ah, but if I do trust him then literally everything in my life is covered by this Psalm. It is also a great way to begin a New Year, contemplating our reliance on God.

That's a thought for you today and loaded with promise - God never forgets and is with us always!

Supporting Scripture:
Matthew 28:18-20

Read through the Bible a Chapter a day

John 10

Day 11

Isaiah 49:15-16

Can a mother forget the baby at her breast
and have no compassion on the child she has borne?
Though she may forget,
*I **will not** forget you!*
*See, **I have engraved you on the palms of my hands**;*
*your walls are **ever** before me.*

We should be comforted when we read words like Isaiah 49:15-16. It is hard to imagine the thought, that of a mother could forget her children, yet I have met parents who have stated: "They were willing to sell their children for the next hit of heroin". Isn't that tragic? We should never forget: God **never** forgets us. We are engraved in the palms of his hands. Keep in mind, that is not just our names - that is us, all of us, our personalities, our stresses, our souls - everything about us! Now let's think on this a bit more. Those hands, they created heaven and earth. They healed countless numbers of people and even gave you and I the opportunity for salvation. Those hands bled holding Jesus on the cross. The very cross where He gave His life as the perfect sacrifice for you and I. Those hands provided the ONLY mechanism for which we can be saved! You and I are engraved in the same hands we can fully trust to fulfill every promise God has made!
Please, do not pin your hopes on a politician, or in the false hopes of the world we live in. They will let you down, every time.
That is not God's way - he will never let you down!

Read through the Bible a Chapter a day

John 11

Day 12

2 Corinthians 1:8-11

*We think you ought to know, dear brothers and sisters, about the trouble we went through in the province of Asia. We were crushed and overwhelmed beyond our ability to endure, and we thought we would never live through it. In fact, we expected to die. But as a result, **we stopped relying on ourselves and learned to rely only on God,** who raises the dead. And he did rescue us from mortal danger, and he will rescue us again. We have placed our confidence in him, and he will continue to rescue us. And you are helping us by praying for us. Then many people will give thanks because God has graciously answered so many prayers for our safety.*

We should not rely on our own confidence, craftiness, ingenuity, smarts - whatever you want to call it. We can rely only on God! No matter what, God will rescue you - now and in the future. This scripture spoke to me today in the midst of all the craziness that is going on right now. We must carry on, relying on God who will deliver us!

Supporting Scripture:
Jeremiah 17:5,7
John 5:21

Read through the Bible a Chapter a day

John 12

Day 13

Galatians 1:15-16

*But even **before** I was born, God chose me and called me by his marvelous grace. Then it pleased him to reveal his Son to me so that I would proclaim the Good News about Jesus to the Gentiles.*
When this happened, I did not rush out to consult with any human being.

In a time when people were basically making it up as they went along (sound familiar?) Paul tells the Galatians that he received the gospel through revelation from Jesus. Look for your self, it was not something man made.

Paul continues this thought, God set him apart at birth and called him by grace (remember Paul's past) and God was pleased to reveal Jesus Christ to him. Why? To preach! But Paul also tells us that he did not receive direction from any man, he received it directly from God! If God called him from birth, he certainly knew his plan for Paul before he was born, and before he was conceived. (**Jeremiah 1:4-5** says: Before I formed you in the womb I knew you, before you were born I set you apart; I appointed you as a prophet to the nations and **Isaiah 49:1** - Before I was born the LORD called me; from my mother's womb he has spoken my name.)

If God did that for Paul and Jeremiah and Isaiah, I wonder what he has planned for you and I?
Keep reading that Bible!

Supporting Scripture:
Jeremiah 1:4-5
Isaiah 49:1
Psalm 139

Read through the Bible a Chapter a day

John 13

Day 14

John 14:6-7

*Jesus answered, "**I am** the way and the truth and the life. **No one** comes to the Father except through me. If you really knew me, you would know my Father as well. From now on, you do know him and have seen him."*

April 8, 2024: The day of the total eclipse. Here in my home town, we got about 4 minutes of darkness. Of course, there were all kinds of theories that came along with the event and as interesting as it got, the words of Jesus here in John 14 are an absolute truth and we cannot lose our prospective of that truth. That goes along with all the other chaos this world is throwing our way. There is no other avenue to reach God, except Jesus!

Supporting Scripture:
John 6:34
John 10:9
Acts 2:36
Ephesians 2:18

Read through the Bible a Chapter a day

John 14

Notes

Day 15

Joel 2:32

*And **everyone** who calls on the name of the Lord **will** be saved.*

This is the scripture that Peter used in Acts 2:21 and Paul in Romans !0:13 proving yet again that God's promises are true and that the whole Bible is true! Today, we hear some say that only the New Testament is valid today - all Scripture speaks to us: old and new! This scripture reminds us that you and I may be the only person to speak to others about God's love through Jesus they may ever hear. Many are not church goers and many still are not going back to church.
Remember God's promise: **Everyone** who calls on the name of the Lord **will** be saved!

Supporting Scripture:
Genesis 4:26
Psalm 105:1
Acts 2:17-21
Romans 10:13

Read through the Bible a Chapter a day

John 15

Day 16

Proverbs 18:21

The tongue can bring death or life;
those who love to talk will reap the consequences.

Boy if there was ever a time we could learn this, it would be now. The words we speak can build up; unfortunately, most of the time they are spent destroying others. So here is something we can do that will bless others and like a huge circle become a blessing as well: Go out and say THANK YOU to someone who has made an impact in your life! Seems small, but it is huge.

Try it out, see what happens.

Supporting Scripture:
Psalm 12:4
Matthew 12:37

Read through the Bible a Chapter a day

John 16

Day 17

2 Chronicles 7:14

*If my people, who are called by my name, will humble themselves and pray and seek my face and turn from their wicked ways, then **I will** hear from heaven, and **I will** forgive their sin and **will** heal their land.*

You and I need to be on our knees seeking God! We have read the promises that Jesus has given us. We know that He can heal our land! This starts with you and I! Look what God says: "I will"! God alone can and will deliver on his promises, not any another god, not science, not an idol. Let us lean into the only solution there actually is, God!

Supporting Scripture:
Numbers 6:27
Isaiah 55:7

Read through the Bible a Chapter a day

John 17

Day 18

Numbers 6:24-27

*'May the LORD bless you
and protect you.
May the LORD smile on you
and be gracious to you.
May the LORD show you his favor
and give you his peace.'
Whenever Aaron and his sons bless the people of Israel in my name, I myself will bless them."*

This prayer of blessing comes directly from the mouth of God! Then the LORD said to Moses, "Tell Aaron and his sons to bless the people of Israel with this special blessing." These words offer blessing, protection, favor and peace and promise! The Israelite's were; and are, God's chosen. As Christians, we are equally blessed as His children. Trust that God's word can continue to deliver corrupted societies as it has from the beginning.

Supporting Scripture:
John 14:27

Read through the Bible a Chapter a day

John 18

Day 19

Matthew 2:16-18

*When Herod realized that he had been outwitted by the Magi, he was furious, and he gave orders to kill **all the boys in Bethlehem** and its vicinity who were two years old and under, in accordance with the time he had learned from the Magi. Then what was said through the prophet Jeremiah was fulfilled:*
"A voice is heard in Ramah,
weeping and great mourning,
Rachel weeping for her children
and refusing to be comforted,
because they are no more."

Throughout history, there have been plots on the lives of Jews and Christians. I did not list the persecution of Christians in the Bible, it is a flat out war against us. Modern times has not changed this, from Hitler to today's abortions and the widespread persecution and antisemitism of Jews and Christians - Satan is doing his best to destroy literally millions of human lives. As of January, 2023 there have been over 64,000,000 abortions since 1974 in the US alone. The worldwide numbers are staggering - 125,000 abortions - PER DAY, over 1.6 Billion since 1980. The Supreme Court has thrown out the legality of Roe VS Wade. Through words, they sent it to the states to decide on their own. I don't think the timing is an accident. Every time there has been a war on the killing of children, something very big is coming. Moses, the birth of God, the rebirth of the Israel. One child changed the world 2000 years ago, and our enemy knows this. He is desperate, time is wrapping up and Satan is desperate to destroy as many lives as possible.

Supporting Scripture:
Exodus 1:22
Esther 3:5-6

Read through the Bible a Chapter a day

John 19

Day 20

Hosea 14:1-4

Return, O Israel, to the LORD your God,
for your sins have brought you down.
Bring your confessions, and return to the LORD.
Say to him,
"Forgive all our sins and graciously receive us,
so that we may offer you our praises.
Assyria cannot save us,
nor can our warhorses.
Never again will we say to the idols we have made,
'You are our gods.'
No, in you alone
do the orphans find mercy."
The LORD says,
"Then I **will** *heal you of your faithlessness;*
my love **will** *know no bounds,*
for my anger **will** *be gone forever.*

Please take one thing from today's scripture: There is no confession like a cry to God for forgiveness. There is no thing, no man-made law, idol, person or government that will save you! No, God is **all** you need, He is the only solution to the craziness that has beset our world today.

Supporting Scripture:
Hosea 14 (Entire chapter)
Hebrews 13:15

Read through the Bible a Chapter a day

John 20

3 Generations and a Linebacker

Three generations and a Linebacker

Let's go back to June 1995.

Having spent several hours driving to Chicago to pick up Jason at football camp, I was unsure what would happen. With me were Jill, my Mom, and Dad. As we watched, a series of awards were being handed out and our players running some scrimmage plays with their counselors. After the demonstration, the two main hosts of the camp began to speak. They discussed what had happened during the week of camp and, of course, football, but they also discussed integrity, faith, and the importance of a relationship with Christ. These two men were Leslie Frazier and Mike Singletary, both great players for the Chicago Bears. I hoped that their message would ring loud and clear to my son, and I felt inspired by their message as well. My Dad, well, my Dad apparently listened too because he was in a bit of a transition, which, frankly, I was unaware of. Before we took off to return to Indianapolis, we had a few minutes to meet Leslie and Mike, and as you can see in the photo op above. I don't know what my Dad was saying to Mike that day; in that moment, but I was later to find out that Dad was impacted by these two men's words of faith. In November (during Thanksgiving weekend), my Dad confirmed his accepting Christ as his Lord and Savior and was baptized. Dad's baptism not only impacted his immediate family but several others, including the Minister who officiated his baptism, George Tooze. George mentioned several times over the years how Dad's baptism affected his faith, and I had many opportunities to speak to George about this. And it made a chapter in a book George had written:

Jeff,

You are very kind to be in touch. Somewhere I have a picture from early on when I dedicated one of the children - there we all are looking quite a bit younger in the nursery where all of those walls had been recently painted with colorful animals.

Your father's baptism I will never forget. In fact, without mentioning his name, I have included that story in a recent book I have written about Baptist Principles. It is in the chapter on Baptism, and I use it to get away from the rigorous demand some have that baptism has to be by total immersion. There is no doubt in my mind but that the Spirit was there and that your father was totally and completely baptized.

I have shared a lot of experiences with your family and been blessed by them.

Blessings.

George

Hi George,

I just got your personal note. I want you to know that Jill and I are praying for you and Connie and the entire family!

You know, this past year we have not been attending FBC, but I had a recent opportunity to revisit some of my past experiences with the Church. There are so many fond memories that will always be in my heart. But one, and it is very strong - was the Baptism of my Dad. I am not sure I ever said thank you for all you did for him (before and after he passed away), but here is what I know: I will see him again, and you are a major reason why!

God has already blessed you, but I know he will never leave you or stop blessing you, my friend!

Thanks for being my Pastor!

Jeff

My Dad passed away in May of 1996. He had a bad heart and it basically just stopped working. Several years before, he had heart failure and I think scared him so badly that he quit smoking and began to realize his mortality. God gave him a few more years before he died. One month after Dad passed away, June took us back to Chicago for another week at the football camp and the same routine afterward. When it was time to speak to the counselors, Mike walked over and asked me, "Where is your dad?" We lost him last month, Mike, was my response. I know I thanked Mike for his ministry with the kids and in the case of my Dad, something rhymed in his head and watching these two players of the Bears may have been exactly what my Dad needed. I will never say that Mike Singletary saved my Dad; that is only possible through the Holy Spirit of God to save someone. But hearing the message of the gospel through these men in a different environment may have helped solidify what he was already processing. Losing my dad was tough, but through time and a pretty hectic lifestyle, I began to push my grief on. There is one more part of this story, and that is in August (same year), I was in the St. Louis airport waiting to board an airplane when I noticed a man walking down the terminal and from a distance, this man looked familiar to me. Yes, you guessed it correctly, Mike Singletary! I could not resist an opportunity to thank him. When I approached and mentioned that I had picked my son up from the camp, he immediately said, "Yes, your father passed away" and then asked me how I was doing. We sat and talked for what seemed 20 minutes or so about parents and families. I will never forget what a fine man Mike Singletary is and those encounters.

What lessons can be learned from this?

One is never too old to accept Christ. Nor is there a time which is too late to give your heart to God. Look at the criminal on the cross with Christ.

Always be waiting and watching and expecting God to move. Don't be afraid of those moments; embrace them.

Never be ashamed to share your faith; in fact, practice telling it. You are being watched, and others around you can be influenced by the Spirit moving.

Day 21

Romans 12:2

*Don't copy the behavior and customs of this world, but **let God** transform you into a new person by changing the way you think. Then you will learn to know God's will for you, which is **good and pleasing and perfect.***

You and I are creations from Almighty God! We were conceived and raised with the presence of God all around us. He planned us with a purpose in mind. As we grow and (hopefully, mature) we spread our knowledge and begin to take in that knowledge from sources all around us. Let me state this in strongest of words: The world is not friendly to those who listen to God. It is destructive and full of falsehoods. God has more, much more planned for you and he will transform you into what He created you to be. Do you need more evidence of this? Check out 2 Corinthians 5:17 - This means that anyone who belongs to Christ **has** become a **new** person. **The old life is gone; a new life has begun!** Spend more time with God and you will experience that friendship **He** wants to have with you!

Supporting Scripture:
2 Corinthians 5:17

Read through the Bible a Chapter a day

John 21

Notes

Day 22

Deuteronomy 30:19-20

*"Today I have given you the choice between **life and death**, between **blessings and curses**. Now I call on heaven and earth to witness the choice you make. **Oh, that you would choose life, so that you and your descendants might live!** You can make this choice by loving the LORD your God, obeying him, and committing yourself firmly to him. **This is the key to your life.** And if you love and obey the LORD, you **will** live long in the land the LORD swore to give your ancestors Abraham, Isaac, and Jacob.*

Take your pick on how you interpret this. To me, it touches so many ways from the conversation we are having about abortion. I don't know if this is discussed enough: Think about the issue from the time stand of a hundred years or more. If it is true that there are approximately 3000 abortions performed daily right here in our own country, That would mean that an entire generation of lives are lost over 100 years. We have lost our way and our minds. This is the exact opposite of what the scripture is telling us. The answer is part two of this scripture: Love the Lord YOUR God, Obey Him, Commit to Him and we WILL live long in the blessing God longs to give us!

Read through the Bible a Chapter a day

Genesis 1

Day 23

Genesis 1:1

In the beginning God created the heavens and the earth.

As I write this morning, I am reminded to take a moment and just contemplate Genesis 1:1. "In the beginning God created the heavens and the earth". As only God can do, order is the rule of the day. Not confusion - everything of God is in order. There is a lot to take in while you read Genesis 1. There is a beginning and guess what, God was already there. He has always been there! Again, I have to think about that one because at the end of the day, much of the entirety of scripture points us right back to this verse, Genesis 1:1. God created everything including the heavens and the earth. He also gave you and I the chance to view what He made and that it is very good! A few years ago, we had a chance to go to Nasa and the Space Center and as we were walking through learning about what is happening at Nasa, I believe God said to me.... Explore, explore all you want - Just remember, I made all this.

Supporting Scripture:
Psalms 19:1-5

Read through the Bible a Chapter a day

Genesis 2

Day 24

Jonah 2:7-10

As my life was slipping away,
I remembered the LORD.
And my earnest prayer went out to you
in your holy Temple.
Those who worship false gods
turn their backs on all God's mercies.
But I will offer sacrifices to you with songs of praise,
and I will fulfill all my vows.
For my salvation comes from the LORD alone."
Then the LORD ordered the fish to spit Jonah out onto the beach.

You and I may not be ministers, prophets, or ordained in any way. We can still tell people and be the people who offer the gospel and the truth of The Bible to others. Our lives are living testimonies of what we experience. We are being watched! I don't say that to creep anyone out, I say it because there is something different about you and people notice that. Let's be sure to be ready as Peter states it: "Instead, you must worship Christ as Lord of your life. And if someone asks about your hope as a believer, always be ready to explain it" (1 Peter 3:15).

Supporting Scripture:
1 Peter 3:15

Read through the Bible a Chapter a day

Genesis 3

Day 25

Genesis 19:26

But Lot's wife looked back as she was following behind him, and she turned into a pillar of salt.

We don't know much about Lot's wife. Yet her story is one that affects us all. Both Lot and his wife were reluctant to leave Sodom and Gomorrah. God mentions in Genesis 18 that He is going to destroy the city and Abraham pleads with Him. As you read that, it turns out that the only ones to be saved are Lot and his family. There is something about Sodom and Gomorrah that is appealing to Lot and his wife, yet the angels sent to destroy the cities tell them to hurry and leave with the warning: "Run for your lives! And don't look back or stop anywhere in the valley! Escape to the mountains, or you will be swept away!" But Lot's wife did look back and she turned into a pillar of salt.

Recent excavations in the plains of Jordan may have discovered the ruins of Sodom and Gomorrah, so time will tell the story of the cities. The lesson of Lot's wife however is this: Sin can be pleasurable! The long term effects of sin however are catastrophic. We are offered forgiveness by God and when we "turn around" and longingly look back at the past we are opening ourselves to stumbling in our own lives. Just like the angels warned Lot and his wife, God's word tells us - DON'T LOOK BACK! Keep going! Lean into God and depend upon Him.

Supporting Scripture:
Genesis 18:22-33
Ecclesiastes 7:10

Read through the Bible a Chapter a day

Genesis 4

Day 26

Luke 10:41-42

*But the Lord said to her, "My dear Martha, you are worried and upset over all these details! There is only **one** thing worth being concerned about. Mary has **discovered** it, and it will not be taken away from her."*

You might remember this story, in preparation of Jesus's visit, sisters Mary and Martha are busy getting things ready, only trouble is when Jesus actually arrives, Mary spends her time with Jesus, leaving all the work for Martha and that upsets her. She confronts Jesus. His response may have surprised her, but it's a response we all need to hear: **Set your focus on Jesus!** The story reminds me of a prayer walk I went on a few years ago. At the beginning of the journey, you were asked to take some luggage you would carry during your walk. Of course mine weighed what seems like 100 pounds. Then you went through a maze with stops along the way to help you remember events of your past. At the end, you dropped off the baggage which represented all the stuff you accumulated during your life (burdens, worries etc...). Finally. as you left and walked out, you came face to face with a sign which simply said: **I am all you need!**

Mary figured it out. How about you and I?

Supporting Scripture:
Psalm 27:4-5

Read through the Bible a Chapter a day

Genesis 5

Day 27

Psalm 19:1-6

The heavens proclaim the glory of God.
The skies display his craftsmanship.
Day after day they continue to speak;
night after night they **make him known.**
They speak without a sound or word;
their voice is never heard.
Yet their message has gone throughout the earth,
and their words to all the world.
God has made a home in the heavens for the sun.
It bursts forth like a radiant bridegroom after his wedding.
It rejoices like a great athlete eager to run the race.
The sun rises at one end of the heavens
and follows its course to the other end.
Nothing can hide from its heat.

I guess it is an obvious verse that I would choose the morning after an eclipse. Those able to watch the eclipse were treated to an amazing event. Only God can set this up and bless us with such precise measurement. That humans can actually predict fifty years with such precision is a testament to God's perfection and order of His creation! The next eclipse is scheduled for 2045. So glad to have been able to see this one.

Read through the Bible a Chapter a day

Genesis 6

Day 28

2 Samuel 22:31-33

"As for God, his way is perfect:
The Lord's word is flawless;
he shields all who take refuge in him.
For who is God besides the Lord?
And who is the Rock except our God?
It is God who arms me with strength
and keeps my way secure".

Another reminder of The Lord's perfect word. That perfect word comes from our perfect God. Look around you today, is there anything as beautiful as our perfect Lord?

Supporting Scripture:
2 Timothy 3:16
Psalm 18:30
Proverbs 30:5

Read through the Bible a Chapter a day

Genesis 7

Notes

Day 29

Romans 8:14-17

For all who are led by the Spirit of God are children of God.
So you have not received a spirit that makes you fearful slaves. Instead, you received God's Spirit when he adopted you as his own children. Now we call him, "Abba, Father." For his Spirit joins with our spirit to affirm that we are God's children. And since we are his children, we are his heirs. In fact, together with Christ we are heirs of God's glory. But if we are to share his glory, we must also share his suffering.

It is interesting when we go outside to take a walk or work in the yard etc.... everything around us continues as normal. The birds are singing, squirrels are running around, the seasons are unfolding before our eyes, the grass is greening and the trees are turning into their beautiful colors. What is going on in our society apparently only affects human beings. Think about that for a minute. It is no wonder why so many are freaked out by events. You and I hopefully have thought through this enough to know - we have not only been given the Spirit of God to free us from fear, but also to testify we are children of the living God, heirs of God and co-heirs with Christ! Let us praise God for what he has done through Jesus Christ!

Supporting Scripture:
Mark 14:36
Galatians 4:6

Read through the Bible a Chapter a day

Genesis 8

Day 30

2 Corinthians 5:17

*This means that **anyone** who belongs to Christ **has** become a **new** person. The old life is gone; a **new** life has begun!*

Many like to think that each new year brings a fresh start. It's nice to think that way, but we know that not much has really changed. If you want a fresh start, look to Jesus Christ! The Bible tells us that anyone who belongs to Christ has become a new person! The old life is gone and a new life has begun! To be honest with you, at my age, I did not even notice this until 7 or 8 years ago. It is so important to read the Bible. Every word, every page - it all has meaning! So if we really want to affect our lives and that of those around us - start a scripture club, or read these gems on your own!

Supporting Scripture:
John 1:13
Galatians 6:15

Read through the Bible a Chapter a day

Genesis 9

Day 31

Acts 3:19

*Now repent of your sins and **turn** to God, so that your sins may be wiped away.*

It sounds and seems so simple.
We don't hear enough about repentance. It is not enough to ask for forgiveness, we must reject and run from that sin - like a U-Turn! Somewhere along the way we have learned to accept sin as part of our lives without addressing the consequences. Peter reminds his audience that we must repent of our sins and turn to God!
Ask God to open your eyes to the sin in your life - Be ready to act. Run from the sin - as fast as you can!

Supporting Scripture:
Psalm 51.1
Isaiah 43:25
Acts 2:38

Read through the Bible a Chapter a day

Genesis 10

Day 32

Deuteronomy 34: 5-12

*And Moses the **servant** of the Lord died there in Moab, as the Lord had said. He buried him in Moab, in the valley opposite Beth Peor, but to this day no one knows where his grave is. Moses was a hundred and twenty years old when he died, **yet his eyes were not weak nor his strength gone**. The Israelites grieved for Moses in the plains of Moab thirty days, until the time of weeping and mourning was over.*
Now Joshua son of Nun was filled with the spirit of wisdom because Moses had laid his hands on him. So the Israelites listened to him and did what the Lord had commanded Moses.
*Since then, no prophet has risen in Israel like Moses, whom the Lord **knew** face to face, who did all those signs and wonders the Lord **sent him to do in Egypt**—to Pharaoh and to all his officials and to his whole land. For no one has ever shown the mighty power or performed the awesome deeds that Moses did in the sight of all Israel.*

How is the death of Moses a promise to us from God? If you read all of chapter 34 God reminds Moses why he is not crossing over the Jordon River with the Israelites. He sinned and dishonored the Lord (Deuteronomy 32:51). God did allowed him to see the promise land. Then Moses died. A careful read of these scriptures tell us Moses was in physically good shape, he just died. Today, we look at our health as a barometer of our lives. Here we see something few are willing to discuss - Moses did not die of natural causes. He was finished with the task of leadership to which God had called him. A person is immortal until God pleases to let his life come to an end. Some may find this controversial, you and I are here to serve God and each of us has an appointed time. Now that is not to say that we should tempt or test God, Jesus himself said this during his temptation in the wilderness. Despite the sin of Moses, he knew the Lord face to face and he accomplished all the Lord sent him to do in Egypt and beyond! Moses is proof that we can truly know God, we are under His protection!

Read through the Bible a Chapter a day

Genesis 11

Day 33

Acts 2:36

*"Therefore let all Israel be **assured** of this: God **has** made this Jesus, whom you crucified, both Lord and Christ."*

We have spent a good amount of time on KNOWING for certain our God and Savior. When Jesus Christ was born, Little did anyone understand what was coming. Oh, God knew every moment and how this would end. Now the message for the rest of time is: God made this Jesus both Lord and Christ. What do we do with that? Some are still crucifying Jesus. Some have chosen Jesus as both Lord, and Christ and others, well they don't know what to do with him. People run from him, he steps in their way trying to get their attention and for a million reasons they choose to run away. We saw that in the story of Jonah as he tried to go in the opposite direction God wanted him to go. There is no running from God. You either accept him or you don't and as Peter states here in the book of Acts not only will all of Israel be **assured** of this, the entire world and everyone in it can be assured of it. Because it is true! He is the Lord and He is Christ. He is Father and best friend. It matters not of the color of your skin, or where you are from - This Jesus is God!
Case Closed.

Supporting Scripture:
Matthew 28:18
Luke 2:11

Read through the Bible a Chapter a day

Genesis 12

Day 34

Hebrews 6:13-20

*When God made his promise to Abraham, since there was no one greater for him to swear by, he swore by himself, saying, "I **will** surely bless you and give you many descendants." And so after **waiting** patiently, Abraham received what **was** promised. Men swear by someone greater than themselves, and the oath confirms what is said and puts an end to all argument. Because God wanted to make the **unchanging** nature of his purpose very clear to the heirs of what was promised, he **confirmed** it with an oath. God did this so that, by two unchangeable things in which it is **impossible for God to lie**, we who have fled to take hold of the hope set before us may be greatly encouraged. We have this hope as an anchor for the soul, firm and secure. It enters the inner sanctuary behind the curtain, where Jesus, who went before us has **entered** on **our** behalf. He has become a high priest forever, in the order of Melchizedek.*

God made a promise to Abraham, one that continues to be fulfilled even today. Abraham's part in this was waiting patiently. Oh, he and Sara worked out a shortcut plan to have children and that has affected history since, but he believed God who gave him Isaac as a son at a very great old age. He received what was promised to him. God's nature never changes. And what I often forget with all the promises in the Bible - **It is impossible for God to lie.** You and I have a hope that is not understood in the world - we have Jesus, who is pleading for us as an intercessor, and the example of this is Melchizedek. (Read Hebrews chapter 7 and Genesis Chapter 14:18-20 for more information on Melchizedek) Jesus himself prays for us!

Isn't this amazing? It's true, every single word!

Supporting Scripture:
Genesis 22:16
Genesis 14:18-20
Luke 1:73-75
Hebrews 7

Read through the Bible a Chapter a day

Genesis 13

Day 35

2 Kings 22:8-13

Hilkiah the high priest said to Shaphan the secretary, "I have found the Book of the Law in the temple of the LORD." He gave it to Shaphan, who read it. Then Shaphan the secretary went to the king and reported to him: "Your officials have paid out the money that was in the temple of the LORD and have entrusted it to the workers and supervisors at the temple." Then Shaphan the secretary informed the king, "Hilkiah the priest has given me a book." And Shaphan read from it in the presence of the king.
*When the king **heard** the words of the Book of the Law, he **tore** his robes. He gave these orders to Hilkiah the priest, Ahikam son of Shaphan, Akbor son of Micaiah, Shaphan the secretary and Asaiah the king's attendant: "Go and inquire of the LORD for me and for the people and for all Judah about what is written in this book that has been found. Great is the LORD's anger that burns against us because those who have gone before us have not obeyed the words of this book; they have not acted in accordance with all that is written there concerning us."*

Everyone probably has a place in their home where things accumulate. A closet, an attic, the junk drawer. We downsized a number of years ago and there are still boxes we have not looked in since that move! I wonder if that is what happened here. **They found the book of the law**. There is no mention where they found it except in the Lord's Temple. I cannot help but to notice Josiah's reaction to the words as they they were read to him. It's as if they are words he has never read. All the customs and sayings that were passed down to him, it took God's word to open his eyes and see he and his nation's true condition. I myself have encountered countless scriptures I had never read much less heard about when I was in Church (I am not blaming Church, God opened my eyes when I took the time to read for myself). What I want to emphasize is this: God's word changes things. Our perceptions, our attitudes, our whole being and if you continue to read 2 Kings you read that the entire nation was reminded of God's word as it was read DIRECTLY to them.

Supporting Scripture:
1 Samuel 3:21
Psalm 46:10

Read through the Bible a Chapter a day

Genesis 14

Notes

Day 36

1 Samuel 17:48

As Goliath moved closer to attack, David quickly ran out to meet him.

One of the most memorable stories of the Bible is that of David and Goliath. This battle shaped up to be one of the most lopsided in all the stories of the Bible. Here you have a hardened warrior - a literal giant against a boy with no battle experience. Yet the appearance is visual only. We quickly find out that Goliath relied only on himself, David relied on God. Words matter in the Bible, and we see how David approached the battle - he ran to meet his opponent. There was no hiding behind trees or trickery - David ran to meet his opponent. We know how this ends, David faced up to his challenger, knowing God was with him. We can do the same! It is all about knowing God!

Supporting Scripture:
John 4:4

Read through the Bible a Chapter a day

Genesis 15

Day 37

Proverbs 3:7-8

Don't be impressed with your own wisdom.
*Instead, **fear the LORD** and **turn away from evil.***
*Then you will have **healing** for your body*
*and **strength** for your bones.*

Here is another scripture that advises us to turn from sin and run from it. In fact, the Bible tells us that we will have healing of our bodies by following the advice. And it makes sense doesn't it? Someone who lies has to continue to lie to cover up his or her original lie and it just grows from there. It literally can make you sick.. We don't have to look far to see the ramifications of the results of sin.
More practical advice to us from God's word!

Supporting Scripture:
Genesis 39: 6-12
Acts 3:19

Read through the Bible a Chapter a day

Genesis 16

Day 38

Obadiah 15

"The day is near when I, the LORD,
will judge all godless nations!
As you have done to Israel,
so it will be done to you.
***All** your evil deeds*
***will** fall back on your own heads".*

The Bible is filled with warnings about nations that mess with Israel. The United States has been the only true friend of Israel since it was re-founded as a nation in 1948. It is a dangerous position to be against God when we are trying to placate the world and not Him. Oh wait, we need to understand whether it is us as individuals or as a nation - Lean into God and depend upon HIM alone! The Bible tells us over and over again: This is about Him and His people. You are His when you accept the free gift of Jesus Christ!

Supporting Scripture:
Genesis 12:2-3
Exodus 23:22

Read through the Bible a Chapter a day

Genesis 17

Day 39

Joshua 1:1-9

*After the death of Moses the LORD's servant, the LORD spoke to Joshua son of Nun, Moses' assistant. He said, "Moses my servant is dead. Therefore, the time has come for you to lead these people, the Israelites, across the Jordan River into the land I am giving them. I **promise** you what I **promised** Moses: 'Wherever you set foot, you will be on land I have given you— from the Negev wilderness in the south to the Lebanon mountains in the north, from the Euphrates River in the east to the Mediterranean Sea in the west, including all the land of the Hittites.' No one will be able to stand against you as long as you live. **For I will be with you** as I was with Moses. I will not fail you or abandon you. "**Be strong and courageous**, for you are the one who will lead these people to possess all the land I swore to their ancestors I would give them. **Be strong and very courageous.** Be careful to obey all the instructions Moses gave you. Do not deviate from them, turning either to the right or to the left. Then you will be successful in everything you do. **Study this Book** of Instruction continually. **Meditate on it day and night** so you will be sure to obey everything written in it. Only then will you prosper and succeed in all you do. This is my command—**be strong and courageous!** Do not be afraid or discouraged. **For the LORD your God is with you wherever you go.**"*

This section of Joshua is filled with mighty promises. God is speaking directly to Joshua and three times God says "Be strong and courageous" and twice reminds Joshua that God is always with us and will never leave us nor forsake us. What more do we need to face uncertainty? Has something changed? Does God not honor his promises any more? These days, people act as if God is not here. They have trusted everything The Lord has asked us not to trust. Maybe The Lord is waiting for us... to just stand and be courageous.

Supporting Scripture:
Matthew 28:20

Read through the Bible a Chapter a day

Genesis 18

Day 40

Acts 10:34-36

*Then Peter replied, "I see very clearly that God shows no favoritism. In every nation he accepts those who fear him and do what is right. This is the message of **Good News** for the people of Israel—that **there is peace** with God through Jesus Christ, who is Lord of all.*

Through all the Apostles had seen and been through, God clearly was not finished teaching them His gospel. Here we see that the Message of God is not exclusive to the people of Israel but to all who fear Him and follow Jesus Christ. God shows no favoritism, what a fantastic promise delivered to us through the Bible!

Supporting Scripture:
Acts 15:9

Read through the Bible a Chapter a day

Genesis 19

Day 41

1 John 5:13-15

*I have written this to you who believe in the name of the Son of God, so that you may **know** you have eternal life. And we are confident that he hears us whenever we ask for anything that pleases him. And since we **know** he hears us when we make our requests, we also **know** that he will give us what we ask for.*

I have been asked how I choose which scriptures to use for these messages. I can tell you that there is no formula, not pattern, no hidden plan. There is an agenda however, and here it is - The entire Bible brings us to one conclusion: We can trust and KNOW: God's love is evident throughout, and he wants you and I to move beyond just hoping it's true and KNOWING Him through these words! I read a chapter a day (it takes about 3 years to get through the entire Bible, and many of the messages are taken during my daily reading. There are times when I am inspired by a message from someone like Greg Laurie or Charles Stanley and sometimes I even close my eyes and close the book and just point to something to write (yes, I do). Here is the thing, EVERY WORD has meaning in this treasure chest of God's Love and at the end of the day, no matter where it is located, God's story is there! Be inspired and KNOW God!

Supporting Scripture:
Job 19:25
Psalm 46:10

Read through the Bible a Chapter a day

Genesis 20

Day 42

Job 19:25-27

*"But as for me, I **know** that my Redeemer lives,
and he **will** stand upon the earth at last.
And after my body has decayed,
yet in my body I **will** see God!
I **will** see him for myself.
Yes, I **will** see him with my own eyes.
I am overwhelmed at the thought!*

The Book of Job is said to be one of the oldest in the Bible. Dating back to sometime between 2000-1500 BC, which means it is probably before the exodus from Egypt. Job's relationship with God was firm. He says: "I know my redeemer lives!" So how can we be sure of God? There are several references in the Bible to the truth of the word of God. Proverbs 30:5 states: "**Every** word of God is pure: He is a shield unto them that put their trust in him". I have come to believe that literally. Looking at the scripture above is the word "know". Read God's word, and you will come to KNOW that every word is there for a purpose. To **know** without doubt of God and
to **know** that you have eternal life because you believe in Jesus Christ is why we have a Bible!

Supporting Scripture:
Proverbs 30:5

Read through the Bible a Chapter a day

Genesis 21

Notes

Day 43

Isaiah 43:18-19

"But forget all that—
it is nothing compared to what I am going to do.
For I am about to do something new.
See, I have already begun! Do you not see it?
I will make a pathway through the wilderness.
I will create rivers in the dry wasteland.

Keep your glance going forward, not on the past. You can't change it and you and I have probably created some real chaos as we walked along this path we call life. Trusting in ourselves seems ok; in fact, we might even begin to think that is what we are suppose to do. Then, as we continue that walk suddenly we realize we have a very short dimension to work with; that is, going forward - and with no knowledge of the future. God however, tells us to trust Him. He has the insight we need and the greatest part of all is that he offers security for the walk. The more we rely on him, the safer we are!

Supporting Scripture:
Ecclesiastes 7:10

Read through the Bible a Chapter a day

Genesis 22

Day 44

Matthew 6:5-6

"And when you pray, do not be like the hypocrites, for they love to pray standing in the synagogues and on the street corners to be seen by others. Truly I tell you, they have received their reward in full. But when you pray, go into your room, close the door and pray to your Father, who is unseen. Then your Father, who sees what is done in secret, **will** *reward you.*

Jesus is very upfront about our prayer habits. Go into a private room when it is only God and you and pour your heart out! Now I have a favor to ask from you today. When you have family, friend or associate needing prayer, go to your private place and pour out your heart to Him.

Supporting Scripture:
2 Kings 19:14

Read through the Bible a Chapter a day

Genesis 23

Day 45

Psalm 5:3

*In the morning, O LORD, you **hear** my voice;*
*in the morning I lay my requests **before** you*
*and **wait** in **expectation**.*

God hears our prayers whenever we say them. God hears everything you say or think. The intentional time you spend with God are the times that are most cherished. Then there is the waiting. There are two words that get my attention this morning: **Wait** and **expectation**. This can be most challenging. If we change our approach from just waiting to waiting with expectation you may move from doubt to hope. Which eventually turns to confidence. There is the story of King Hezekiah's response when Judah was being threatened by the King of Assyria. 2 Kings 19:14 says Hezekiah took the letter and spread it out before the Lord and then Hezekiah prayed to the Lord. Do you see the intentionality behind his actions. He prayed to God knowing God was with him. Have you done this? Is there something you are praying for - debt, children, spouse, family, nation - virtually anything! You can do this as well. The point is: Pray with intention. Prepare and find a quiet, private spot to reach out to God. He will honor your intentions - That's a promise from God!

Supporting Scripture:
2 Kings 19:14

Read through the Bible a Chapter a day

Genesis 24

Day 46

Acts 13:38-41

*"**Brothers, listen!** We are here to proclaim that through this man Jesus there is forgiveness for your sins. **Everyone who believes in him is made right in God's sight**—something the law of Moses could never do. Be careful! Don't let the prophets' words apply to you. For they said,*
'Look, you mockers,
be amazed and die!
For I am doing something in your own day,
something you wouldn't believe
even if someone told you about it.'"

When we are asked to listen - *pay attention!*
Paul and his companions were traveling on the island of Cyprus and were preaching the Gospel. Their message? Everyone who believes in Him (Jesus) is made right in God's sight. We have read these words before in John 6:29: Jesus told them, **"This is the only work God wants from you: Believe in the one he has sent."** Those in the synagogues thirst for more from Paul, the word of God is like fresh water to those who will listen, even today. As we know from the book of Hebrews: For the word of God is alive and powerful. It is sharper than the sharpest two-edged sword, cutting between soul and spirit, between joint and marrow. It exposes our innermost thoughts and desires. Nothing in all creation is hidden from God. Everything is naked and exposed before his eyes, and he is the one to whom we are accountable. (Hebrews 4:12-13)
Our work is to believe in the one God sent!

Supporting Scripture:
John 6:29
John 3:15
Hebrews 4:12-13

Read through the Bible a Chapter a day

Genesis 25

Day 47

Proverbs 13:11

Wealth from get-rich-quick schemes quickly disappears;
wealth from hard work grows over time.

The Bible advises us on every issue in our lives. In this instance, it advises you and I to save for the future. It also tells us that the right method - hard work and consistent saving, little by little is the right way. Get rich quick schemes are not the best when it comes to longevity and the Bible says wealth from such ways disappear quickly.
Sound advice directly from the Bible!

Supporting Scripture:
Proverbs 10:2

Read through the Bible a Chapter a day

Genesis 26

Day 48

Isaiah 26:2-4

Open the gates
that the righteous nation may enter,
the nation that keeps faith.
*You **will** keep in **perfect** peace*
*him whose mind **is** steadfast,*
because he trusts in you.
Trust in the LORD forever,
*for the LORD, the LORD himself, **is** the Rock eternal.*

We can look at this theme from Isaiah two different ways, praying for our nation. I am not sure in its entire history where this turmoil sits, but I know in my lifetime it's pretty bad. With that in mind, the scripture also relates to us as individuals. God promises those who trust in him peace, not just any peace - perfect peace. Look what Paul tells us at the end of 2 Corinthians (13:11) Finally, brothers, good-by. Aim for perfection, listen to my appeal, be of one mind, live in peace. **And the God of love and peace will be with you.**
Greet one another with a holy kiss. All the saints send their greetings.
May the grace of the Lord Jesus Christ, and the love of God, and the fellowship of the Holy Spirit be with you all.

Supporting Scripture:
2 Corinthians 13:11

Read through the Bible a Chapter a day

Genesis 27

Day 49

Acts 17:11

And the people of Berea were more open-minded than those in Thessalonica, and they listened eagerly to Paul's message. They searched the Scriptures day after day to see if Paul and Silas were teaching the truth.

What was it that convinced you to believe in Jesus Christ? How did you decide if it was true? It has taken me decades to finally investigate what I was told. I admit to all of you this morning I really did not understand much of what I was hearing in church or what I was reading, I basically just went along for the ride. I finally decided I was tired of my journey of confusion and started a solid investigation - I read the Bible. I learned early on: The Bible speaks about its authority as the word of God on its own. Certain scripture like: **Every word** of God proves true. He **is** a shield to all who come to him for protection. **Proverbs 30:5.** God's word is available to you and I to investigate what you hear and process. Every time you open it with solid intention I am convinced God's honors your labor!

Supporting Scripture:
Proverbs 30:5
2 Timothy 3:16

Read through the Bible a Chapter a day

Genesis 28

Notes

Day 50

Mark 7:6-8

Jesus replied, "You hypocrites! Isaiah was right when he prophesied about you, for he wrote, 'These people honor me with their lips, but their hearts are far from me. Their worship is a farce, for they teach man-made ideas as commands from God.' For you ignore God's law and substitute your own tradition."

What Jesus is saying has been true for really long time. He spoke of the "religious" Jews and priests who were looking for any reason they could find to discredit Jesus or use him to work a system in Jerusalem. Today, Unfortunately, the same thing happens. There are churches where God's word is not preached and they settle for whatever the hot topic is brewing. Partial blame may be the decline of worshippers in church and leadership decides to stop preaching the Bible because of its ability to as Hebrews 4:12 states: *"sharper than any double-edged sword, it penetrates even to dividing soul and spirit, joints and marrow; it judges the thoughts and attitudes of the heart."* Many cannot stand the truth and leave.

Churches should consider doubling down on using the Bible as the only source they use. Forget the headlines, forget what social media says and teach the only real source of truth: The Bible!

Supporting Scripture:
Isaiah 29:13

Read through the Bible a Chapter a day

Genesis 29

Day 51

Acts 8:1

*Saul was one of the witnesses, and he agreed completely with the killing of Stephen. A great wave of persecution began that day, sweeping over the church in Jerusalem; and **all the believers** except the apostles were **scattered** through the regions of Judea and Samaria.*

After the killing of Stephen, there was a great wave of persecution against the Christians in Jerusalem. As tragic as this was, it was the event which scattered the believers to begin to spread throughout the region. And this was foretold by Jesus himself. Acts 1:8 tells us this: **"But you will receive power when the Holy Spirit comes upon you. And you will be my witnesses, telling people about me everywhere— in Jerusalem, throughout Judea, in Samaria, and to the ends of the earth."**
God can use every event that happens around us to His glory and His purpose!

Supporting Scripture:
Acts 1:8

Read through the Bible a Chapter a day

Genesis 30

Day 52

Zechariah 8:16-17

But this is what you must do: Tell the truth to each other. Render verdicts in your courts that are just and that lead to peace. Don't scheme against each other. Stop your love of telling lies that you swear are the truth. I hate all these things, says the LORD."

Look how God expects us to act among each other. Speak the truth and be fair! Don't scheme and plot evil against each other. Stop telling lies that you swear are the truth. When you look out and around the world today, these are words we need to heed if not for any other reason than God hates them! We should as well. Just as we see in this perfect word, living by these standards sets us apart and the world is watching....

How will we respond?

Supporting Scripture:
Psalm 15:2-5

Read through the Bible a Chapter a day

Genesis 31

Day 53

Genesis 32:24-30

So Jacob was left alone, and a man wrestled with him till daybreak. When the man saw that he could not overpower him, he touched the socket of Jacob's hip so that his hip was wrenched as he wrestled with the man. Then the man said, "Let me go, for it is daybreak."
But Jacob replied, "I will not let you go unless you bless me."
The man asked him, "What is your name?"
"Jacob," he answered.
*Then the man said, "**Your name will no longer be Jacob, but Israel,** because you have struggled with God and with humans and have overcome."*
Jacob said, "Please tell me your name."
But he replied, "Why do you ask my name?" Then he blessed him there.
So Jacob called the place Peniel, saying, "It is because I saw God face to face, and yet my life was spared."

During this time we are walking together, it can be a bit confusing and troubling. It might help to think about Peter during Jesus trial and crucifixion. Upon his resurrection the angel who appeared to Mary said **"But go, tell his disciples and Peter, (Mark 16:7) 'He is going ahead of you into Galilee. There you will see him, just as he told you.'"** "And Peter" - God knows our names! How do we know this for sure? How can we know for sure God's promises are for us, you and I? Take a peek at **Isaiah 43:1**:

Call out to God - HE KNOWS YOUR NAME!

Supporting Scripture:
Genesis 35:9-11
Mark 16:7
Isaiah 43:1

Read through the Bible a Chapter a day

Genesis 32-33

Day 54

Esther 3:5-6

When Haman saw that Mordecai would not kneel down or pay him honor, he was enraged. Yet having learned who Mordecai's people were, he scorned the idea of killing only Mordecai. Instead Haman looked for a way to destroy all Mordecai's people, the Jews, throughout the whole kingdom of Xerxes.

We don't have to look too far to see how this story resembles where we are in today's world. The story of Haman is a graphic illustration of our enemy's goal: to steal, kill and destroy God's people (John 10:10). He will first try to get us out of relationship with God, and then he will seek to destroy us. Sin can seem so alluring, but once it has its claws in us, it will pull us down so fast that we won't know what hit us. Satan's end game is always destruction, misery and death.
By contrast, Jesus, wants to give us "a rich and satisfying life" (John 10:10). The Shepherd's primary objective for his flock is that they flourish, be well fed and cared for. content and satisfied. A rich and satisfying life is not necessarily a long one, but it certainly is a full one. Medical science seeks to add years to our lives, but only Christ can add life to our years!

By the way, Haman's wicked plan backfired, and he ended up hanging on the very same gallows he erected for others. God's will prevails no matter what Satan may plot for our destruction.

Supporting Scripture:
John 10:10

Read through the Bible a Chapter a day

Genesis 34

Day 55

Esther 4:14

For if you remain silent at this time, relief and deliverance for the Jews **will** *arise from another place, but you and your father's family will perish. And who knows but that you have come to royal position for such a time as this?*

If you have a few minutes, read this chapter of Esther. There are no mistakes in God's plan. You have been given everything you need to live the successful life God has given you. As we have been reading this, God's word - you will read hundreds of promises that are yours to act on. **Yet who knows whether you have come to the kingdom for such a time as this?"**

It's your time!

Supporting Scripture:
Esther 4
Genesis 45:7

Read through the Bible a Chapter a day

Genesis 35

Day 56

Habakkuk 2:3

*For the revelation awaits an appointed time;
It speaks of the end
and will not prove false.
Though it linger, **wait for it;**
It will certainly come and will not delay*

Whenever we go through a time in our lives of hardship and probably even a more pronounced period as the entire nation and world stumbles along, the tendency is to think we are closing in on the appointed day God has chosen to bring the end. The scripture was pointing out the time that the Babylonian empire would fall. This scripture however, also speaks for us - today. We are approaching THAT time. It will happen, God has promised it. There is a day, a day for your blessing, a day for revival, and even though things may look bleak, THAT day is fast approaching.

Supporting Scripture:
Psalm 27:13-14

Read through the Bible a Chapter a day

Genesis 36

Notes

Day 57

1 Thessalonians 5:19-24

Do not quench the Spirit. Do not treat prophecies with contempt but test them all; hold on to what is good, reject every kind of evil.
*May God himself, the God of peace, sanctify you through and through. May your whole spirit, soul and body be kept blameless at the coming of our Lord Jesus Christ. The one who calls you **is** faithful, and **he will** do it.*

Another of God's promises, The one who calls you **IS** faithful, and **HE WILL** do it. You and I are invited to test the prophecies. Investigate them. Any time we open the Bible and read we subject ourselves to God's truth he pours into us. God alone is able to do this. Look, we are talking about the very same God who created the universe with a command! When I read this, I am reminded: TV or talk shows or the internet or the newspaper are not going to fill you with confidence for today - nope, the opposite of that. God's word is the only place you are going to receive the promises of God.

Supporting Scripture:
Ephesians 5:20

Read through the Bible a Chapter a day

Genesis 37

Day 58

Psalm 1

***Blessed** is the man*
who does not walk in the counsel of the wicked
or stand in the way of sinners
or sit in the seat of mockers.
But his delight is in the law of the Lord,
and on his law he meditates day and night.
He is like a tree planted by streams of water,
which yields its fruit in season
and whose leaf does not wither.
Whatever he does prospers.
Not so the wicked!
They are like chaff
that the wind blows away.
Therefore the wicked will not stand in the judgment,
nor sinners in the assembly of the righteous.
For the Lord watches over the way of the righteous,
but the way of the wicked will perish.

Don't just study the Bible, apply its truth to your life. While it is excellent to read, study and memorize the Scriptures, the truth of God's word must also sink in. Apply what you have learned into your lives. It's not just the way we mark our Bibles that's important, it's how our Bibles mark us. Let's let what we meditate on affect how we live our lives.

Supporting Scripture:
James 1:22

Read through the Bible a Chapter a day

Genesis 38

Day 59

James 2:21-24

*Don't you remember that our ancestor Abraham was shown to be right with God by his actions when he offered his son Isaac on the altar? You see, his faith and his actions worked together. His actions made his faith complete. And so it happened just as the Scriptures say: "Abraham believed God, and God counted him as righteous because of his faith." He was even called the **friend of God**. So you see, we are shown to be right with God by what we do, not by faith alone*

Faith that does not move you to action may not be a mature faith. I would not say that if I don't experience it myself. Who takes the time to go out and start your car and then just sits there? You have to put the car in drive to start moving and that is the way our faith is. Move on your faith! There have been times (if I am being honest), that I am almost paralyzed by fear when I need to act in faith. Once I have moved in that right direction - God has been by my side every time! Move on your faith, it's like flexing a muscle - there is no other way to gain faith strength!

Supporting Scripture:
Hebrews 11:32-33

Read through the Bible a Chapter a day

Genesis 39

Day 60

Ephesians 3:20-21

Now all glory to God, who is able, through his mighty power at work within us, to accomplish infinitely more than we might ask or think. Glory to him in the church and in Christ Jesus through all generations, forever and ever! Amen.

When you are taking a poll, you are might be asked to rate something from 1-10. On a scale of God's measurements, it might start at one - but there is no limit to the topside because it is infinite. Don't limit God, trust him and he may do far more than anything you can think of.

Don't give up, ever!

Supporting Scripture:
Romans 16:25
Jude 24

Read through the Bible a Chapter a day

Genesis 40

Day 61

Acts 17:24-29

The God who made the world and everything in it is the Lord of heaven and earth and does not live in temples built by human hands. And he is not served by human hands, as if he needed anything. **Rather, he himself gives everyone life and breath and everything else.** *From one man he made all the nations, that they should inhabit the whole earth; and* **he marked out their appointed times in history and the boundaries of their lands.** *God did this so that they would* **seek him** *and perhaps* **reach out for him and find him,** *though* **he is not far from any one of us. 'For in him we live and move and have our being.'** *As some of your own poets have said,* **'We are his offspring.'**
"Therefore since **we are** *God's offspring, we should not think that the divine being is like gold or silver or stone—an image made by human design and skill.*

From Paul's own lips... There are no accidents, no coincidence, no luck. It is all known by God, and like Paul's example these things are done so that we may:
>Seek Him
>Reach out to Him
>Find Him

For truly, he is not far from any of us! We live and move and in fact everything we do, we do in the presence of God.

You are a child of God - his offspring - YOU REALLY ARE, stop with the doubt and live!

Supporting Scripture:
Deuteronomy 10:14

Read through the Bible a Chapter a day

Genesis 41

Day 62

1 Timothy 1:15-17

Here's a word you can take to heart and depend on: Jesus Christ came into the world to save sinners. I'm proof—Public Sinner Number One— of someone who could never have made it apart from sheer mercy. And now he shows me off—evidence of his endless patience—to those who are right on the edge of trusting him forever.
Deep honor and bright glory
to the King of All Time—
One God, Immortal, Invisible,
ever and always. Oh, yes!

Because this is true, it is a promise received. Christ came into this world to save sinners - You and I! Paul is very clear that he is being used as an example - Let's be clear here: God uses us as examples as well! Make no mistake, You and I are being watched by others! He displays his mercy and patience to those who will believe in him and receive eternal life! Praise him for what he has done and is going to do - It's a done deal!

Supporting Scripture:
John 3:17

Read through the Bible a Chapter a day

Genesis 42

Day 63

2 Timothy 3:16-17

All Scripture is inspired by God and is useful to teach us what is true and to make us realize what is wrong in our lives. It corrects us when we are wrong and teaches us to do what is right. God uses it to prepare and equip his people to do every good work.

God's word is perfect and every word is useful. Please, don't take my word for it, look what the Bible says about itself:

Supporting Scripture:
2 Samuel 22:31
1 Thessalonians 2:13
2 Peter 1:21
Proverbs 30:5
Psalm 18:30
Psalm 119:160
1 Samuel 3:21

Read through the Bible a Chapter a day

Genesis 43

Notes

Day 64

Hebrews 4:12 -13

For the word of God is alive and powerful. It is sharper than the sharpest two-edged sword, cutting between soul and spirit, between joint and marrow. It exposes our innermost thoughts and desires. Nothing in all creation is hidden from God. Everything is naked and exposed before his eyes, and he is the one to whom we are accountable.

Continuing on from yesterday, my goodness, what an encouragement this is and frankly something we need to be reminded of daily, especially these days! This God of ours is true and faithful and his word is living and active. He will never lead us wrong or forsake us! If you struggle with that or are struggling at all, keep these verses and read them again and again.

Supporting Scripture:
2 Samuel 22:31
1 Thessalonians 2:13
2 Peter 1:21
Proverbs 30:5
Psalm 18:30
Psalm 119:160
1 Samuel 3:21
2 Timothy 3:16-17

Read through the Bible a Chapter a day

Genesis 44

Day 65

James 1:12-15

*God blesses those who patiently endure testing and temptation. Afterward they will receive the **crown of life** that God has **promised** to those who love him. And remember, when you are being tempted, do not say, "God is tempting me." God is never tempted to do wrong, and he never tempts anyone else. Temptation comes from our own desires, which entice us and drag us away. These desires give birth to sinful actions. And when sin is allowed to grow, it gives birth to death.*

James is rather straight forward in his advice to us. Early in the chapter he discusses wisdom and later tells us: "Don't just read God's word, you must do what it says". Here he discusses patience and temptation. Temptation, in his words are self induced - by our own desires. No, the good stuff from God is never temptation but whatever is good and perfect, starting with His word (James 1:18)

Supporting Scripture:
James 1:18

Read through the Bible a Chapter a day

Genesis 45

Day 66

John 3:16-17

*"For **this is** how God loved the world: He **gave** his one and only Son, so that **everyone** who believes in him **will not** perish but **have** eternal life. God sent his Son into the world not to judge the world, but to **save** the world through him.*

John 3:16 is arguably the most recognizable scripture in the Bible. As people read the Bible, they recognize that God had a plan to restore man long before there was any thing else. Before Adam and Eve, before the flood, before Moses (remember Alpha and Omega, the beginning and the end?). In fact, there was just God. We know that the Bible is an illustration of the love of God, it is God's love story for us. So it makes complete sense that God would have a plan for a permanent solution to the sin separation problem. He would do it himself. I struggled with Jesus being God's son for a long time until I realized, The Trinity (Father, Son, Holy Spirit) are all one, Jesus being Son. He is God! Isn't that great? Our friend, Our Savior who is a man - is God! Our God! During these days. we have to learn to lean into God and depend upon him. After all, he is in complete control. This plan was fulfilled during Easter. Let's put a personal touch on this. For this is how God loved _____ (put your name in the spot), He gave his one and only Son for _____ (your name). If you and I were the only people to be saved - Jesus would have still died for us! That is what God really thinks of you - check out Isaiah 49:16, then read John 4 or Luke 15.

Supporting Scripture:
Isaiah 49:16
John 4
Luke 15

Read through the Bible a Chapter a day

Genesis 46

Day 67

1 Peter 5:6-11

*Humble yourselves, therefore, under God's mighty hand, that **he may lift you up** in due time. Cast **all** your anxiety on him because he cares for you. Be self controlled and alert. Your enemy the devil prowls around like a roaring lion looking for someone to devour. Resist him, standing firm in the faith, because you know that your brothers throughout the world are undergoing the same kind of sufferings.*
*And the God of all grace, **who called you** to his eternal glory in Christ, after you have suffered a little while, **will himself restore you** and make you strong, firm and steadfast. To him be the power for ever and ever. Amen.*

Today's promise is that God will restore you. You can be sure that you are never far from God, and your circumstances never out of God's care - lean into him for all your troubles (I like the word cast, because it literally means to throw off and throw them to God). Know that he absolutely loves and care about you and for you. Be comforted by the fact that whatever you are going through, you are not the only one to have gone the route you are on, even though it may feel like it. As the Bible states: know that the family of believers throughout the world is undergoing the same kinds of suffering!

Supporting Scripture:
Psalm 37:5

Read through the Bible a Chapter a day

Genesis 47

Day 68

Psalm 37:23-24

The LORD directs the steps of the godly.
*He delights in **every** detail of their lives.*
*Though they stumble, they will **never** fall,*
for the LORD holds them by the hand.

Running to God **is** the answer to **all** things.
I like that quote. It is true, when we turn to God's Word and declare it over our circumstances it will bring real power and peace.
There is literally **nothing** that stands in our place between us and God if we hand it over to God. He delights in EVERY detail!

Ah yes, running to God is the answer to all things!

Supporting Scripture:
Numbers 14:8

Read through the Bible a Chapter a day

Genesis 48

Day 69

Matthew 27:50-51

Then Jesus shouted out again, and he released his spirit. At that moment the curtain in the sanctuary of the Temple was torn in two, from top to bottom.

The Veil of the Temple was torn from top to bottom. What does this mean? We have to go back to Exodus 26:31-33 to realize that the curtain separated the most Holy place from everything else. But now, the veil is torn, nothing separates us from the direct presence with God. Hebrews 10:19-20 explains a bit further: **Therefore, brothers and sisters, since we have confidence to enter the Most Holy Place by the blood of Jesus, by a new and living way opened for us through the curtain, that is, his body,**

Supporting Scripture:
Exodus 26:30-33
Hebrews 10:19-20

Read through the Bible a Chapter a day

Genesis 49

Day 70

Matthew 28:20

*Teach these new disciples to obey all the commands I have given you. And be **sure** of this:* ***I am with you always, even to the end of the age.***

As we walk into day 70 of this devotion, we might be thinking about next year, or maybe next month, next week - heck you just want to get through today. There is a lot thrown at us these days. I don't know about you, but I am comforted knowing that Jesus has drawn a circle and you and I are in it - with HIM! He has promised to be with us ALWAYS - even to end of the age! He is the author of our lives and so it does not matter if it's the end of our physical lives here on earth, or the end of all time as we know it - we can be sure of this: Christ is with us! **I AM** is with us!

Supporting Scripture:
John 14:26ß

Read through the Bible a Chapter a day

Genesis 50

Notes

Day 71

Genesis 50:19-20

But Joseph said to them, "Don't be afraid. Am I in the place of God? You intended to harm me, **but God** *intended it for good to accomplish what is now being done, the saving of many lives.*

The phrase "But God" indicates how a different idea to a circumstance ended. Whether it was a flood or the resurrection of Jesus, God took what looked like a dismal end and provided the ultimate hope. Here we see Joseph and his explanation to his brothers of how God provided his "But God" moment. Here, (at least in my view) is a personal response to a life that was both filled with sorrow and a life that was truly touched by God. At the end of his story he realized that no matter what life brought him, it was God who was working, not only for his good but to save countless lives. I hope we all can see how God is moving in our lives; if not, ask him to show you - he will!

Supporting Scripture:
Romans 8:28

Read through the Bible a Chapter a day

Matthew 1

Day 72

Amos 5:4

Now this is what the LORD says to the family of Israel:
"Come back to me and live!

That's it folks, God tells us: Seek me and live. No where else in our crazy world do we hear such a simple message. The light of the world is telling you and I to seek him - him alone. I am not going to say nothing else matters..... it does, its just not as urgent. I am not going to say - it's easy..... it is not. No, the message to seek God is a simple message and we should focus like a laser on it. There is life in God, everything else gets blown away.
Keep reading the Bible, God's voice to us.

Supporting Scripture:
Deuteronomy 4:29
Jeremiah 29:13

Read through the Bible a Chapter a day

Matthew 2

Day 73

Psalm 3

O LORD, I have so many enemies;
so many are against me.
So many are saying,
"God will never rescue him!"
But you, O LORD, are a shield around me;
you are my glory, the one who holds my head high.
I cried out to the LORD,
and he answered me from his holy mountain.
I lay down and slept,
yet I woke up in safety,
for the LORD was watching over me.
I am not afraid of ten thousand enemies
who surround me on every side.
Arise, O LORD!
Rescue me, my God!
Slap all my enemies in the face!
Shatter the teeth of the wicked!
Victory comes from you, O LORD.
May you bless your people.

As we continue looking at some assuring prayer in the Bible, Psalm 3 gives us an insight into what David was facing as his own son, Absalom pursued him. Read carefully how he knew that God was protecting him. May we all feel that confidence as God protects us - Physically, Spiritually and Mentally!

Supporting Scripture:
Genesis 15:1

Read through the Bible a Chapter a day

Matthew 3

Day 74

Genesis 15:1-6

*After this, the **word** of the LORD came to Abram in a vision:*
"Do not be afraid, Abram.
I am your shield,
your very great reward.*"*
But Abram said, "Sovereign LORD, what can you give me since I remain childless and the one who will inherit my estate is Eliezer of Damascus?" And Abram said, "You have given me no children; so a servant in my household will be my heir."
*Then the **word** of the LORD came to him: "This man will not be your heir, but a son who is your own body **will** be your heir." He took him outside and said, **"Look up at the heavens and count the stars —if indeed you can count them."** Then he said to him, "So shall your offspring be."*
*Abram **believed** the LORD, and he **credited it to him as righteousness**.*

The word of the LORD came to Abram in a vision. We don't know how God actually spoke to Abram, audible or spoke to his heart...... but he did indeed speak to him. These days, God still speaks but we have a third source: The Bible. Abram believed God, and he credited it to him as righteousness. God drilled down to the issue Abram was worried about.... an heir. So that is probably as personal as it gets. So let me ask the question: what's troubling you? What is keeping you from the relationship that God wants to have with you? Give it up to God, he already knows what it is.... this is for your benefit!

Supporting Scripture:
John 4:50

Read through the Bible a Chapter a day

Matthew 4

Day 75

Joshua 5:13-15

When Joshua was near the town of Jericho, he looked up and saw a man standing in front of him with sword in hand. Joshua went up to him and demanded, "Are you friend or foe?"
"Neither one," he replied. "I am the commander of the LORD's army." At this, Joshua fell with his face to the ground in reverence. "I am at your command," Joshua said. "What do you want your servant to do?"
The commander of the LORD's army replied, **"Take off your sandals, for the place where you are standing is holy."** *And Joshua did as he was told.*

Here we see the Israelites as they neared the town of Jericho, Joshua encounters a man standing in front of him with a drawn sword. Is this a case of a Christophany? It may well be, we see Jesus in many forms throughout the Bible including Genesis when he wrestled with Jacob (Genesis 32:22-30), In Revelation we see a completely different Jesus - a warrior (19:11-21). The clue to this man standing in front of Jacob is: **"Take off your sandals, for the place where you are standing is holy."** We have seen this before, when Moses encountered the burning bush in Exodus (3:5). God is standing near us - right now - Teach these new disciples to obey all the commands I have given you. And be sure of this: I am with you always, even to the end of the age." (Matthew 28:20)

Supporting Scripture:
Genesis 32:22-30
Revelation 19:11-21
Exodus 3:5
Matthew 28:20

Read through the Bible a Chapter a day

Matthew 5

Day 76

1 Peter 1:23-25

*For **you have been born again,** but not to a life that will quickly end. **Your new life will last forever** because it comes from the **eternal, living word of God.** As the Scriptures say,*
"People are like grass;
their beauty is like a flower in the field.
The grass." withers and the flower fades.
*But the **word of the Lord remains forever."***
And that word is the Good News that was preached to you.

Today's scripture has three very important elements:
1. The transforming change of our lives we have looked at recently - You have been born again!
2. The reaffirmation of the power of the word of God.
3. God's promise of safekeeping over our lives - forever!
This is a fantastic reminder of the love that our God has for His children.

Supporting Scripture:
2 Corinthians 5:17
Galatians 2:20

Read through the Bible a Chapter a day

Matthew 6

Day 77

Isaiah 44:24

*This is what the Lord says - your Redeemer, who **formed you** in the womb:*
*I am the Lord, who has **made all things**,*
*who alone **stretched out the heavens**,*
*who **spread out the earth** by myself*

I would like to take you back to **Genesis 1:31** which says: God saw all that he had made and **it was very good.**
Last night we were checking out God's heaven and it (once again) made me realize that the very same God who created the universe - formed you and I.
We are not lost to God, he is with us always and if he can form all this with his voice, the troubles we have right here and now are nothing.

Keep putting your trust in God, you will never go wrong!

Supporting Scripture:
Genesis 1:31

Read through the Bible a Chapter a day

Matthew 7

Notes

Day 78

Matthew 8:2-3

A man with leprosy came and knelt before him and said, "Lord, if you are willing, you can make me clean."
*Jesus reached out his hand and touched the man. "I **am** willing," he said. **"Be clean!"** Immediately he **was** cleansed of his leprosy.*

This story about a man with leprosy may not be all that different than our need for Jesus. He acknowledged his deficiency, he knew his illness and still he came forward to ask for Jesus to help. He knew Jesus had the ability to perform this miracle, but he was a leper, the lowest of low in the present society. Yes Jesus could do this, but will he bother to heal me? Jesus responds and says "I am willing" and he healed him. You and I can take from this story: Jesus turns no one away, and he gives his very best to each of us. His best is always better than anything we can do. Here is the other conclusion to consider: Depend on God and he will respond!

Supporting Scripture:
Leviticus 13:45
Luke 5:12

Read through the Bible a Chapter a day

Matthew 8

Day 79

Matthew 19:16-26

Someone came to Jesus with this question: "Teacher, what good deed must I do to have eternal life?"
"Why ask me about what is good?" Jesus replied. "There is only One who is good. But to answer your question—if you want to receive eternal life, keep the commandments."
"Which ones?" the man asked.
And Jesus replied: "'You must not murder. You must not commit adultery. You must not steal. You must not testify falsely. Honor your father and mother. Love your neighbor as yourself.'"
"I've obeyed all these commandments," the young man replied. "What else must I do?"
Jesus told him, "If you want to be perfect, go and sell all your possessions and give the money to the poor, and you will have treasure in heaven. Then come, follow me."
But when the young man heard this, he went away sad, for he had many possessions.
Then Jesus said to his disciples, "I tell you the truth, it is very hard for a rich person to enter the Kingdom of Heaven. I'll say it again—it is easier for a camel to go through the eye of a needle than for a rich person to enter the Kingdom of God!"
The disciples were astounded. "Then who in the world can be saved?" they asked.
Jesus looked at them intently and said, "Humanly speaking, it is impossible. But with God everything is possible."

Look at the Ten Commandments. If you break one; your busted, and I dare say "I am guilty" - We all are! Notice what Jesus does not do here, He does not list the sin's this rich young man struggles with. Jesus tells him plainly, get rid of your idols man. Pack it all up and give it away! But he walked away sadly, because he just could not give it all up. You and I encounter folks who are in the same position. It might be you, I know it's me. Jesus is asking for one thing from you and I. He is asking us to give it all to Him. What he might do with it, well that is a Jesus decision.
With God, everything is possible!

Supporting Scripture:
Leviticus 18:4-5

Read through the Bible a Chapter a day

Matthew 9

Day 80

Ecclesiastes 12:13-14

That's the whole story. Here now is my final conclusion: Fear God and obey his commands, for this is everyone's duty. God will judge us for everything we do, including every secret thing, whether good or bad.

Although it is not known for sure, there is evidence in Ecclesiastes that it was written by King Solomon. If you recall, King Solomon was considered the wisest person to ever live. The Book of Ecclesiastes is a journal of sorts as the writer looks back on a lifetime of experience.

Some of you may know that I host a weekly radio program. On the last Weekend of the school year I interview all the graduating students from the radio station and it is an interesting conversation. They have such short prospective to draw from their lives. Many of them have seen and done more than many others in those 17-18 years. I ask them three questions:
1. What are your plans after high school?
2. What will you remember about your experience?
3. What mark have you left for your school (legacy)

I am not sure it is fair to ask those questions because at 18 years old, it is difficult to see how those life lessons might have impacted you. The final question, frankly should be asked when they are Sophomores and then followed up when they graduate. Here is the thing, we can ask these questions of ourselves as well.

We all can learn from these two verses we read today. It offers us a lifetime of wisdom, probably from the wisest man to ever walk the planet. When we talk about God's promises, generally it is encouraging - here it is sobering. To FEAR God is to respect him and hold him in awe at who he is. No one escapes the gaze of God. Thank goodness God provided a way to be saved that is permanent and perfect. If you have not invited Christ into your heart.... Today would be a great day to do that. Remember what he said in **Revelation 3:20** - Here I am! I stand at the door and knock. If anyone hears my voice and opens the door, I **will** come in and eat with him, and he with me. (NIV)

Supporting Scripture:
Revelation 3:20

Read through the Bible a Chapter a day

Matthew 10

Day 81

Joshua 21:43-45

So the LORD gave to Israel all the land he had sworn to give their ancestors, and they took possession of it and settled there. And the LORD gave them rest on every side, just as he had solemnly promised their ancestors. None of their enemies could stand against them, for the LORD helped them conquer all their enemies. Not a single one of all the good promises the LORD had given to the family of Israel was left unfulfilled; everything he had spoken came true.

God's promises were fulfilled - EVERY single one. Now to be sure, it did not all happen at once, it took 40 years for some of those promises to be fulfilled. God is the promise keeper! One thing I notice here is: Not only were the promises kept, they were given rest on every side! I like rest and peace - how about you?

Supporting Scripture:
1 Kings 8:56

Read through the Bible a Chapter a day

Matthew 11

Day 82

1 Corinthians 6:18-20

Run from sexual sin! No other sin so clearly affects the body as this one does. For sexual immorality is a sin against your own body. **Don't you realize that your body is the temple of the Holy Spirit, who lives in you and was given to you by God? You do not belong to yourself,** *for* **God bought you with a high price. So you must honor God with your body.**

If only we would live by these words - our society would be different and I dare say we would not have the scar in our land from 65,000,000 abortions and other lifestyle confusions. Both men and women are subject to these words. Clearly this has been with us for thousands of years, but truth is truth - even if it is hard to listen to.
Something to consider...

Supporting Scripture:
Galatians 5:19

Read through the Bible a Chapter a day

Matthew 12

Day 83

Hosea 6:6

For I desire mercy, not sacrifice, and acknowledgment of God rather than burnt offerings.

Remember when Jesus said that the Ten Commandments are summed up with 2 Commandments? Love the Lord your God with all your heart, soul and mind, and love your neighbor as yourself. It is increasingly harder to show love these days, even when we read that protesters are burning flags and Bibles in some of our cities. Yet this is exactly what we must do. Remember, that we are learning to have a mind focused on Jesus and a Biblical worldview and not a worldly worldview. Perhaps I am mistaken, but this scripture screams what God is telling us to do.

Jesus says: Go and learn what this means. We see it is God's intention for us to know Him better. The process never ends, it grows more intense!

Supporting Scripture:
Matthew 9:12
Matthew 22:27-30

Read through the Bible a Chapter a day

Matthew 13

Day 84

Ephesians 2:8-10

God saved you by his grace when you believed. And you can't take credit for this; it is a gift from God. Salvation is not a reward for the good things we have done, so none of us can boast about it. For we are God's masterpiece. He has created us anew in Christ Jesus, so we can do the good things he planned for us long ago.

Paul tells us a secret. You and I have the cards stacked against us. Until me met Jesus Christ on a personal basis, there is nothing we can do to saves ourselves. That is the work of God through the death and resurrection of Jesus Christ! It is God's powerful, perfect grace that has saved us. Why would God do this? Go back and read Genesis, You are the climax of the Genesis story! Nothing else in creation can claim to be made in the image of God - You are!

Supporting Scripture:
Genesis 1:26

Read through the Bible a Chapter a day

Matthew 14

Notes

Day 85

Acts 27:21-26

No one had eaten for a long time. Finally, Paul called the crew together and said, "Men, you should have listened to me in the first place and not left Crete. You would have avoided all this damage and loss. But take courage! None of you will lose your lives, even though the ship will go down. **For last night an angel of the God to whom I belong and whom I serve stood beside me,** *and he said, 'Don't be afraid, Paul, for you will surely stand trial before Caesar! What's more, God in his goodness has granted safety to everyone sailing with you.' So take courage! For* **I believe God.** *It will be just as he said. But we will be shipwrecked on an island."*

I want to encourage you today. Paul, when faced with physical danger reminds the 276 people on board the ship he was sailing on, despite hurricane force winds that they would all survive. Paul was on a mission, he was to stand trial before Caesar and God had protected himself and all the others on board the ill-fated ship they were on. We are fortunate to be living in such a time that we not only may hear in our hearts the voice of God, we also have The Bible. That word is perfect and we can trust it, and believe God (Hebrews 4:12)! Lean into Him!

Supporting Scripture:
Hebrews 4:12-13

Read through the Bible a Chapter a day

Matthew 15

Day 86

Deuterony 31:6

*So be strong and courageous! Do not be afraid and do not panic before them. For the LORD your God **will** personally go ahead of you. **He will neither fail you nor abandon you**.*

So picture this, Moses has lead the Israelites to this point, and he announces he will not be crossing the Jordan river to the promise land, that they will be under the new leadership of Joshua. Everything they know will be changing. New land, new leader; a lot of doubt and fear must have overcome them. Moses reminds them that on the surface things looks terrifying but in reality, God is still with them so they need to be strong and have courage. He will never leave them nor forsake them - and the same can be said for us as we look towards the future. No matter what happens an uncertain future is always certain when we trust God, He will never fail us nor abandon us.

Supporting Scripture:
Joshua 1:5-9
Matthew 28:18-20

Read through the Bible a Chapter a day

Matthew 16

Day 87

Judges 17:6

In those days Israel had no king; everyone did as they saw fit.

This scripture in Judges is repeated at least 4 time in the book of Judges. I bring this scripture up because it mirrors where we are in our society today. Everyone did as they saw fit. Things are weird today, things we always thought were good are now considered not good and things that were always considered not good are considered good. Isaiah describes it in 5:20-21
Woe to those who call evil good
and good evil,
who put darkness for light
and light for darkness,
who put bitter for sweet
and sweet for bitter.
Woe to those who are wise in their own eyes
and clever in their own sight.
Translated for us in today's world and you have everyone doing their own thing, Everyone has their own version of truth. If you are a Christian, then be a Christian. Be a follower of Jesus and glorify and cling to God with your life. If you don't want to be a committed Christian, then do whatever is right in your own eyes and face the consequences. But living in between is a miserable experience of compromise - you have too much of Jesus to be happy in the world and too much of the world to be happy in Jesus. This is similar to a verse in Joshua, *Do what you want, but as for me and my family, we will serve the Lord.* (Joshua 24:15)
Draw a line in the sand and take a side.

Supporting Scripture:
Isaiah 5:20-21
Joshua 24:15

Read through the Bible a Chapter a day

Matthew 17

Day 88

John 18:37-38

"You are a king, then!" said Pilate. Jesus answered, "You are right in saying I am a king. In fact, for this reason I was born, and for this I came into the world, to testify to the truth. Everyone who is on the side of truth listens to me." "What is truth?" Pilate asked. With this, he went out again to the Jews and said, "I find no basis for a charge against him.

There is so much in this brief encounter. Pilot confirms who Jesus is without even realizing it. And we see Jesus confirming to everyone the very reason he was born. God planned the Gospel long before the birth of Jesus. I read an article recently that talks about the probability of Jesus being the Messiah from the prophecies in the Old Testament. There are over 400 prophesies in the Old Testament about Jesus, but let's say that there were only 8. With only 8 prophecies being exactly true in the New Testament the chances are 10X17 zeroes. what the heck does that look like? 1 in 100,000,000,000,000,000. Now, say we get gutsy and say the probabilities of 48 of the prophecies were right, now the odds of that happening are 10 X 157 zeroes. Folks, I will repeat there are over 400 which fit perfectly. The promise here is that Jesus came for one reason - To save that which was lost - you and I. Finally, Pilot asks the eternal question, one that is still being asked by millions around us every day - What is truth?
Something to ponder today.....

Read through the Bible a Chapter a day

Matthew 18

Day 89

John 1:1-5

In the beginning the Word already existed.
*The Word was **with** God,*
*and the Word **was** God.*
*He existed in the beginning **with** God.*
*God created **everything** through him,*
and nothing was created except through him.
The Word gave life to everything that was created,
and his life brought light to everyone.
The light shines in the darkness,
*and the darkness can **never** extinguish it.*

I love John 1:1-5 and the promise it holds. It reveals who Jesus Christ is, Almighty God! He came as a man for one purpose, to save us and all people who make that choice. It also reaffirms the validity and importance of the Word of God in our lives!

Darkness can never extinguish Him, what a promise!

Supporting Scripture:
Genesis 1:1

Read through the Bible a Chapter a day

Matthew 19

Day 90

Malachi 3:6

*I **am** the Lord and I do **not** change.*

Today's promise is from the prophet Malachi, the last chapter of the Old Testament. James and Paul support that verse and gives us even more. We are told not to be mislead. Every where around us are lies. The world is upside down! What is true is being labeled as false, what is right is being called wrong and lies being called truth. Of all the promises we read about in the Bible, The fact that God does not change is huge, especially these days. You and I could probably write volumes on things changing around us, so it is nice to know that our rock never changes!

Supporting Scripture:
Hebrews 13:8
James 1:16-18

Read through the Bible a Chapter a day

Matthew 20

The Storm of all Storms

It was in January 1998, and at the time, I worked in the printing industry as a product manager. I was scheduled to travel to a large facility in Canada (well east of Montreal), a place called Bromont. An alpine resort area. A few days before the trip, I was faced with a decision, and that was to travel to the region in spite of a huge and awesome ice storm which had ravaged the area.

The storm also had a bad impact on the northern eastern third of the US. I was going round and round trying to work out the last minutes of the plans for the trip, including whether I should go at all. was assured that the installation of the client was going forward
and that it would not be a waste of time. What I had to prepare myself for was the aftermath of this storm. I made the decision to go and flew out with a connection through Cincinnati.

I can remember flying into Montreal very early in the morning, and that the airport and, in fact, the entire area was trapped in darkness. There was very little light at the airport, and it seemed that the runway was lined with candles to guide the pilots in. I don't think those were candles, but it was not your typical lighting you see on a runway. Upon landing, I was taken to my hotel for the remainder of the evening. The hotel had some power, but everything was at best reserved.

My ride picked me up for the two-hour ride east to Bromont, which took nearly 4 hours. As I am moving along, I am questioning my decision to travel to this area this week, month, or year. Everything was encased in ice, and as you passed under trees and bridges, you hoped and prayed that the limbs and ice spears which had developed didn't break off as your car passed through. In fact, as we are driving, I am reminded of the fact that the day before, a woman had been killed by one of these mammoth ice spears breaking off and striking her as she crossed a bridge. Dangerous stuff.

So we arrive in Bromont. A very pretty area with a ski lodge and lifts (closed of course today). We decided to go ahead and stop at the plant to get a sense of what was going on at the printing plant. And no shock here…. Closed! Well, not completely. We were able to go in and scout out where the installation was going to occur and check status on everything. But a reminder - NO POWER. With that, we opted to go and check into the hotel, which I had mentioned earlier was a ski lodge. It was a beautiful place, and when you walked into the lobby, I was struck with comfort. A huge roaring fire was burning, and I decided that I would conduct a training program in this very room in front of that very fireplace (not only was my task to install this system but also train our Canadian team on the equipment and technology involved).

But before all that, I needed to check into the hotel/lodge. Giving the nice lady behind the desk my credit card, she stamped it in a machine that ate my card – OK, not really, but the timing on my part was really bad because the minute she stamped the card, the power in the lodge went out forever, sealing the fate of my card. Not to worry, she said, as soon as the power came back, I would get my card back. Fortunately, she had already given me the keys to the room, and so I could move forward to unpacking and training our employees by the nice warm fire! Since there was no power, I was using the power supplied by the battery during training and finished with just a few minutes left.

Dinner that evening was in the lobby of the hotel, and the food was very basic – cooked and warmed by Sterno heaters. It was all turning into a comedy of coincidences, and it was until I decided to go to bed that I realized the severity of the situation. It started with the room key not working because of the power outage, but even before I could try that, the hallway was pitch black, requiring an escort and assistance to get into my room. Once in the room and realizing there was no heat, no lights, and no TV or internet (this was all dial-up – 1998). There was no heat, no phone, no email, no lights. But it was cold – 20 below zero outside!

Not having a good feeling about this, I began to go through my suitcase and layering. I put on virtually everything I had packed with me, which turned out to be 4 separate sets of clothes. It was about this time that a nice warm candle would have helped a great deal. But two problems existed – the candles and getting back into the room. Taking my chances, I went to the front desk. The attendant was a nice woman but did not speak English, so I had a tough time explaining my predicament to her. I needed more blankets and candles, of which she had neither except tiny candles – I would call them tea candles. I was allotted 3 of them.

She escorted me back to my room to let me in, and I laid down the candles on the table, trying to warm my hands. I honestly began to wonder about my safety. Is this it? Is this where it all ends for me tonight, and they find me lying in bed in April – frozen? Panic began to fill my mind as I had no place to turn or could not contact my wife to tell her I loved her and the kids. By now, it was around 2:00 a.m. and I could not sleep a wink. I remember getting up to use the restroom and wondering if the pipes were frozen; I was not going to find out. I had one candle left, and I began looking in the drawers for a Bible. That was the beginning of the turnaround. I have no idea what book I opened in the Bible; I only know that the minute the Bible was opened, the power came back on. Heat quickly filled the room, and the rest of the evening progressed with no incident. The next morning, I checked out and told the escorting employee to take me back to Montreal because there was no way I was going to stay. He argued with me concerning his install, so I agreed to go back to the plant. The management at the client told us to go home - this was a national emergency, and the last thing they would do is provide power for an install when there were hundreds of thousands without power in this part of the country.

That install did not finish for 2 more months after this event.

Day 91

Matthew 21:28-32

"What do you think? There was a man who had two sons. He went to the first and said, 'Son, go and work today in the vineyard.'
"'I will not,' he answered, but later he changed his mind and went.
"Then the father went to the other son and said the same thing. He answered, 'I will, sir,' but he did not go.
"Which of the two did what his father wanted?"
"The first," they answered.
Jesus said to them, "I tell you the truth, the tax collectors and the prostitutes are entering the kingdom of God ahead of you. For John came to you to show you the way of righteousness, and you did not believe him, but the tax collectors and the prostitutes did. And even after you saw this, you did not repent and believe him.

You and I are sinners. I know that sounds harsh, but it's the truth. Jesus came to save sinners. Perhaps that is why this resonates within us. Many don't feel they need to be saved, they asked saved from what? I am a good person. Or perhaps they have other beliefs or they believe in God but just never took salvation seriously, in other words they may have the wrong motives. I can remember training for a sales position early in my career and the trainer said to me - join a church there are lots of good prospects in church. Needless to say, selling that product was not for me. Others simply don't want to believe because their perception is giving up their worldly beliefs. What ever it is, thank God for Christmas.... He was born a baby to become a man to save sinners - just like us!

Supporting Scripture:
Luke 7:29

Read through the Bible a Chapter a day

Matthew 21

Notes

Day 92

Luke 24:13-32

Now that same day two of them were going to a village called Emmaus, about seven miles from Jerusalem. They were talking with each other about everything that had happened. As they talked and discussed these things with each other, Jesus himself came up and walked along with them; but they were kept from recognizing him. He asked them, "What are you discussing together as you walk along?"
They stood still, their faces downcast. One of them, named Cleopas, asked him, "Are you the only one visiting Jerusalem who does not know the things that have happened there in these days?" "What things?" he asked. "About Jesus of Nazareth," they replied. "He was a prophet, powerful in word and deed before God and all the people. The chief priests and our rulers handed him over to be sentenced to death, and they crucified him; but we had hoped that he was the one who was going to redeem Israel. And what is more, it is the third day since all this took place. In addition, some of our women amazed us. They went to the tomb early this morning but didn't find his body. They came and told us that they had seen a vision of angels, who said he was alive. Then some of our companions went to the tomb and found it just as the women had said, but they did not see Jesus." He said to them, "How foolish you are, and how slow to believe all that the prophets have spoken! Did not the Messiah have to suffer these things and then enter his glory?" And beginning with Moses and all the Prophets, he explained to them what was said in all the Scriptures concerning himself.
As they approached the village to which they were going, Jesus continued on as if he were going farther. But they urged him strongly, "Stay with us, for it is nearly evening; the day is almost over." So he went in to stay with them. When he was at the table with them, he took bread, gave thanks, broke it and began to give it to them. Then their eyes were opened and they recognized him, and he disappeared from their sight. They asked each other, ***"Were not our hearts burning within us while he talked with us on the road and opened the Scriptures to us?"***

Not much is said about Saturday, the day between Good Friday and Easter Sunday....We have probably all read about the two disciples who encountered the risen Christ on the road to Emmaus. Here are the two in deep emotional stress about what has happened to Jesus, they do not even recognize him. This was after his resurrection but I wonder if this would also be how they felt on Saturday. The day in-between. Look at how their attitudes changed after their encounter, their hearts were burning within when he opened up the scriptures to them!
Jesus will do the same for us - let's ask him to fill our hearts and minds with the very scriptures he told these two. Strive to dig deeper into the scriptures.

Read through the Bible a Chapter a day

Matthew 22

Day 93

Matthew 16:13-15

When Jesus came to the region of Caesarea Philippi, he asked his disciples, "Who do people say that the Son of Man is?"
"Well," they replied, "some say John the Baptist, some say Elijah, and others say Jeremiah or one of the other prophets."
Then he asked them, "But who do you say I am?"

Today's reading is great because Jesus asks his disciples a really great question. He is asking the same of us today. "But what about you?" he asked. "Who do you say I am?" Folks, this is really important because we have the world against us. In the past week, I have read articles about Easter and was Jesus really God? I even saw a headline from the NYT on Good Friday - Let's get rid of God. Are you kidding me? So, the time that you spend reading the Bible is so crucial for us to know who Jesus Christ really is. Remember, the disciples had the benefit of spending every day with the Lord. So do we, by reading his trustworthy and faithful word.

Supporting Scripture:
John 1:21

Read through the Bible a Chapter a day

Matthew 23

Day 94

Daniel 3:16-25

Shadrach, Meshach, and Abednego replied, "O Nebuchadnezzar, we do not need to defend ourselves before you. If we are thrown into the blazing furnace, the God whom we serve is able to save us. He will rescue us from your power, Your Majesty. But even if he doesn't, we want to make it clear to you, Your Majesty, that we will never serve your gods or worship the gold statue you have set up."
Nebuchadnezzar was so furious with Shadrach, Meshach, and Abednego that his face became distorted with rage. He commanded that the furnace be heated seven times hotter than usual. Then he ordered some of the strongest men of his army to bind Shadrach, Meshach, and Abednego and throw them into the blazing furnace. So they tied them up and threw them into the furnace, fully dressed in their pants, turbans, robes, and other garments. And because the king, in his anger, had demanded such a hot fire in the furnace, the flames killed the soldiers as they threw the three men in. So Shadrach, Meshach, and Abednego, securely tied, fell into the roaring flames.
But suddenly, Nebuchadnezzar jumped up in amazement and exclaimed to his advisers, "Didn't we tie up three men and throw them into the furnace?"
"Yes, Your Majesty, we certainly did," they replied.
"Look!" Nebuchadnezzar shouted. "I see four men, unbound, walking around in the fire unharmed! And the fourth looks like a god!"

I love the story of Shadrach, Meshach, and Abednego. How they maintained their faith in such adversity is inspiring to me. Of course we all know who the "fourth man" is and not only is it a Christophany, Jesus came in the literal heat of the moment. This moment not only saved Shadrach, Meshach, and Abednego, it had a huge impact on Nebuchadnezzar. And that is what happens when folks pay attention to Jesus Christ. People are watching.

Read through the Bible a Chapter a day

Matthew 24

Day 95

2 Kings 4:1-7

One day the widow of a member of the group of prophets came to Elisha and cried out, "My husband who served you is dead, and you know how he feared the LORD. But now a creditor has come, threatening to take my two sons as slaves." "What can I do to help you?" Elisha asked. "Tell me, what do you have in the house?" "Nothing at all, except a flask of olive oil," she replied. And Elisha said, "Borrow as many empty jars as you can from your friends and neighbors. Then go into your house with your sons and shut the door behind you. Pour olive oil from your flask into the jars, setting each one aside when it is filled." So she did as she was told. Her sons kept bringing jars to her, and she filled one after another. Soon every container was full to the brim! "Bring me another jar," she said to one of her sons. "There aren't any more!" he told her. And then the olive oil stopped flowing. When she told the man of God what had happened, he said to her, "Now sell the olive oil and pay your debts, and you and your sons can live on what is left over."

This morning, for several reasons I was in a mood, and not a good one. As I frequently do, I started to "unload" as I drove to work this morning. Suddenly, the Spirit of God spoke to me and reminded me about Elisha and the Widow and the oil. As I recounted the story, I am reminded of the supply of Grace that God has and yes, it settled me. It never runs out. Just keep bringing those jars!

Supporting Scripture:
Romans 12:3

Read through the Bible a Chapter a day

Matthew 25

Day 96

2 Peter 1:12-21

Therefore, I will always remind you about these things—even though you already know them and are standing firm in the truth you have been taught. And it is only right that I should keep on reminding you as long as I live. For our Lord Jesus Christ has shown me that I must soon leave this earthly life, so I will work hard to make sure you always remember these things after I am gone.

For we were not making up clever stories when we told you about the powerful coming of our Lord Jesus Christ. We saw his majestic splendor with our own eyes when he received honor and glory from God the Father. The voice from the majestic glory of God said to him, ***"This is my dearly loved Son, who brings me great joy." We ourselves heard that voice from heaven when we were with him on the holy mountain.*** *Because of that experience, we have even greater confidence in the message proclaimed by the prophets. You must pay close attention to what they wrote, for their words are like a lamp shining in a dark place—until the Day dawns, and Christ the Morning Star shines in your hearts.* ***Above all, you must realize that no prophecy in Scripture ever came from the prophet's own understanding, or from human initiative. No, those prophets were moved by the Holy Spirit, and they spoke from God.***

Peter tells us the transfiguration of Jesus was a critical moment in his ministry and here's why: They remembered it! That and the words of the prophets of the Old Testament increased their faith. You and I are no different, there are moments in our lives when God speaks to us and those moments (if we were listening and waiting and watching) are for us to look back and remember. Don't forget that Bible you read, Peter reaffirms the importance of paying close attention to what is written. He describes those words as a lamp shining in a dark place.... hmm, where have I heard this before. There is one thing I would encourage you to do - Each time you open your Bible ask God to speak to you. You might seek His wisdom, His inspiration and how He wants to use that word in your life.
He will never turn you away!

Supporting Scripture:
Matthew 17:2-6

Read through the Bible a Chapter a day

Matthew 26

Day 97

Matthew 17:1-5

After six days Jesus took with him Peter, James and John the brother of James, and led them up a high mountain by themselves. **There he was transfigured before them. His face shone like the sun, and his clothes became as white as the light.** *Just then there appeared before them* **Moses and Elijah**, *talking with Jesus.*
Peter said to Jesus, "Lord, it is good for us to be here. If you wish, I will put up three shelters—one for you, one for Moses and one for Elijah."
While he was still speaking, a bright cloud covered them, and a voice from the cloud said, "This is my Son, whom I love; with him I am well pleased. **Listen to him!**"

This is a "The Big One" Moment. We see Jesus in what is his real state - God! But what of Moses and Elijah? What is the significance of the two Old Testament giants appearing and speaking with Jesus? Could it be an affirmation that Jesus came to fulfill the words of the Old Testament? That Moses represents the law and Elijah the prophets? The Old Testament points to the coming Christ, and not only the coming of Christ but the glory of his Kingdom. The truth is, not one word of the prophecies about Jesus was wrong, every one was fulfilled. With that in mind, we are assured that every word about the return of Christ will be fulfilled. Listen to his word, we need to listen and be watching!

Supporting Scripture:
2 Peter 1:17-18

Read through the Bible a Chapter a day

Matthew 27

Day 98

John 4:4

*Now he **had** to go through Samaria.*

I want to give you an incredible passage today. You probably know the story of the woman at the well. She was in Samaria and as Jesus was traveling from Judea to Galilee, the most direct route was through Samaria. Thing is, Jews did not associate with Samaritans. He was probably under pressure to go around. The Disciples most likely didn't want to go through there, yet he **had** to go through and of course, he met the woman at the well. We know how the story goes, He was on a mission... He had an appointment with her. She just did not realize it at the time. She was transformed by her experience. She was most likely an outcast (remember, she was there around noon when no one else would be there). By the end of her visit with Jesus, she was telling everyone about Jesus - The first female evangelist! Here is the thing, she was pretty much a nobody except she was probably known in her village - for all the wrong reasons. Jesus still meets us (we are just like the woman at the well) when we need him. There is nothing that separates us. Think back to a time when you were in desperate need, did Jesus meet with you?

As we go along these days, it's a trying time... Jesus wants to meet with you, he has an appointment with you - don't miss that opportunity.

Supporting Scripture:
Matthew 10:5

Read through the Bible a Chapter a day

Matthew 28

Notes

Day 99

Matthew 14:34-36

After they had crossed the lake, they landed at Gennesaret. When the people recognized Jesus, the news of his arrival spread quickly throughout the whole area, and soon people were bringing all their sick to be healed. They begged him to let the sick touch at least the fringe of his robe, and **all who touched him were healed.**

Soon after Jesus walks on water, the Bible says they got to their destination and crowds began to build and bring all their sick, who were convinced that they could just touch His cloak and they would be healed. All this for the final statement: ALL who touched Him were healed. All who touched Him were healed! No one who journeys to Jesus is disappointed when they touch Him with sincerity - All who touch Him are healed! Reach out to Him today with your illness and your needs. All who touched Him were healed!

Thank you God!

Supporting Scripture:
Matthew 9:20-21

Read through the Bible a Chapter a day

Exodus 1

Day 100

1 Chronicles 28:9-10

*And Solomon, my son, learn to **know** the God of your ancestors intimately. Worship and serve him with your whole heart and a willing mind. For the Lord sees **every** heart and knows **every** plan and thought. If you seek him, you **will** find him. But if you forsake him, he **will** reject you forever. **So, take this seriously.** The Lord has chosen you to build a temple as his sanctuary. Be strong, and do the work."*

Here are David's final words to to his son, Solomon. There is an important message that speaks to us as well. Our first and most most important objective in this life we live is to **know** God intimately! Seek Him and you will find him. This is not the only place this statement is found: Deuteronomy 4:29, Proverbs 8:17, Jeremiah 29:13, Matthew 7:7, Luke 11:9, Acts 17:24-28 all say the same thing. This is a fantastic promise from God. The other part of this is really not what we want to hear, but it is equally true and a promise: if we forsake the Lord he will reject us. This is a similar promise from Jesus who said "I never knew you" (Matthew 7:21-23) - We indeed need to take this very seriously!

Supporting Scripture:
Deuteronomy 4:29
Proverbs 8:17
Jeremiah 29:13
Matthew 7:7
Luke 11:9
Acts 17:24-28
Matthew 7:21-23

Read through the Bible a Chapter a day

Exodus 2

Day 101

Joshua 24:14-15

Now fear the Lord and serve him with all faithfulness. Throw away the gods your forefathers worshiped beyond the River and in Egypt, and serve the Lord. But if serving the Lord seems undesirable to you, then choose for yourselves this day whom you will serve, whether the gods your forefathers served beyond the River, or the gods of the Amorites, in whose land you are living. But as for me and my household, we will serve the Lord."

As I read today's scripture it occurs to me that each of us have decisions we must make. Some of those are not complicated, they may be what coffee to buy, what cereal to eat in the morning etc etc... Some decisions however are not so simple and can bring about a life changing response. Today, we can decide that God is in control over the universe, our world, our nation (in fact - all nations) and our own lives. Each person must decide his or her own mind on what to believe. So much of what we have been told as we grew up has been founded on man made science. Many of these ideas are exactly opposite of what God tells us in the Bible. You have to make a decision on what you believe. When you are reading this morning, think a simple thought: where did I come from? Am I just a product of millions of years of evolution from a cell, to a fish, and then from an animal, or am I created by a loving God who watched me develop in that secret place (Psalm 139: 13-15)? Am I going to believe that somehow mankind has lofted himself into the role of God and can somehow determine the fate of this planet and the universe or can I simply rest in the knowledge that God is in control of all things and is working his master plan out and there is not a blasted thing I can do to change that (or would want to)? You have to decide for yourself - Jesus put it this way - He who is not with me is against me (Matthew 12:30) - there is no gray area here.   Joshua also said it like this - "Now fear the Lord and serve him with all faithfulness. Throw away the gods your ancestors worshiped beyond the Euphrates River and in Egypt, and serve the Lord. But if serving the Lord seems undesirable to you, then choose for yourselves this day whom you will serve, whether the gods your ancestors served beyond the Euphrates, or the gods of the Amorites, in whose land you are living. But as for me and my household, we will serve the Lord" (Joshua 24: 14-15).
Each of us must make that decision.

Supporting Scripture:
Psalm 139:13-15
Matthew 12:30

Read through the Bible a Chapter a day

Exodus 3

Day 102

Hebrews 11:1-3

Now faith is confidence in what we hope for and assurance about what we do not see. This is what the ancients were commended for.
*By faith we understand that the universe was formed at God's **command**, so that what is seen was not made out of what was visible.*

Why would the writer of Hebrews remind us of the creation of the universe in this opening verse of Hebrews 11? Personally, I believe it is to affirm the most obvious miracle of God - His Creation. God whispered, and the universe was created. What we see was made from what we cannot see! These days, this truth is exactly opposite what the world is telling us. We hear words like "believe the science". For a lot of people, science has become an idol, and as a result - making of mankind into a God. This is very dangerous!
Just like Jesus said: He who is not with me is against me, and he who does not gather with me scatters (Matthew 12:30). You and I have a choice to make: God or the world.

Supporting Scripture:
Matthew 12:30

Read through the Bible a Chapter a day

Exodus 4

Day 103

Psalm 33:4

*For the word of the Lord holds true,
and we **can** trust everything he does.*

What the Bible says about itself is all the evidence we need to believe it. So if that is the case, we **know** we can trust God with everything in our lives!
Short and sweet - and true!

Supporting Scripture:
Psalm 19:8
Psalm 119:142
Revelation 19:9
Revelation 22:6

Read through the Bible a Chapter a day

Exodus 5

Day 104

Ezra 8:21-23

*There, by the Ahava Canal, I proclaimed a fast, so that **we might humble ourselves before our God and ask him for a safe journey for us and our children,** with all our possessions. I was ashamed to ask the king for soldiers and horsemen to protect us from enemies on the road, because we had told the king, "The gracious hand of our God is on everyone who looks to him, but his great anger is against all who forsake him." **So we fasted and petitioned our God about this, and he answered our prayer.***

So why fast?
Well, Ezra explains why we should consider fasting. We are to humble ourselves before God. I could be wrong here, but I envision fasting as prayer on steroids. It costs something. Fasting may not just include food, it could include anything that you find valuable in your environment. You could fast from your cellphone if during your prayer and focus you find it to be a distraction. Fasting is our action to demonstrate God's claim over everything. Now in the Ezra's situation, they were concerned about their security and Ezra had proclaimed to the King the protection from God. They fasted and God answered their prayer! Fasting may not always result in the answering of prayer we want, but it will always give us the proper prospective God wants for us.

Supporting Scripture:
Daniel 10:2-3

Read through the Bible a Chapter a day

Exodus 6

Day 105

John 6:26-29

Jesus replied, **"I tell you the truth, you want to be with me because I fed you, not because you understood the miraculous signs. But don't be so concerned about perishable things like food. Spend your energy seeking the eternal life that the Son of Man can give you. For God the Father has given me the seal of his approval."**
They replied, "We want to perform God's works, too. What should we do?"
*Jesus told them, "This is the **only work** God wants from you: **Believe in the one he has sent.**"*

It seems reasonable, to believe in the one God has sent. But it also seems way too simple. Surely God has something more for us to do than just to believe in Jesus. Surely we need to be busy getting ready for "that" day! No, Jesus himself says it..... Just believe in the one God has sent. What a great place to start, focusing on The Son and looking to Him instead of all the chaos and distractions around us. You and I have our marching orders....
Let's go!

Supporting Scripture:
Isaiah 55:2
1 John 3:23

Read through the Bible a Chapter a day

Exodus 7

Notes

Day 106

Isaiah 55:8-9

"My thoughts are nothing like your thoughts," says the LORD.
"And my ways are far beyond anything you could imagine.
For just as the heavens are higher than the earth,
so my ways are higher than your ways
and my thoughts higher than your thoughts.

Some amazing words to contemplate this today. As we have discussed before, God's ways and His thoughts are a mystery to us. God has given us His words, and just as Jesus told His disciples after His resurrection that He was sending the Holy Spirit to give them power from heaven, we see He opened their minds (Luke 24:45). The Bible gives us what God wants to give us. Keep reading because there is more than we can handle already in our quest to know God!

Supporting Scripture:
Luke 24:45
Philippians 2:5

Read through the Bible a Chapter a day

Exodus 8

Day 107

Psalm 139:17-18

How precious are your thoughts about me, O God.
They cannot be numbered!
I can't even count them;
they outnumber the grains of sand!

Let's think for just a second on what God thinks of us. You, yes, YOU are his treasured possession. You - he loves so much that he thinks about you all the time. Psalm 139:17-18 says he thinks about you as the grains of sand (paraphrase) - he never stops thinking of you. But wait, he is also so crazy about you that he SINGS over you (Zephaniah 3:17) wow, he literally sings over us. God takes this relationship seriously, even to a whole new level. The really cool part is he has already given us the tools to meet him there!

Sing with all your heart friend, you are loved by your Daddy!

Supporting Scripture:
Zephaniah 3:17

Read through the Bible a Chapter a day

Exodus 9

Day 108

Zephaniah 3:17

For the Lord your God is living among you.
*He **is** a mighty savior.*
*He **will** take delight in you with gladness.*
*With his love, he **will** calm **all** your fears.*
*He **will** rejoice over you with **joyful songs**.*

Have you ever been in one of those moods where you just have to sing? Something wonderful is going on and the best way to express it is in song! Well that is how God feels about you!
God rejoices over you and I with joyful songs!
As wonderful as that is, this verse also promises that God WILL calm ALL your fears! But wait, there's even more, we have assurance that he is right here, among us - RIGHT NOW!
Not sure why God would feel that way about me, but I am sure glad he does.

Supporting Scripture:
Isaiah 63:1
Joel 2:21

Read through the Bible a Chapter a day

Exodus 10

Day 109

Daniel 4:35

*His rule **is** everlasting, and his kingdom **is** eternal. All the people of the earth are nothing compared to him. He does **as** he pleases among the angels of heaven and among the people of the earth. No one can stop him or say to him, 'What do you mean by doing these things?'*

This quote was not by an Apostle, or a Prophet or follower of Christ. This quote is from King Nebuchadnezzar. To see the full context of his statement look at **verse 34**: After this time had passed, I, Nebuchadnezzar, looked up to heaven. My sanity returned, and I praised and worshiped the Most High who lives forever. Nebuchadnezzar was one bad dude. Yet he is described by God in the Bible as his servant (**Jeremiah 27:6** - With my great power and outstretched arm I made the earth and its people and the animals that are on it, and I give it to anyone I please. Now I will give all your countries into the hands of **my servant** Nebuchadnezzar king of Babylon; I will make even the wild animals subject to him).

Kings, Presidents, Prime Ministers - all leaders are under the control of God. While we may not understand God's movements or motives, he is working all things out towards his conclusion. In the case of Nebuchadnezzar, he recognized the control of God in his life and ended up worshiping God. May our leaders understand God's control in our world and universe, and worship him, the only true God!.

Supporting Scripture:
Jeremiah 27:6
Daniel 4:34

Read through the Bible a Chapter a day

Exodus 11

Day 110

Ecclesiastes 7:10

Don't long for "the good old days."
This is not wise.

We have read of Lot's wife who looked back and turned into a pillar of salt. You and I are reminded not to look back with longing to remember the "good old days". The Bible says that is not wise. It certainly understandable why we would look back these days. We live in a chaotically dangerous world. It's what we have to remember. As children of God however, we should be looking up and living as if God is in control - because He is. The Bible promises that God has set us apart and while we live in this world, we are not of this world (John 17:14-17, Romans 12:2). Take a couple of minutes and check out those two verses. Let's keep charging forward, remembering that God is a step ahead, waiting for us.

Supporting Scripture:
John 17:14-17
Romans 12:2
Genesis 19:26

Read through the Bible a Chapter a day

Exodus 12

Day 111

2 Timothy 3:1-5

You should know this, Timothy, that in the last days there will be very difficult times. For people will love only themselves and their money. They will be boastful and proud, scoffing at God, disobedient to their parents and ungrateful. They will consider nothing sacred. They will be unloving and unforgiving; they will slander others and have no self control. They will be cruel and hate what is good. They will betray their friends, be reckless, be puffed up with pride, and love pleasure rather than God. They will act religious, but they will reject the power that could make them godly. **Stay away from people like that!**

We don't have to look very far to see this scripture coming true in our world today. We are loaded with it! I think that social media may be one of the worst, or maybe I should say one of the best examples, disagree with someone and you are lambasted. People say things and repeat things that they would never say in person. **BEWARE!**

Supporting Scripture:
1 Timothy 4:1

Read through the Bible a Chapter a day

Exodus 13

Day 112

Jeremiah 1:4-12

The LORD gave me this message:
"I knew you before I formed you in your mother's womb.
Before you were born I set you apart
and appointed you as my prophet to the nations."
"O Sovereign LORD," I said, "I can't speak for you! I'm too young!"
The LORD replied, "Don't say, 'I'm too young,' for you must go wherever I send you and say whatever I tell you. And don't be afraid of the people, for I will be with you and will protect you. I, the LORD, have spoken!" Then the LORD reached out and touched my mouth and said,
"Look, I have put my words in your mouth!
Today I appoint you to stand up
against nations and kingdoms.
Some you must uproot and tear down,
destroy and overthrow.
Others you must build up
and plant."
Then the LORD said to me, "Look, Jeremiah! What do you see?"
And I replied, "I see a branch from an almond tree."
*And the LORD said, "That's right, and it means that I am watching, and I **will** certainly carry out **all** my plans."*

I keep hearing that this time we are going through is unprecedented. Yet while I believe what we are seeing is unprecedented, there is more outreach to an unbelieving world than possibly ever before. What an amazing time to be alive! And that is exactly what today's scripture is all about, God telling us BEFORE I FORMED YOU IN THE WOMB I KNEW YOU. Think of that, God planned for you and I before he formed the universe! Not everyone is going to be a prophet (yet in many ways, we all are). Many of us are going to be bus drivers, teachers, printers, painters, electricians, pilots and CEO's etc.... yet what we all share in common today is that we are all here, right now sharing in a time that the world may have never seen before. God is not absent, he is right here, watching just as he told Jeremiah he would be. There are no accidents, we are here exactly as we are suppose to be! Each of us has a unique role right here, right now!

Supporting Scripture:
Psalm 139: 13-14

Read through the Bible a Chapter a day

Exodus 14

Notes

Day 113

Psalm 37:3-5

Trust in the Lord and do good;
dwell in the land and enjoy safe pasture.
Take delight in the Lord,
*and he **will** give you the **desires of your heart.***
Commit your way to the Lord;
*trust in him and he **will** do this:*

God will give you the desire of your heart when you are in and working in his will for your life. You are in HIS will when you:
>Trust him!
>Live right!
>Delight in God!

Supporting Scripture:
Deuteronomy 30:20
Numbers 13:17-25

Read through the Bible a Chapter a day

Exodus 15

Day 114

Hebrews 13:1-9

***Keep on** loving each other as brothers and sisters. Don't forget to show hospitality to strangers, for some who have done this have **entertained angels** without realizing it!*
***Remember those in prison**, as if you were there yourself. Remember also those being mistreated, as if you felt their pain in your own bodies.*
***Give honor to marriage**, and remain faithful to one another in marriage. God will surely judge people who are immoral and those who commit adultery.*
***Don't love money;** be satisfied with what you have.*
For God has said,
"I will never fail you.
I will never abandon you."
So we can say with confidence,
"The LORD is my helper,
so I will have no fear.
What can mere people do to me?"
Remember your leaders who taught you the word of God. Think of all the good that has come from their lives, and follow the example of their faith.
*Jesus Christ is the **same yesterday, today, and forever. So do not be attracted by strange, new ideas**. Your strength comes from God's grace, not from rules about food, which don't help those who follow them.*

There is some disagreement as to who wrote the Book of Hebrews. Regardless, It is good for us to see this advice and be reminded of God's promise to never leave us or forsake us. To remind us of the help of God's presence gives us confidence!
I need to hear that right now, how about you?

Supporting Scripture:
Matthew 28:20

Read through the Bible a Chapter a day

Exodus 16

Day 115

Psalm 148

Praise the LORD!
Praise the LORD from the heavens!
Praise him from the skies!
Praise him, all his angels!
Praise him, all the armies of heaven!
Praise him, sun and moon!
Praise him, all you twinkling stars!
Praise him, skies above!
Praise him, vapors high above the clouds!
Let every created thing give praise to the LORD,
for he issued his command, and they came into being.
He set them in place forever and ever.
His decree will never be revoked.
Praise the LORD from the earth,
you creatures of the ocean depths,
fire and hail, snow and clouds,
wind and weather that obey him,
mountains and all hills,
fruit trees and all cedars,
wild animals and all livestock,
small scurrying animals and birds,
kings of the earth and all people,
rulers and judges of the earth,
young men and young women,
old men and children.
Let them all praise the name of the LORD.
For his name is very great;
his glory towers over the earth and heaven!
He has made his people strong,
honoring his faithful ones—
the people of Israel who are close to him.
Praise the LORD!

Each of us have decisions we must make. Some are not complicated, they may be what coffee to buy, what cereal to eat in the morning etc etc... Some decisions however are not so simple and can bring about a life changing response. Today's Psalm confirms God control over the universe, our world, our nation (in fact - all nations) and our own lives. Each person must decide in his or her own mind on what they believe. So much of what we have been told as we grew up has been founded on man made science and beliefs. Many of these ideas are exactly opposite of what God tells us in the Bible. You have to make a decision on what you believe. When you are reading this morning, think a simple thought - where did I come from? Am I just a product of millions of years of evolution from a cell, to a fish, and then from an animal, or am I created by a loving God who watched me develop in that secret place (Psalm 139:13-15)? Am I going to believe that somehow mankind has lofted himself into the role of God and can somehow determine the fate of this planet and the universe or can I simply rest in the knowledge that God is in control of all things and is working his master plan out and there is not a blasted thing I can do to change that (or would want to)? You have to decide for yourself - Jesus put it this way - He who is not with me is against me (Matthew 12:30) - there is no gray area here. Joshua also said it like this - "Now fear the Lord and serve him with all faithfulness. Throw away the gods your ancestors worshiped beyond the Euphrates River and in Egypt, and serve the Lord. But if serving the Lord seems undesirable to you, then choose for yourselves this day whom you will serve, whether the gods your ancestors served beyond the Euphrates, or the gods of the Amorites, in whose land you are living. But as for me and my household, we will serve the Lord" (Joshua 24:14-15).

Each of us must make that decision.

Supporting Scripture:
Psalm 139:13-15
Matthew 12:30
Joshua 24:14-15

Read through the Bible a Chapter a day

Exodus 17

Day 116

Deuteronomy 7:9

***Know** therefore that the Lord your God **is** God; he **is** the faithful God, keeping his covenant of love to a thousand generations of those who love him and keep his commandments.*

Good Morning!
Every morning is a good morning when we **remember AND know** that The Lord God is God and that he is the faithful God. Everything sort of takes a back seat to this doesn't it? We all know about faith, but it is God who is faithful! You and I can struggle with faith, but God (there it is: But God) is always faithful.

Know this with certainty today!

Supporting Scripture:
Psalm 18:25

Read through the Bible a Chapter a day

Exodus 18

Day 117

Joshua 8:34-35

*Joshua then read to them all the **blessings and curses** Moses had written in the Book of Instruction. **Every** word of **every** command that Moses had ever given was read to the entire assembly of Israel, including the women and children and the foreigners who lived among them.*

This is what makes the Bible so real, so believable. In this series of books we have the very best and the very worst. It's all here and whether we like what we hear or not, God's word is alive and powerful. It is sharper than the sharpest two-edged sword, cutting between soul and spirit, between joint and marrow. It exposes our innermost thoughts and desires. Nothing in all creation is hidden from God. Everything is naked and exposed before his eyes, and he is the one to whom we are accountable (Hebrews 4:12-13). Literally, there is nothing like the Bible!

Supporting Scripture:
Deuteronomy 31:11
Hebrews 4:12-13

Read through the Bible a Chapter a day

Exodus 19

Day 118

Matthew 6:33

Seek the Kingdom of God above all else, and live righteously, and He will give you everything you need.

Today we read about the constant care of God over His people. There are two additional scriptures about the depth of God's care for us. He always has our best intentions in mind. He looks past the narrow vision you and I have and sees what our souls really desire and he gives us those desires! When you and I fill our lives up with God, he places those desires in us, what a wonderful gift he has given us! If we truly consider His ways, we will be blown away as God shapes us into the people he designed us to be.

Supporting Scripture:
Psalm 37:5-7
Isaiah 49:16

Read through the Bible a Chapter a day

Exodus 20

Day 119

Matthew 6:31-33

"So don't worry about these things, saying, 'What will we eat? What will we drink? What will we wear?' These things dominate the thoughts of unbelievers, but your heavenly Father already knows all your needs. Seek the Kingdom of God above all else, and live righteously, and he will give you everything you need.

A continuation from yesterday:
How much time do we spend worrying? How much time do we spend trying to resolve an answer to our worries? How much energy and wasting of our resources do we exhaust worrying? Jesus refers to some very basic necessities here, and no doubt we have expressed the same concerns at points in our lives. Look what he calls folks who search for these things: unbelievers. You mighty be worried about something far deeper and more confusing to you. You might be saying: This involves my family, my spouse or child or my house or car, far more than the basics of life. Read what Jesus is saying to you and I today, your Heavenly Father knows what you need! Seek **first** his kingdom and his righteousness. **Seek him out**, be aggressive about it! (**Psalm 34:10** - The lions may grow weak and hungry, but those who seek the LORD lack no good thing.) don't bear this burden by yourself - God **will** help you. Open up that Bible and search his word and cry out to HIM!

Supporting Scripture:
Psalm 34:10

Read through the Bible a Chapter a day

Exodus 21

Notes

Day 120

Matthew 10:28-34

"Don't be afraid of those who want to kill your body; they cannot touch your soul. Fear only God, who can destroy both soul and body in hell. What is the price of two sparrows—one copper coin? But not a single sparrow can fall to the ground without your Father knowing it. ***And the very hairs on your head are all numbered.*** *So don't be afraid; you are more valuable to God than a whole flock of sparrows.*
"Everyone who acknowledges me publicly here on earth, I will also acknowledge before my Father in heaven. But everyone who denies me here on earth, I will also deny before my Father in heaven.
"Don't imagine that I came to bring peace to the earth! I came not to bring peace, but a sword.

There is so much here! I feel it is better you read this through a couple of times than for me to let you know how important you are in God's plans.

Supporting Scripture:
Isaiah 8:12

Read through the Bible a Chapter a day

Exodus 22

Day 121

Luke 21:13-19

*But **make up your mind** not to worry beforehand how you will defend yourselves. For I **will** give you words and wisdom that none of your adversaries will be able to resist or contradict. You will be betrayed even by parents, brothers and sisters, relatives and friends, and they will put some of you to death. All men will hate you because of me. But not a hair of your head **will** perish. Stand firm, and you **will** gain life.*

Promises of God many times require action from us. Do you remember Daniel 1:8? Daniel resolved in his heart. Make up your mind NOT to worry. This is faith, that we trust God to do what he says he will do! The John 5:6 is good because many times we are stuck in a rut, we are completely capable of action but sometimes it is easier to make excuses when all we need is a response - put the left foot forward, then the right foot. Your faith may require action.
As Jesus asks: "Do you want to get well"?

Supporting Scripture:
John 5:6
Daniel 1:8

Read through the Bible a Chapter a day

Exodus 23

Day 122

Psalm 78:5-6

*He decreed statutes for Jacob
and established the law in Israel,
which he commanded our forefathers
to teach their children,
so the next generation would know them,
even the **children yet to be born**,
and they in turn would tell their children.*

You and I are recorded in the Bible! Look it up!

Supporting Scripture:
Psalm 102:18
Numbers 12:6
John 17:20
Psalm 22:31

Read through the Bible a Chapter a day

Exodus 24

Day 123

Joshua 3:9-10

*Joshua said to the Israelites, "Come here and **listen to the words of the LORD your God**. This is how you will **know** that the **living God** is among you and that he **will** certainly drive out before you the Canaanites, Hittites, Hivites, Perizzites, Girgashites, Amorites and Jebusites.*

Elohim Chayim, The Living God is just one of several names that refer to our Glorious God. This story refers to when the Israelites had finally come to the promise land and were preparing to cross. Look at the words carefully today, this has everything we can possibly want in the promises of God. **Listen to the words of the Lord your God** - that's our Bible! And Joshua tells the people that's how we will KNOW that the Living God (there it is - Elohim Chayim) is here. Look what it says about the menacing obstacles in our way - He WILL drive them out! Finally, notice how many of the peoples the Lord will drive out - Go ahead, I'll wait... seven - that God's number. God's promises are better than gold - It's God's word!

Supporting Scripture:
Deuteronomy 5:26

Read through the Bible a Chapter a day

Exodus 25

Day 124

Joel 2:12-14

That is why the LORD says,
"Turn to me now, while there is time.
Give me your hearts.
Come with fasting, weeping, and mourning.
Don't tear your clothing in your grief,
but tear your hearts instead."
Return to the LORD your God,
*for he is **merciful and compassionate**,*
slow to get angry and filled with unfailing love.
He is eager to relent and not punish.
Who knows? Perhaps he will give you a reprieve,
*sending you a **blessing** instead of this curse.*
Perhaps you will be able to offer grain and wine
to the LORD your God as before.

Here is the thing about God, He is gracious and compassionate! He is full of love and he wants our attention - all of our heart, not some lukewarm, halfway faith. We see this in the book of Revelation 3:15-16 where Jesus is talking to the church in Laodicea - **I know your deeds, that you are neither cold nor hot. I wish you were either one or the other! So, because you are lukewarm—neither hot nor cold—I am about to spit you out of my mouth.** So it is time for us to show some life as the church of believers. I believe God is looking for folks who are ready to stand up and give an Isaiah response: Send me! **(Isaiah 6:8 - Then I heard the voice of the Lord saying, "Whom shall I send? And who will go for us? " And I said, "Here am I. Send me!")**
Note the exclamation point, proving yet again, that it is not only every word of the Bible that has meaning - so does the punctuation!
This is good stuff!

Supporting Scripture:
Revelation 3:15-16
Isaiah 6:8

Read through the Bible a Chapter a day

Exodus 26

Day 125

Luke 5:27-28

Later, as Jesus left the town, he saw a tax collector named Levi sitting at his tax collector's booth. "Follow me and be my disciple," Jesus said to him. So Levi got up, left everything, and followed him.

When Jesus invites - how do we respond? Jesus saw the despised tax collector Levi and gave him the invitation, "follow me and be my disciple." Of course, Levi was not despised by Jesus. To the Pharisees and Teachers of the law however, tax collectors were despised. And what was Levi's response? He literally left everything and followed him. I remember a prayer walk I went through a number of years ago and it started by picking luggage for your adventure. Of course the luggage must have weighed 75 pounds. You are lugging this suitcase your entire journey until the end and as you leave there was a sign: **I am all you need!** The relief at leaving that baggage was incredible. Levi got it, he understood, **Jesus is all you need!** So he literally left everything he had and followed The Lord. So how about you, what is your response to the invitation by Jesus?

Supporting Scripture:
Psalm 35:3
Revelation: 3:20

Read through the Bible a Chapter a day

Exodus 27

Day 126

Daniel 1:8-9

*But Daniel **purposed in his heart** that he would not defile himself with the portion of the king's delicacies, nor with the wine which he drank; therefore he requested of the chief of the eunuchs that he might not defile himself. Now God had brought Daniel into the favor and goodwill of the chief of the eunuchs.*

It is very easy for us to fall into destructive habits in our lives. These days, it is even easier to find fault and blame others for our own ways.   The fastest way way out of said areas is to accept blame and resolve our hearts not to continue down the destructive path. God will surely help us when we **REPENT** and turn away and go the opposite direction!

Supporting Scripture:
Genesis 39:21

Read through the Bible a Chapter a day

Exodus 28

Notes

Day 127

Joshua 10:7-15

So Joshua and his entire army, including his best warriors, left Gilgal and set out for Gibeon. "Do not be afraid of them," the LORD said to Joshua, "for I have given you victory over them. Not a single one of them will be able to stand up to you."
Joshua traveled all night from Gilgal and took the Amorite armies by surprise. The LORD threw them into a panic, and the Israelites slaughtered great numbers of them at Gibeon. Then the Israelites chased the enemy along the road to Beth-horon, killing them all along the way to Azekah and Makkedah. As the Amorites retreated down the road from Beth-horon, the LORD destroyed them with a terrible hailstorm from heaven that continued until they reached Azekah. The hail killed more of the enemy than the Israelites killed with the sword.
On the day the LORD gave the Israelites victory over the Amorites, Joshua prayed to the LORD in front of all the people of Israel. He said,
*"Let the sun **stand still** over Gibeon,*
and the moon over the valley of Aijalon."
So the sun stood still and the moon stayed in place until the nation of Israel had defeated its enemies.
Is this event not recorded in The Book of Jashar? The sun stayed in the middle of the sky, and it did not set as on a normal day. There has never been a day like this one before or since, when the LORD answered such a prayer. Surely the LORD fought for Israel that day!
Then Joshua and the Israelite army returned to their camp at Gilgal.

The sun stood still and the moon stayed in place! Normally, I would want to know the how and why of this story. To my knowledge, this has never happened before. Ah, no doubt someone would have blamed global warming or climate change for such an event. The beauty here is: I don't have to know the why or the details, just that God can stop the earth literally to answer a prayer if He chose to do that. There is nothing impossible for God when we ask in His will. And what is His will? To know and Love Him and lean into Him.
God is Great!

Supporting Scripture:
Isaiah 38:8

Read through the Bible a Chapter a day

Exodus 28

Day 128

Psalm 23

Here is one of the most quoted of scriptures and certainly one of the most popular of all the Psalms. Read it carefully as it an affirmation of God's presence in our lives. These words have it all: Waiting for God, God is our sustainer, God is faithful and God's constant friendship. He does not just help us get by, he provides the very best care we could ever ask for!

Psalm 23
The LORD is my shepherd;
I shall not want.
He makes me to lie down in green pastures;
He leads me beside the still waters.
He restores my soul;
He leads me in the paths of righteousness
For His name's sake.
Yea, though I walk through the valley of the shadow of death,
I will fear no evil;
For You are with me;
Your rod and Your staff, they comfort me.
You prepare a table before me in the presence of my enemies;
You anoint my head with oil;
My cup runs over.
Surely goodness and mercy shall follow me
All the days of my life;
And I will dwell in the house of the LORD
Forever.

Read through the Bible a Chapter a day

Exodus 30

Day 129

Luke 22:31-34

*And the Lord said, "Simon, Simon! Indeed, Satan **has** asked for you, that he may sift you as wheat. But I have prayed for you, that your faith should not fail; and **when** you have returned to Me, strengthen your brethren."*
But he said to Him, "Lord, I am ready to go with You, both to prison and to death."
*Then He said, "I tell you, Peter, the rooster shall not crow this day before you **will** deny three times that you know Me."*

My eyes have been opened to this interesting interaction between Jesus and Peter. Like we see in the book of Job, Satan has no authority over you and I unless he has been given it. God surrounds us, nothing can get to you and I unless it goes through God first. I have always thought this verse meant, Peter I have prayed for you that your faith may not fail, you have a choice in this. But Jesus may be saying to Peter is, it's already done, you are going to stumble and fall, but in faith, get back up and lead the others by example and brotherly love. Jesus prays for us! Isn't that amazing? Romans 8:34 says: Who is he who condemns? No one. Christ Jesus who died —more than that, who was raised to life —is at the right hand of God and is also interceding for us. We are most assuredly going to stumble and fall, but it is Christ who praying for us! One more verse - Job 16:20-21: My intercessor is my friend as my eyes pour out tears to God; on behalf of a man he pleads with God as one pleads for his friend.

Supporting Scripture:
Job 1:6-12
Job 16:20-21
Romans 8:34

Read through the Bible a Chapter a day

Exodus 31

Day 130

Romans 8:11

*And if the Spirit of him who raised Jesus from the dead is living in you, he who raised Christ from the dead **will also give life** to your mortal bodies through the Spirit, who lives in you.*

Want to hear some great news? I don't know about you, but I could use some great news. Romans 8 is filled with fantastic news for you and I. This little nugget is a reminder of the fact the same Holy Spirit of God that raised Jesus from the dead - will give you and I a new life not only at our rebirth, but also right here and right now. How does that happen? When you believe Jesus Christ as your Lord and Savior, when you cry out to God - The Holy Spirit comes to reside in your soul. The Bible says that you are sealed with the Holy Spirit. I hope this news makes your soul jump for joy, because it is the greatest news you will ever hear!

Supporting Scripture:
Galatians 6:15
2 Corinthians 5:17

Read through the Bible a Chapter a day

Exodus 32

Day 131

1 John 4:2-3

This is how we know if they have the Spirit of God: If a person claiming to be a prophet acknowledges that Jesus Christ came in a real body, that person has the Spirit of God. But if someone claims to be a prophet and does not acknowledge the truth about Jesus, that person is not from God. Such a person has the spirit of the Antichrist, which you heard is coming into the world and indeed is already here.

We see this all the time, it is very important to test the spirit of every message and every messenger, even in our churches. It all revolves around Jesus Christ.

Pay attention to what you watch and read!

Supporting Scripture:
John 1:14

Read through the Bible a Chapter a day

Exodus 33

Day 132

Luke 12:54-56

Then Jesus turned to the crowd and said, "When you see clouds beginning to form in the west, you say, 'Here comes a shower.' And you are right. When the south wind blows, you say, 'Today will be a scorcher.' And it is. You fools! You know how to interpret the weather signs of the earth and sky, but you don't know how to interpret the present times.

I wonder if Jesus would be telling us the same these days. On one hand, there has never (at least in my life time) a more divided time than what we see today. The lines seem divided between a Biblical worldview and a worldly world view. One the other hand; recently, the movement to God has been extraordinary with outbreaks of evangelism all over the world! We live in a fascinating time!

Supporting Scripture:
Matthew 16:2

Read through the Bible a Chapter a day

Exodus 34

Day 133

James 1:5-8

*If any of you lacks wisdom, you should ask God, **who gives generously** to all without finding fault, and **it will** be given to you. But when you ask, you **must believe and not doubt**, because the one who doubts is like a wave of the sea, blown and tossed by the wind. That person should not expect to receive anything from the Lord. Such a person is double-minded and unstable in all they do.*

Talk about God's promises! If we lack wisdom, God will give all we can handle! But there are a couple of catches to this:
1. You gotta ask!
2. You gotta believe!

Supporting Scripture:
1 Kings 3:9-10

Read through the Bible a Chapter a day

Exodus 35

Notes

Day 134

Psalm 119:73

With your very own hands you formed me;
now breathe your wisdom over me so I can understand you.

Psalm 119 is a treasure of God's promises and His word. In fact, it is the longest chapter in the Bible and every verse has a reference to God's word! Here we confirm that our very existence is determined by God, we are made by Him! There must be a reason each of us is so wonderfully made, so much so that the writer asks God himself to breath wisdom over his life so that he can know Him better and more deeply! We may not always know and understand why God wants to have such a close relationship with us, He just does and that is a promise we can always depend on!

Supporting Scripture:
Jeremiah 1:5
Genesis 2:7
Psalm 139

Read through the Bible a Chapter a day

Exodus 36

Day 135

Micah 6:5-8

Don't you remember, my people,
how King Balak of Moab tried to have you cursed
and how Balaam son of Beor blessed you instead?
And remember your journey from Acacia Grove to Gilgal,
when I, the LORD, did everything I could
to teach you about my **faithfulness."**
What can we bring to the LORD?
Should we bring him burnt offerings?
Should we bow before God Most High
with offerings of yearling calves?
Should we offer him thousands of rams
and ten thousand rivers of olive oil?
Should we sacrifice our firstborn children
to pay for our sins?
No, O people, the LORD has told you what is good,
and this is what he requires of you:
to do what is right, to love mercy,
and to walk humbly with your God.

God's faithfulness! At the end of our lives, we will finally understand the depth of what God has done. God's faithfulness has carried us all along. Our response is to somehow give back to God for what He has done, offering everything we have. God requires none of those things, He wants us to do what is right, love mercy and like Enoch - Walk humbly with our God.

Supporting Scripture:
Genesis 5:22
1 Samuel 15:22

Read through the Bible a Chapter a day

Exodus 37

Day 136

1 Corinthians 3:6-9

After all, who is Apollos? Who is Paul? We are only God's servants through whom you believed the Good News. Each of us did the work the Lord gave us. I planted the seed in your hearts, and Apollos watered it, but it was God who made it grow. It's not important who does the planting, or who does the watering. What's important is that God makes the seed grow. The one who plants and the one who waters work together with the same purpose. And both will be rewarded for their own hard work. For we are both God's workers. And you are God's field. You are God's building.

I love this. Jesus tells us in chapter 4 of John to look around. The fields are ripe for harvest. Just open your eyes and your heart, never before has the harvest been so ready. Over the past year we have been witness to the Spirit of God moving in our nation. I read of a meeting out west just this weekend. Out of 7600 hundred people, hundreds committed their lives to Christ. The Times, they are a Changin (Bob Dylan 1965)!

Supporting Scripture:
John 4:34-38

Read through the Bible a Chapter a day

Exodus 38

Day 137

1 Timothy 4:4-5

Since everything God created is good, we should not reject any of it but receive it with thanks. For we know it is made acceptable by the word of God and prayer.

Genesis 1 tells us several times that everything God created was good. He made it for us and for others and it truly is good. And we are not suppose to reject God's creation, but rather embrace it and thank him for what he has done.

Supporting Scripture:
Genesis 1:31

Read through the Bible a Chapter a day

Exodus 39

Day 138

Romans 10:9-15

*If you openly declare that Jesus is Lord and believe in your heart that God raised him from the dead, **you will be saved.** For it is by **believing in your heart** that you are made **right** with God, and it is by **openly declaring your faith that you are saved**. As the Scriptures tell us, **"Anyone who trusts in him will never be disgraced."** Jew and Gentile are the same in this respect. They have the same Lord, who gives generously to all who call on him. For **"Everyone who calls on the name of the LORD will be saved."** But how can they call on him to save them unless they believe in him? And how can they believe in him if they have never heard about him? And how can they hear about him unless someone tells them? And how will anyone go and tell them without being sent? That is why the Scriptures say, "How beautiful are the feet of messengers who bring good news!"*

Who remembers Operation Desert Shield back in the early 90's? Well how about some shock and awe this morning of our own? Romans 10:9-15 is filled with awesome news! News we need to remember. News we need to share. Others need this as well.....

Supporting Scripture:
Matthew 10:32

Read through the Bible a Chapter a day

Exodus 40

Day 139

Proverbs 3:5-6

*Trust in the Lord with **all** your heart
and **lean not** on your own understanding;
in **all** your ways submit to him,
and he **will** make your paths straight.*

Total obedience to God is not easy; however learning to lean into him is what he wants us to do. God does make your path straight and that's good because the ways of the world will try to set you on a different course, and that is not good.

Supporting Scripture:
Psalm 4:5

Read through the Bible a Chapter a day

Mark 1

Day 140

Revelation 1:1-8

The revelation from Jesus Christ, which God gave him to show his servants what must soon take place. He made it known by sending his angel to his servant John, who testifies to everything he saw—that is, **the word of God** *and the testimony of Jesus Christ.* **Blessed** *is the one who reads aloud the words of this prophecy, and* **blessed** *are those who hear it and take to heart what is written in it, because the time is near.*
John,
To the seven churches in the province of Asia:
Grace and peace to you from him **who is**, *and* **who was,** *and* **who is to come**, *and from the seven spirits before his throne, and from Jesus Christ,* **who is the faithful witness**, *the firstborn from the dead, and the* **ruler of the kings of the earth.**
To him who **loves us** *and has* **freed us** *from our sins by his blood, and has made us to be a kingdom and priests to serve his God and Father —to him be glory and power for ever and ever! Amen.*
"Look, he is coming with the clouds,"
and "every eye will see him,
even those who pierced him";
and all peoples on earth "will mourn because of him."
So shall it be! Amen.
"I am the Alpha and the Omega," says the Lord God, "who is, and who was, and who is to come, the Almighty."

A lot of people get hung up about the book of Revelation. It can be complex, but there is amazing revelation just by reading the book. The opening scripture for example, we find several remarkable items. The first being, those who read this book will be blessed! I am not absolutely sure of this, but it seems to me that this is the only book to promise a blessing by reading. Another promise is a reminder that the book comes from God and that God is promised to us today, yesterday and tomorrow. It also reminds us who Jesus is. As the faithful witness, it's a reminder that every word of the Bible is true..... take a look at John 1 and 1 John 1.
Jesus is the ruler of the kings of earth. These passages also reminds us - GOD LOVES US and FREED US! Lastly, it is a firm reminder that God is the beginning and the end, with confirmation that he was always and is always to come. These words are truly promising!

Read through the Bible a Chapter a day

Mark 2

Notes

Day 141

2 Corinthians 3:16-18

But whenever someone turns to the Lord, the veil is taken away. **For the Lord is the Spirit, and wherever the Spirit of the Lord is, there is freedom.** *So all of us who have had that veil removed can see and reflect the glory of the Lord. And the Lord—who is the Spirit—makes us more and more like him as we are changed into his glorious image.*

A good day to read this might be Independence Day - 4th of July!
I hope you all have a chance to read this scripture carefully. Our freedom is a gift - given to us by God. Our true freedom is in our relationship with God. Our freedom is realized that God is shaping us more and more into his glorious image. When we finally recognize this, we are one step closer to helping others as well and maybe, just maybe this nation will begin to turn into what our founding fathers envisioned almost 250 years ago.

Supporting Scripture:
Mark 15:38
Isaiah 61:1-2

Read through the Bible a Chapter a day

Mark 3

Day 142

Isaiah 40:28-31

Have you never heard?
Have you never understood?
The LORD is the everlasting God,
*the **Creator of all the earth.***
He never grows weak or weary.
No one can measure the depths of his understanding.
He gives power to the weak
and strength to the powerless.
Even youths will become weak and tired,
and young men will fall in exhaustion.
But those who trust in the LORD will find new strength.
They will soar high on wings like eagles.
They will run and not grow weary.
They will walk and not faint.

This is considered by many to be a "Best of" scripture. And for good reason. Here we see that not only did God create everything, He empowers you and I to change our lives. No matter what blocks us in our view, God see beyond what we see. Cry out to him today and watch what happens!

Supporting Scripture:
Psalm 37:9

Read through the Bible a Chapter a day

Mark 4

Day 143

Revelation 22:12-15

*"**Look, I am coming soon,** bringing my reward with me to repay all people according to their deeds. **I am the Alpha and the Omega**, the **First and the Last,** the **Beginning and the End."***
*Blessed are those who wash their robes. They will be permitted to enter through the gates of the city and eat the fruit from the tree of life. **Outside the city are the dogs—the sorcerers, the sexually immoral, the murderers, the idol worshipers, and all who love to live a lie.***

Talk about an awesome promise! Here we have Jesus, once again, admitting - he is God! He was there at the beginning and he will be there at the end. Some may ask what am I suppose to be doing in these days? Jesus gives us the answer in John 6: They replied, "We want to perform God's works, too. What should we do?" Jesus told them, "This is the only work God wants from you: Believe in the one he has sent." Not only is that a great start, it's in the Bible!

Supporting Scripture:
Matthew 16:27
John 6:29

Read through the Bible a Chapter a day

Mark 5

Day 144

Genesis 1:26-27

*Then God said, "Let **us** make mankind in our image, in **our** likeness, so that they may rule over the fish in the sea and the birds in the sky, over the livestock and all the wild animals, and over all the creatures that move along the ground."*
So God created mankind in his own image,
*in the **image of God** he created them; male and female he created them.*

As I mentioned yesterday, there are many references of Jesus Christ in the Old Testament. Early on, during the creation we see that God the Father was not alone. "Let us make mankind in our likeness". This meant both physically and soul filled. He made man and breathed spirit into his being. Father/ Son/ Holy Spirit were all there. That has never changed and it will never will. What an awe inspiring thought.

Supporting Scripture:
Psalm 100:3

Read through the Bible a Chapter a day

Mark 6

Day 145

Galatians 1:11-12

*Dear brothers and sisters, I want you to understand that the gospel message I preach is not based on mere human reasoning. I received my message from no human source, and no one taught me. Instead, I received it by **direct revelation** from Jesus Christ.*

As we read on day 13, this scripture has a partner. Here Paul is explaining to the Galatian Church that what he has learned about Jesus and His gospel came as a direct revelation from Jesus himself! This cannot be man made, it is far too glorious to be given by a person. You have already heard about importance of reading your Bible, this just re-enforces how important your study is!

Hang in there!

Supporting Scripture:
Galatians 1:15-16

Read through the Bible a Chapter a day

Mark 7

Day 146

Psalm 81:10-12

For it was I, the LORD your God,
who rescued you from the land of Egypt.
Open your mouth wide, and I will fill it with good things.
"But no, my people wouldn't listen.
Israel did not want me around.
So I let them follow their own stubborn desires,
living according to their own ideas.

There is a danger to a nation who decides they don't want to follow God. Now when I say "nation" that can be God's children such as Israel and Christians as well as nations who certainly relied on God from its beginnings. Yep, I mean the United States. We see similar behavior in the book of Romans 1:18-32. Are we a lost cause? No, I don't think so. God is filled with love for His people and if you notice in the Bible - that never ends! But we do need to make changes for it does not go well for the nation that demonstrates "all the people did whatever seemed right in their own eyes." Judges 21:25

It starts with us.

Supporting Scripture:
Romans 1:18-32
Judges 21:25

Read through the Bible a Chapter a day

Mark 8

Day 147

John 20:24-29

Now Thomas (also known as Didymus), one of the Twelve, was not with the disciples when Jesus came. So the other disciples told him, "We have seen the Lord!"
But he said to them, "Unless I see the nail marks in his hands and put my finger where the nails were, and put my hand into his side, I will not believe."
A week later his disciples were in the house again, and Thomas was with them. Though the doors were locked, Jesus came and stood among them and said, "Peace be with you!" Then he said to Thomas, "Put your finger here; see my hands. Reach out your hand and put it into my side. Stop doubting and believe." Thomas said to him, "My Lord and my God!"
Then Jesus told him, "Because you have seen me, you have believed; blessed are those who have not seen and yet have believed.

I relate to Thomas. I am a skeptic. I have to investigate things myself before I jump on the wagon of belief. A couple of other notes here in Thomas's presence: Jesus and stood among them even though the doors were locked, nothing keeps Jesus from you and I! Thomas rightly claims: My Lord and my God! All those years they spent with Jesus, it took His death and resurrection to finally understand. Even after that - some doubted!

Supporting Scripture:
Matthew 28:17

Read through the Bible a Chapter a day

Mark 9

Notes

Day 148

Jeremiah 17:7-9

*"But blessed are those who trust in the LORD
and have made the LORD their hope and confidence.
They are like trees planted along a riverbank,
with roots that reach deep into the water.
Such trees are not bothered by the heat
or worried by long months of drought.
Their leaves stay green,
and they never stop producing fruit."
The human heart is the most deceitful of all things,
and desperately wicked.
Who really knows how bad it is?*

Wow, we were really feeling good about this scripture and suddenly we made a sharp turn and it went bad. Actually, we have to stop with the emotions and and face the truth: Trust in God and lean not on the emotions of the heart.

Supporting Scripture:
Matthew 13:15
Mark 7:21-22

Read through the Bible a Chapter a day

Mark 10

Day 149

Philippians 4:4-7

Always be full of joy in the Lord. I say it again—rejoice! Let everyone see that you are considerate in all you do. Remember, the Lord is coming soon.
Don't worry *about anything; instead,* ***pray about everything.*** *Tell God what you need, and thank him for all he has done. Then you will experience God's peace, which exceeds anything we can understand. His peace will guard your hearts and minds as you live in Christ Jesus.*

Another wonderful promise from God.
Here, Paul says that in every situation, go to God with your concerns and requests. There is nothing too small, silly or gigantic that we cannot go to God. Remember the saying: Big problems = Little God, Little problems = Big God. In return, God promises us peace, but not just any peace, Godly peace. Just like the ads on TV - But wait, there's more: He also promises to guard our hearts and minds in Christ Jesus. We are never alone - ever!

Supporting Scripture:
Habakkuk 3:18

Read through the Bible a Chapter a day
Mark 11

Day 150

John 3:18-21

"There is no judgment against anyone who believes in him. But anyone who does not believe in him has already been judged for not believing in God's one and only Son. And the judgment is based on this fact: God's light came into the world, but people loved the darkness more than the light, for their actions were evil. All who do evil hate the light and refuse to go near it for fear their sins will be exposed. But those who do what is right come to the light so others can see that they are doing what God wants."

This scripture comes on the tail of John 3:16-17, arguably the most identified scripture in the entire Bible. While we are basking in the promise of God's love in 16-17, we are also sobered by the reality of the lack of faith in verses 18-21. Jesus seems to be saying that the lack of belief comes from sin and the fear of exposure of that sin. This is what makes the Bible so remarkable, it exposes The Good, The Bad and The Ugly in our relationship with The God of the Universe. Drop what you are doing and cry out to God!

Supporting Scripture:
John 3:16
1 John 3:19
Psalm 52:3

Read through the Bible a Chapter a day

Mark 12

Day 151

1 Samuel 8:6-9

*But when they said, "Give us a king to lead us," this displeased Samuel; so he prayed to the LORD. And the LORD told him: "Listen to all that the people are saying to you; it is not you they have rejected, but they **have rejected me** as their king. As they have done from the day I brought them up out of Egypt until this day, forsaking me and serving other gods, so they are doing to you. Now listen to them; but warn them solemnly and let them know what the king who will reign over them will do."*

Can you imagine how this must have grieved God? Yet, as we follow in the Bible, king after king came and went, God forgave them. You and I face the same dilemma constantly. Do we trust God, or rely on our own devices to resolve our needs and decisions? I cannot help but apply this lesson to where we are as a society today. We trust in ourselves, we are looking for someone to lead us, we have our own gods and idols in our jobs, "things", sciences, lifestyles, etc...... How God longs for us to lean into him and trust him.

And they say the Bible isn't relevant.

Supporting Scripture:
Matthew 12:30

Read through the Bible a Chapter a day

Mark 13

Day 152

2 Corinthians 1:18-22

*But as surely as God **is** faithful, our message to you is not "Yes" and "No." For the Son of God, Jesus Christ, who was preached among you by us—by me and Silas and Timothy —was not "Yes" and "No," but in him it has **always** been "Yes." **For no matter how many promises God has made, they are "Yes" in Christ.** And so through him the "Amen" is spoken by us to the glory of God. Now it is God who makes both us and you stand firm in Christ. **He anointed us, set his seal of ownership on us**, and **put his Spirit in our hearts as a deposit, guaranteeing what is to come.***

What an amazing promise! All of God's promises are true and available to you and I because of Jesus Christ. It is hard to process that, but it is true! But the good news does not end there, the Bible tells us that God has put a seal upon us. We belong to him. To show us his claim, he put his Spirit in our hearts as a deposit - with a promise of eternity to come. If that doesn't give us encouragement for this new day, I am not sure what will.

Supporting Scripture:
Romans 15:8

Read through the Bible a Chapter a day

Mark 14

Day 153

Joshua 23:14-16

Now I am about to go the way of all the earth. You know with all your heart and soul that not one of all the good promises the LORD your God gave you has failed. Every promise has been fulfilled; not one has failed. But just as all the good things the LORD your God has promised you have come to you, so he will bring on you all the evil things he has threatened, until the LORD your God has destroyed you from this good land he has given you. If you violate the covenant of the LORD your God, which he commanded you, and go and serve other gods and bow down to them, the LORD's anger will burn against you, and you will quickly perish from the good land he has given you."

Ok picture this, Joshua is (putting it in today's terms) retiring. He has this proclamation to make: God has delivered on every promise he has made. Not one has failed! However, just because he has fulfilled every promise you still have to live right. Here is where the water gets murky, Joshua tells them that those promises will all be yanked from them if they sin and follow idols and other gods. Here is a question for you all this morning: We love and should trust all the promises God has made (2 Corinthians 1:20) but what about this judgement thing? Is it possible that what is happening in our country today is judgement? I am just asking, do we really think we can explain away 64,000,000 abortions? Do we think we can turn away from needless violence on each other? Do we think we can follow idols and other gods and everything will be ok? This scripture tells us something different. Maybe we need to remember God's standard and not our own.

Supporting Scripture:
2 Corinthians 1:20

Read through the Bible a Chapter a day

Mark 15

Day 154

Romans 1:1-7

*This letter is from Paul, a slave of Christ Jesus, **chosen by God** to be an apostle and sent out to preach his Good News. God promised this Good News long ago **through his prophets in the holy Scriptures.** The Good News is **about his Son**. In his earthly life he was born into King David's family line, and he was shown to be the Son of God when he was raised from the dead by the power of the Holy Spirit. He is Jesus Christ our Lord. Through Christ, God has given us the privilege and authority as apostles to tell Gentiles everywhere what God has done for them, so that they will believe and obey him, bringing glory to his name.*
*And **you are included** among those Gentiles who have been called to belong to Jesus Christ. I am writing to all of you in Rome who are loved by God and are called to be his own holy people.*
May God our Father and the Lord Jesus Christ give you grace and peace.

In Paul's introduction of the Book of Romans we can see that there are no mistakes when it comes to God. He planned for Paul, He planned for Jesus and at the end of verse seven He planned for you and I. God has prepared the Gospel from the very beginning as He introduces us to His prophets through His Holy Word! It is awesome and frankly frightening to think that you and I have been given such a lofty position that God knew us before He created the universe.

What will you do with such news?

Supporting Scripture:
Galatians 1:15

Read through the Bible a Chapter a day

Mark 16

Notes

Day 155

Exodus 7:10-13

So Moses and Aaron went to Pharaoh and did what the LORD had commanded them. Aaron threw down his staff before Pharaoh and his officials, and it became a serpent! Then Pharaoh called in his own wise men and sorcerers, and these Egyptian magicians did the same thing with their magic. They threw down their staffs, which also became serpents! But then Aaron's staff swallowed up their staffs. Pharaoh's heart, however, remained hard. He still refused to listen, just as the LORD had predicted.

As the Israelite's were held captive by Pharaoh in Egypt, God was working His plan to get them released. The first time Moses and Aaron went to confront Pharaoh, Aaron threw down his staff and it became a snake. Notice that Pharaoh had magicians who could do the same thing. Also notice that Aaron's staff swallowed up the magicians staffs. The enemy has copies where he can. He also has distractions, and there are distractions - lot's of them. They can and will rob you of the intimacy of your time with the Baby born in a manger. The simple and pure message of love and hope of a Savior born unto us still shines through. Nothing can rob you of God's message. Not the enemy or the world as long as you fill yourself with God's word and love.

Supporting Scripture:
Daniel 1:20

Read through the Bible a Chapter a day

Leviticus 1

Day 156

John 20:30-31

The disciples saw Jesus do many other miraculous signs in addition to the ones recorded in this book. But these are written so that you may continue to believe that Jesus is the Messiah, the Son of God, and that by believing in him you will have life by the power of his name.

There is power in the name of Jesus! Many many people say His name without a clue as to what they are saying or doing. Look at it this way, God said to not use his name in vain, yet many still do. If nothing else, let us recall the power that is in the name of God and respect that. There is power in the name of Jesus Christ!

Supporting Scripture:
Matthew 4:3

Read through the Bible a Chapter a day

Leviticus 2

Day 157

Ecclesiastes 7:29

But I did find this: God created people to be virtuous, but they have each turned to follow their own downward path."

According to the Bible, there have only been two people who never experienced death, Enoch and Elijah. But we certainly have lived as though we will never die, especially in our youth. God has provided for each of us, but for many, that is not enough and we can come up with some wild schemes in our effort to move ahead, when God is telling us to wait for him.

Supporting Scripture:
Psalm 46:10
Genesis 3:1-3

Read through the Bible a Chapter a day

Leviticus 3

Day 158

Romans 3:20-22

*For **no one** can ever be made right with God by doing what the law commands. The law simply shows us how sinful we are. **But** now God has shown us a way to be made right with him without keeping the requirements of the law, as was promised in the writings of Moses and the prophets long ago. We are **made right** with God by **placing our faith in Jesus Christ.** And this is true for everyone who believes, no matter who we are.*

You and I live with standards. We have to, it's really the only way to mark our progress. When we were growing up, there was always that mark on the wall to see how much we had grown. If you are in the sales world, you have quotas and you have past performance sales to mark your performance. In our lives, we have the 10 Commandments. By themselves, we could never be made complete. They are the standard by which God wants for us to live our lives. There are 2 problems.
1. We can never live up to those standards.
2. You break one and you break them all.
So God gave us a way to be made right: Placing our faith in Jesus. And no one is exempt from this, it applies to everyone. We still have the 10 Commandments because they are the standard for determining sin. Thanks be to God for what he has done!

Supporting Scripture:
Isaiah 46:13

Read through the Bible a Chapter a day

Leviticus 4

Day 159

Romans 4:20-25

*Abraham never wavered in believing God's promise. In fact, his faith grew stronger, and in this he brought glory to God. He was fully convinced that God is **able** to do whatever he **promises**. And because of Abraham's faith, God counted him as righteous. And when God counted him as righteous, it wasn't just for Abraham's benefit. It was recorded for **our** benefit, too, assuring us that God will also count us as righteous if we believe in him, the one who raised Jesus our Lord from the dead. He was handed over to die because of our sins, and he was raised to life to make us right with God.*

Take a second and ponder this. Here is another mention of you and I in the Bible! When God counted Abraham as righteous, it was not just for Abraham's benefit, it was for ours as well! And it was the fulfillment of a promise from God!

Keep reading those promises, God never forgets them!

Supporting Scripture:
Hebrews 11:11

Read through the Bible a Chapter a day

Leviticus 5

Day 160

1 Kings 19:9-18

But the LORD said to him, "What are you doing here, Elijah?"
Elijah replied, "I have zealously served the LORD God Almighty. But the people of Israel have broken their covenant with you, torn down your altars, and killed every one of your prophets. I am the only one left, and now they are trying to kill me, too."
"Go out and stand before me on the mountain," the LORD told him. **And as Elijah stood there, the LORD passed by, and a mighty windstorm hit the mountain. It was such a terrible blast that the rocks were torn loose, but the LORD was not in the wind. After the wind there was an earthquake, but the LORD was not in the earthquake. And after the earthquake there was a fire, but the LORD was not in the fire. And after the fire there was the sound of a gentle whisper.** When Elijah heard it, he wrapped his face in his cloak and went out and stood at the entrance of the cave.
And a voice said, "What are you doing here, Elijah?"
He replied again, "I have zealously served the LORD God Almighty. But the people of Israel have broken their covenant with you, torn down your altars, and killed every one of your prophets. I am the only one left, and now they are trying to kill me, too."
Then the LORD told him, "Go back the same way you came, and travel to the wilderness of Damascus. When you arrive there, anoint Hazael to be king of Aram. Then anoint Jehu grandson of Nimshi to be king of Israel, and anoint Elisha son of Shaphat from the town of Abel-meholah to replace you as my prophet. Anyone who escapes from Hazael will be killed by Jehu, and those who escape Jehu will be killed by Elisha! Yet I will preserve 7,000 others in Israel who have never bowed down to Baal or kissed him!"

I love this story of Elijah and how God spoke to him. Many expect God will come to them in the middle of their storms. But He came as a whisper and that really got his attention. The Apostle Paul has something to say about this story as well. Read Paul's account in Romans 11. Pay attention to those whispers!

Supporting Scripture:
Romans 11:8-9

Read through the Bible a Chapter a day

Leviticus 6

Day 161

Jeremiah 29:11

*For I **know** the plans I have for you," declares the Lord, "plans to **prosper** you and not to harm you, plans to give you hope and a **future**.*
*We know that in **all** things God works for the **good** of those who love him, who have been called according to his purpose. (Romans 8:28)*

We know that God knew us even before we were formed in the womb, he had set us apart for a very special purpose. Today's scripture tells us even more. God wants us to succeed, not fail. He has planned every day of your life! That does not mean that we won't have setbacks... quite the contrary, with God by our side, living within us he will turn it all (good and bad) into a good he has purposed for our lives.
Now I would recommend that you crack open your Bible and read the full scripture in both cases, but here we can clearly see that God has a plan for each of us, and he will see us through. Be strengthened by these words, they come from the very lips of God!

Supporting Scripture:
Romans 8:28
Psalm 139:16

Read through the Bible a Chapter a day

Leviticus 7

Notes

Day 162

Romans 7:21-25

I have discovered this principle of life—that when I want to do what is right, I inevitably do what is wrong. I love God's law with all my heart. But there is another power within me that is at war with my mind. This power makes me a slave to the sin that is still within me. Oh, what a miserable person I am! Who will free me from this life that is dominated by sin and death? Thank God! The answer is in Jesus Christ our Lord. So you see how it is: In my mind I really want to obey God's law, but because of my sinful nature I am a slave to sin.

What I love about Paul is his honesty. We see this wisdom he acquired from the Holy Spirit. He discovered a principle for his life - it's almost as if there was another person residing in Paul driving him in all the wrong ways. That is sin that lives within us. You and I don't stand a chance if it were not for Jesus Christ! He is our only answer! Like Paul, join with me and THANK GOD for what He has done!

Supporting Scripture:
Galatians 5:17

Read through the Bible a Chapter a day

Leviticus 8

Day 163

Psalm 139:13-16

*You made all the delicate, inner parts of my body
and knit me together in my mother's womb.
Thank you for making me so wonderfully complex!
Your workmanship is marvelous—how well I know it.
You watched me as I was being formed in utter seclusion,
as I was woven together in the dark of the womb.
You saw me before I was born.
Every day of my life was recorded in your book.
Every moment was laid out
before a single day had passed.*

If you have a few minutes today, read Psalm 139, it is really amazing.
As one who instructs high school students, it is very easy to see confusion in their lives. I have been confronted with pregnancy, homosexuality, bi-sexuality and gender confusion with kids not even 18 years old. I am not going to get into the fact that 70% of these kids do not have a father figure in their lives. Like the rest of us, they are searching and they have not yet discovered that like a jigsaw puzzle, the hole in their hearts can only be filled with God. I thought that this was unique to our school, but it is not. A quick scan of any media outlet and you will see this thinking has infiltrated our society. God created **every** individual in his image. We are not evolved animals and every aspect of our bodies are energy burning miracles. He created us to be in communion with him. This a truth and promise that is unique to the Bible and the only way we are going to see the truth is by saying no to the media around us and saying yes to Jesus Christ of the Bible. Not everybody reads the Bible; for some, you are the closest thing to a Bible. Share that love with others!

Supporting Scripture:
Isaiah 44:24

Read through the Bible a Chapter a day

Leviticus 9

Day 164

Psalms 85:8-9

I will listen to what God the LORD says;
*he **promises** peace to his people, his faithful servants -*
but let them not turn to folly.
Surely his salvation is near those who fear him,
that his glory may dwell in our land.

I am so thankful to have the word of God that I can open and read freely. Not everyone has that opportunity, and who knows how long we have that. The devil roams this planet and would love to take it from us. Fortunately, he does not possess the ability to do that unless it is allowed by God. In fact, I have heard that Satan hates the Bible, and cannot stand in the presence of an open Bible. Probably because of John 17:17 (Sanctify them by the truth; your word is truth). Anyway, the point of this is the promises that God makes to us. Today he promises his peace! Turn to him for peace, ask God for it and KNOW he hears you and will respond!

I need this today, how about you?

Supporting Scripture:
Leviticus 26:6

Read through the Bible a Chapter a day

Leviticus 10

Day 165

Romans 11:33-36

Oh, how great are God's riches and wisdom and knowledge! How impossible it is for us to understand his decisions and his ways!
For who can know the LORD's thoughts?
Who knows enough to give him advice?
And who has given him so much
that he needs to pay it back?
For everything comes from him and exists by his power and is intended for his glory. All glory to him forever! Amen.

Our infinite God! God is beyond measurement. We cannot define Him by proportion or magnitude. He has no beginning, no end, and no limits. Not only is He not bound by limits, there is no possible way for you and I to fully understand God's universe he has created.

Supporting Scripture:
Psalm 92:5
Job 5:9

Read through the Bible a Chapter a day

Leviticus 11

Day 166

Psalm 114

*When the Israelites escaped from Egypt—
when the family of Jacob left that foreign land—
the land of Judah became God's sanctuary,
and Israel became his kingdom.
The Red Sea saw them coming and hurried out of their way!
The water of the Jordan River turned away.
The mountains skipped like rams,
the hills like lambs!
What's wrong, Red Sea, that made you hurry out of their way?
What happened, Jordan River, that you turned away?
Why, mountains, did you skip like rams?
Why, hills, like lambs?
Tremble, O earth, at the presence of the Lord,
at the presence of the God of Jacob.
He turned the rock into a pool of water;
yes, a spring of water flowed from solid rock.*

Here is a great scripture for The Fourth of July!

We hold these truths to be self-evident, that
all men are created equal, that they are endowed
by their Creator with certain unalienable
Rights, that among these are Life, Liberty and
the pursuit of Happiness.

You and I know these words. They come from the Declaration of Independence. These words as well as our nations Constitution were derived from the Bible. No matter what we see around us, God is the creator the Forefathers spoke of in our founding documents. As we see in Psalm 114, even nature serves God. Let us remember as we celebrate, true freedom comes from Jesus Christ, the author of these words. Let us boldly live as a truly free people!

Supporting Scripture:
2 Corinthians 3:16-17

Read through the Bible a Chapter a day

Leviticus 12

Day 167

Isaiah 48:12-13

*"Listen to me, O family of Jacob,
Israel my chosen one!*
I alone am God,
*the **First and the Last.***
*It was my hand that laid the foundations of the earth,
my right hand that spread out the heavens above.*
When I call out the stars,
they all appear in order."

As if we need a reminder, God again claims to be all we need. He alone is God! He is The First and the Last. Doesn't this is also show us that this chaos we see in our society is not from Him, He is a God of order, not chaos. He also is bringing this whole mess to its conclusion. Check out what Revelation has to say about this: "I am the First and the Last. I am the living one. I died, but look—I am alive forever and ever! And I hold the keys of death and the grave".
Our focus should be HIM. Keep your eyes on Jesus!

Supporting Scripture:
Revelation 1:17-18

Read through the Bible a Chapter a day

Leviticus 13

Day 168

John 17:3

*And this is the way to have eternal life—**to know you, the only true God, and Jesus Christ**, the one you sent to earth.*

I encourage you to read the words of John 17. I have not noticed verse 3 as it stands alone. Look at the words of Jesus, this is the way to have eternal life - to know God! We have studied the topic of knowing God and Jesus Christ, but here Jesus is saying to know God IS eternal life. It of course makes sense. What is interesting to me is that everyone will live an eternal life, just in different locations. It's heaven or hell. And that is a devastating thought, absolute isolation from God - all while knowing that it did not need to be that way. Being tormented by memories of the times a person could have said yes, but chose no. At some point, as Philippians 2 shows us - everyone will know that this is all true, and everyone will honor Jesus Christ as Lord:
Please bear in mind that I have no insight into how those in Hell will be tormented, I just imagine it would be hell having nothing but the memories of stubbornness, anger, denial and ridicule all with the absolute absence of God.

Supporting Scripture:
Jeremiah 9:23-25
Philippians 2:9-11

Read through the Bible a Chapter a day

Leviticus 14

Notes

Day 169

Jeremiah 30:18-22

This is what the LORD says:
"When I bring Israel home again from captivity
and restore their fortunes,
*Jerusalem **will** be rebuilt on its ruins,*
and the palace reconstructed as before.
*There **will** be joy and songs of thanksgiving,*
*and I **will** multiply my people, not diminish them;*
*I **will** honor them, not despise them.*
*Their children **will** prosper as they did long ago.*
I will establish them as a nation before me,
and I will punish anyone who hurts them.
*They **will** have their own ruler again,*
*and he **will** come from their own people.*
*I **will** invite him to approach me," says the LORD,*
"for who would dare to come unless invited?
You will be my people,
*and **I will be your God**."*

Do you see the promises of God here? The nation Israel is in a difficult struggle right now. I have no doubt that its leadership is the right one for this time. That seems to be a point of contention for some; yet, if we read these words from Jeremiah (and others) we see that God is clearly protecting them. We should support them, not undermine them.

Supporting Scripture:
Deuteronomy 30:3

Read through the Bible a Chapter a day

Leviticus 15

Day 170

Malachi 4:4

"Remember to obey the Law of Moses, my servant—all the decrees and regulations that I gave him on Mount Sinai for all Israel.

Closing out the Old Testament are these words of Malachi 4:4. Jesus re-emphasis the Ten Commandments in Matthew 22:37-40 when He said: "You must love the LORD your God with all your heart, all your soul, and all your mind.' This is the first and greatest commandment. A second is equally important: 'Love your neighbor as yourself.' The entire law and all the demands of the prophets are based on these two commandments." When we are obsessed with love for God, we will continually be thinking about Him. That is how we squeeze the enemies of our soul out.

Supporting Scripture:
Matthew 22:27-40
Exodus 20

Read through the Bible a Chapter a day

Leviticus 16

Day 171

Ephesians 6:17

*Put on salvation as your helmet, and take the **sword of the Spirit, which is the word of God.***

Today, focusing on the word, sword. In Ephesians the sword is the only offensive part of the full armor of God. I don't mean the word offensive as we hear so often today, it is used to strike out, it is a weapon. All the other parts of the armor are defensive and meant to protect the wearer. The word of God is the device that can surely make a difference. We can depend on the mighty word of God! These words we use are the most powerful and awesome - The word of God means business!

Supporting Scripture:
Revelation 19:15
Hebrews 4:12-13

Read through the Bible a Chapter a day

Leviticus 17

Day 172

Proverbs 1:33

"But all who listen to me will live in peace, untroubled by fear of harm."

Wow, look at this promise! We have to learn how to lean into God. Not only are we too listen, we need to do what it says. God's word are words we can live by.

Supporting Scripture:
James 1:22

Read through the Bible a Chapter a day

Leviticus 18

Day 173

Deuteronomy 6:4-9

"Listen, O Israel! **The LORD is our God, the LORD alone**. *And you must love the LORD your God with* **all** *your heart,* **all** *your soul, and* **all** *your strength. And you must* **commit** *yourselves wholeheartedly to these commands that I am giving you today. Repeat them again and again to your children. Talk about them when you are at home and when you are on the road, when you are going to bed and when you are getting up. Tie them to your hands and wear them on your forehead as reminders. Write them on the doorposts of your house and on your gates.*

The book of Deuteronomy is a surprise, at least to me. Moses reminds us that our focus, our attention should be on God. We need to consider God's words all the time. I am reminded this morning of the statement: The devil cannot stay in a room where there is an open Bible. It's the same for our minds. We can push out those thoughts that are destructive when we constantly think about God and His word. How can we do this? Ask God. Have that conversation. He's waiting for you!

Supporting Scripture:
Deuteronomy 11:20

Read through the Bible a Chapter a day

Leviticus 19

Day 174

Genesis 3:15

*"And I will cause hostility between you and the woman,
and between your offspring and her offspring.
He will strike your head,
and you will strike his heel."*

Today, we go back to the beginning. There was a tremendous battle and Satan lost. He was hurtled to the earth and ever since he has been doing his best to destroy the nation Israel and the children of God. Take a few minutes (if you have the time) and recount the times in the Bible that the Israelites faced destruction. Genesis, Exodus, Esther, Matthew all have recounted a time when the Israelites faced their destruction. In recent times the nation Israel has faced annihilation. Hitler, Russia, Iran and even today Israel is surrounded by those who would destroy her. Today antisemitism is flourishing around the world. This hatred began with the God of the world, and it is aimed at God's children. Anything that promotes Jesus Christ is hated. Back in Biblical times, Satan tried to stop anything that would halt the coming of the Christ. I believe this last sentence best describes where we are today: Then the dragon was enraged at the woman and went off to wage war against the rest of her offspring —those who keep God's commands and hold fast their testimony about Jesus. (Revelation 12:17)
Genesis 3:15 is significant. It is the first mention of Jesus Christ as the answer to the sin problem. It is John 5:44 where Jesus announces that some of those following Him were followers of Satan. He exposes him as a liar and a murderer. John also tells us in 1 John 3:8 that the very reason Jesus came was to destroy the devils work. We see that God throughout history had planned for a permanent solution to sin.

For more on this topic check out the supporting scriptures:
Acts 13:10
Genesis 16:11
Judges 13:5
Isaiah 7:14, 8:3, 9:6
Matthew 1:23
Luke 1:31
Galatians 4:4

Read through the Bible a Chapter a day

Leviticus 20

Day 175

Isaiah 35:4

Say to those with fearful hearts,
"Be strong, and do not fear,
for your God is coming to destroy your enemies.
He is coming to save you."

God's promises fill the pages of the Bible. Even so, not everyone reads the Bible. For many, you are the closest to a Bible they may ever get. Shout out the good news of the gospel! For it is true, God is coming back, He is making everything new! He will save you!

Supporting Scripture:
Revelation 21:5

Read through the Bible a Chapter a day

Leviticus 21

Notes

Day 176

Mark 7:14-23

Then Jesus called to the crowd to come and hear. "All of you listen," he said, "and try to understand. It's not what goes into your body that defiles you; you are defiled by what comes from your heart."

Then Jesus went into a house to get away from the crowd, and his disciples asked him what he meant by the parable he had just used. "Don't you understand either?" he asked. "Can't you see that the food you put into your body cannot defile you? Food doesn't go into your heart, but only passes through the stomach and then goes into the sewer." (By saying this, he declared that every kind of food is acceptable in God's eyes.)

And then he added, "It is what comes from inside that defiles you. For from within, out of a person's heart, come evil thoughts, sexual immorality, theft, murder, adultery, greed, wickedness, deceit, lustful desires, envy, slander, pride, and foolishness. All these vile things come from within; they are what defile you."

Have you ever noticed all the commercials involving food, stomach medicines and diet programs on TV? We are obsessed with what we put in our bodies. Here, Jesus tells us that is probably the least of our problems when it comes to our behavior. The real serious stuff is what comes out of our hearts that can ruin us. We can really produce some wicked stuff in our minds and our hearts. I am not saying everything we eat is good or bad for you, just that we need to really to be mindful of the junk we take in with our eyes and minds. That is where the real damage happens!

Supporting Scripture:
Romans 14:1-12

Read through the Bible a Chapter a day

Leviticus 22

Day 177

Judges 2:1-5

The angel of the LORD went up from Gilgal to Bokim and said to the Israelites, "I brought you out of Egypt into this land that I swore to give your ancestors, and I said I would never break my covenant with you. For your part, you were not to make any covenants with the people living in this land; instead, you were to destroy their altars. But you disobeyed my command. Why did you do this? So now I declare that I will no longer drive out the people living in your land. They will be thorns in your sides, and their gods will be a constant temptation to you."
When the angel of the LORD finished speaking to all the Israelites, the people wept loudly. So they called the place Bokim (which means "weeping"), and they offered sacrifices there to the LORD.

There are a couple of interesting points with this mornings scripture. Whenever you see the name of the angel of the Lord, it could very well mean Jesus Christ. We have seen Him before. On one occasion, he stood before Joshua before Israel took Jericho. On numerous occasions Israel disregarded God's commands as they did here in Judges. As a result, He gave them the trouble they sought. We have read about this before, in Romans as a direct result of the nations sin, he gave them over to the desire of their sin - Romans 1:21-32. We have plenty of evidence of God's patience and God's frustration with His children. I pray that we will learn from their lessons and we don't fall the same way.

Supporting Scripture:
Romans 1:21-32

Read through the Bible a Chapter a day

Leviticus 23

Day 178

Hebrews 3:4

For every house is built by someone, but God is the builder of everything.

Isn't it amazing, we know that God's promises are good - look what else he has made!

Mirror Lake in Utah

Supporting Scripture:
Isaiah 42:11

Read through the Bible a Chapter a day

Leviticus 24

Day 179

Jonah 2:1-2

From inside the fish Jonah prayed to the Lord his God. He said:
"In my distress I called to the Lord,
*and **he answered** me.*
From deep in the realm of the dead I called for help,
*and **you listened** to my cry".*

Perhaps one of the greatest promises we have from God is the assurance of answered prayer. God always hears our prayer and answers them (although not always the way we expect or the timing we expect or hope for and when our heart is not centered on God - **Psalm 66:18)** In Jonah's case, God got his attention quickly! So how can we even be assured of the message of Jonah? By reading Jesus himself who said in **Matthew 12:40:** For as Jonah was three days and three nights in the belly of a huge fish, so the Son of Man will be three days and three nights in the heart of the earth.

It really happened, it said so in The Bible.

Supporting Scripture:
Matthew 12:40
Psalm 66:18

Read through the Bible a Chapter a day

Leviticus 25

Day 180

1 Samuel 17:37

*The Lord who **rescued** me from the paw of the lion and the paw of the bear **will** rescue me from the hand of this Philistine."*
Saul said to David, "Go, and the Lord be with you."

Set the scene here......
David is a young man, probably a teenager and he is asked by Jesse his father to take some food to his other three brothers who were with King Saul waiting on one side of a valley and the Philistines on the other. Goliath would come out twice a day to challenge the army of Israel. It is during one of his challenges that David heard Goliath. Now, we know how this story ends, but there are a couple of things I would like to point out. Saul was on his decline as a king. Technically, he should have been the one to take on Goliath. That being said, he had no problem with David and the challenge. Look how God had prepared David for this battle. He (David) was very confident that God would be victorious here as well. David knew that God was at his side!

So what is your Goliath?

Supporting Scripture:
2 Chronicles 1:10

Read through the Bible a Chapter a day

Leviticus 26

Day 181

Judges 6:16-24

*The LORD said to him, "I **will** be with you. And you **will** destroy the Midianites as if you were fighting against one man."*
Gideon replied, "If you are truly going to help me, show me a sign to prove that it is really the LORD speaking to me. Don't go away until I come back and bring my offering to you."
He answered, "I will stay here until you return."
Gideon hurried home. He cooked a young goat, and with a basket of flour he baked some bread without yeast. Then, carrying the meat in a basket and the broth in a pot, he brought them out and presented them to the angel, who was under the great tree.
The angel of God said to him, "Place the meat and the unleavened bread on this rock, and pour the broth over it." And Gideon did as he was told. Then the angel of the LORD touched the meat and bread with the tip of the staff in his hand, and fire flamed up from the rock and consumed all he had brought. And the angel of the LORD disappeared. When Gideon realized that it was the angel of the LORD, he cried out, "Oh, Sovereign LORD, I'm doomed! I have seen the angel of the LORD face to face!"
*"It is all right," the LORD replied. "Do not be afraid. You will not die." And Gideon built an altar to the LORD there and named it **Yahweh-Shalom** (which means **"the LORD is peace"**). The altar remains in Ophrah in the land of the clan of Abiezer to this day.*

Today we call God: Jehovah-shalom. This name means "the God of peace." Just look around you this morning. Everywhere is turmoil and chaos, Our God is a God of order and we can have the peace that God gives. In fact, we are meant to know the fullness of God's perfect peace, or His "shalom." God's peace surpasses all understanding and sustains us even through difficult times. It is the product of fully being what we were created to be. Cry out to God and ask for his peace today!

Supporting Scripture:
Joshua 1:5

Read through the Bible a Chapter a day

Leviticus 27

Day 182

Mark 9:17-24

A man in the crowd answered, "Teacher, I brought you my son, who is possessed by a spirit that has robbed him of speech. Whenever it seizes him, it throws him to the ground. He foams at the mouth, gnashes his teeth and becomes rigid. I asked your disciples to drive out the spirit, but they could not."
"O unbelieving generation," Jesus replied, "how long shall I stay with you? How long shall I put up with you? Bring the boy to me."
So they brought him. When the spirit saw Jesus, it immediately threw the boy into a convulsion. He fell to the ground and rolled around, foaming at the mouth.
Jesus asked the boy's father, "How long has he been like this?"
"From childhood," he answered. "It has often thrown him into fire or water to kill him. But if you can do anything, take pity on us and help us."
"'If you can'?" said Jesus. "Everything is possible for one who believes."
Immediately the boy's father exclaimed, "I do believe; help me overcome my unbelief!"

The promises of God may have to have you involved. Belief is the key. Look at Jesus's promise: "Everything is possible for one who believes". But what if you are struggling with that belief, God will help you overcome. He wants you to be successful, he wants to bless you! Lean into God trusting He is the answer!

Supporting Scripture:
John 11:40

Read through the Bible a Chapter a day

Luke 1

Notes

Yes, They Really do Have an Airshow in Dayton!

It was July 1989, and John Balena and I were in a Piper Archer flying between Cincinnati and Dayton, preparing for the Dayton Airshow. Of course, there is a story here, and this was no small venture. John and I were part of a new chapter for Pilots for Christ International, and this was our first outreach of the new chapter. We were excited because many things had occurred for us to take part in this event. Starting with the Dayton Air Show itself. Having reached out to inquire how much a small booth might cost, we were completely stunned to find out that the airshow was willing to donate our booth. John's flight school donated the use of the Piper Archer for the weekend (for display purposes, of course), which was a huge addition. We even took part in the big dinner and celebration the evening before the show began, with many of aviation's top names and stunt pilots attending. There was a black cloud hanging over the airshow, however. United 232, a DC10, had crashed in Sioux City, Iowa, on Wednesday, July 19, killing many of the passengers on board.

Friday came, and our team went out to set up our tent and start preparations for the airshow. One observation was that we were so far away from the other participants, who seemed to be a mile away at the other end of the airfield. We were concerned we would be all by ourselves and not able to attract the crowd we had hoped for. Oh well, it was a donated space.

Saturday arrived, and as we were getting ready for the airshow to begin, some of the heavies began to arrive. As we watched the different planes land, they all parked on the other side of the field, leaving me with a bit of despair. We watched as the Navy flew over with their F-14 Tomcats, and when they landed, they slowly taxied and kept moving— ever so closer to our end of the runway. And they kept coming until they parked 100 feet from our tent. These awesome flying machines were right next to us. A bit later, the Air Force flew their F-16's over, and yes, they landed, and much to my amazement, they parked on the opposite side of our tent , just a few feet away. We were in between what would be the biggest exhibit of the airshow with our little tent right in the middle! For people to go from one exhibit to the next, they had to walk right through the Pilots for Christ display. Of course, we were ready with water, Bibles, and literature. As cool as that was, it was when the Navy and Air Force Pilots came over to us, telling us how great it was we were there, that made my day! All this was really overwhelming.

Saturday afternoon would bring a fresh sense of purpose to our weekend at the airshow. A lady stopped in to our booth, and she was emotional. It turns out that she had a relative who was on United Flight 232. I don't really remember all the detail of this, but I do remember all of our members circling with hands-on praying for her. I am not sure, but others may have joined in as well. It was an amazing weekend, and I have always believed that God orchestrated all of it for His glory—all of it!

Day 183

Judges 10:6-16

Then the children of Israel again did evil in the sight of the LORD, and served the Baals and the Ashtoreths, the gods of Syria, the gods of Sidon, the gods of Moab, the gods of the people of Ammon, and the gods of the Philistines; and they forsook the LORD and did not serve Him. So the anger of the LORD was hot against Israel; and He sold them into the hands of the Philistines and into the hands of the people of Ammon. From that year they harassed and oppressed the children of Israel for eighteen years—all the children of Israel who were on the other side of the Jordan in the land of the Amorites, in Gilead. Moreover the people of Ammon crossed over the Jordan to fight against Judah also, against Benjamin, and against the house of Ephraim, so that Israel was severely distressed.

And the children of Israel cried out to the LORD, saying, "We have sinned against You, because we have both forsaken our God and served the Baals!"

So the LORD said to the children of Israel, "Did I not deliver you from the Egyptians and from the Amorites and from the people of Ammon and from the Philistines? Also the Sidonians and Amalekites and Maonites oppressed you; and you cried out to Me, and I delivered you from their hand. Yet you have forsaken Me and served other gods. Therefore I will deliver you no more. "Go and cry out to the gods which you have chosen; let them deliver you in your time of distress."

And the children of Israel said to the LORD, "We have sinned! Do to us whatever seems best to You; only deliver us this day, we pray." So they put away the foreign gods from among them and served the LORD. And His soul could no longer endure the misery of Israel.

We have seen this over and over again. God's people doing evil in the eyes of the Lord. In response, God hands them over in the sin they live. This is not an Old Testament vs New Testament comparison, we know that through the book of Romans chapter One. The good news here for us, as it was for Israel is the ultimate Love of God. Our Savior loves us and that love will never change. That is the most wonderful news of all!

Supporting Scripture:
Jeremiah 18:8

Read through the Bible a Chapter a day

Luke 2

Day 184

Hosea 4:1-3

Attention all Israelites! GOD's Message!
GOD indicts the whole population:
"No one is faithful. No one loves.
No one knows the first thing about God.
All this cussing and lying and killing, theft and loose sex,
sheer anarchy, one murder after another!
And because of all this, the very land itself weeps
and everything in it is grief-stricken—
animals in the fields and birds on the wing,
even the fish in the sea are listless, lifeless.

You and I have a responsibility. I write these words every morning hoping I don't offend someone but trying to relay that we have very little control over what is going on in our environment, and less control of others lifestyles and behaviors. Nope, we have a hard enough time controlling ourselves! The good news in all this is this - God knows this; instead, He is asking for you and I to focus our attention on Him. PRAISE and GRATITUDE and Holy Living through our **faith** in Jesus Christ. Remember what Jesus says in John 14:6-7: "I am the way, the truth, and the life. No one can come to the Father except through me. If you had really known me, you would know who my Father is. From now on, you do know him and have seen him!"
Our responsibility is simply this: Know God, and respond to HIM!

Supporting Scripture:
2 Chronicles 7:14
John 14:6-7

Read through the Bible a Chapter a day

Luke 3

Day 185

John 15:5-8

*"I am the vine; you are the branches. If a man remains in me and I in him, he **will** bear much fruit; apart from me you can do nothing. If anyone does not remain in me, he is like a branch that is thrown away and withers; such branches are picked up, thrown into the fire and burned. If you remain in me and **my words remain in you**, ask whatever you wish, and it **will** be given you. This is to my Father's glory, that you bear much fruit, showing yourselves to be my disciples.*

This word from God shows how we are connected to him. Like a vine and its branches, if they are cut or severed, they die. It really as simple as that. Jesus reminds us that the best life has to offer is when we depend upon him for every aspect of our lives. That lifeline is the word of God.

Supporting Scripture:
Ezekiel 15:4-5

Read through the Bible a Chapter a day

Luke 4

Day 186

Malachi 1

A Message. GOD's Word to Israel through Malachi:
GOD said, "I love you."
You replied, "Really? How have you loved us?"
"Look at history" (this is GOD's answer). "Look at how differently I've treated you, Jacob, from Esau: I loved Jacob and hated Esau. I reduced pretentious Esau to a molehill, turned his whole country into a ghost town."
When Edom (Esau) said, "We've been knocked down, but we'll get up and start over, good as new," GOD-of-the-Angel-Armies said, "Just try it and see how far you get. When I knock you down, you stay down. People will take one look at you and say, 'Land of Evil!' and 'the GOD-cursed tribe!'
*"Yes, take a good look. Then you'll see how **faithfully** I've loved you and you'll want even more, saying, 'May GOD be even greater, beyond the borders of Israel!'*
"Isn't it true that a son honors his father and a worker his master? So if I'm your Father, where's the honor? If I'm your Master, where's the respect?" GOD-of-the-Angel-Armies is calling you on the carpet: "You priests despise me!
"You say, 'Not so! How do we despise you?'
"By your shoddy, sloppy, defiling worship.
"You ask, 'What do you mean, "defiling"? What's defiling about it?'
"When you say, 'The altar of GOD is not important anymore; worship of GOD is no longer a priority,' that's defiling. And when you offer worthless animals for sacrifices in worship, animals that you're trying to get rid of—blind and sick and crippled animals—isn't that defiling? Try a trick like that with your banker or your senator—how far do you think it will get you?" GOD-of-the-Angel-Armies asks you.
"Get on your knees and pray that I will be gracious to you. You priests have gotten everyone in trouble. With this kind of conduct, do you think I'll pay attention to you?" GOD-of-the-Angel-Armies asks you.
"Why doesn't one of you just shut the Temple doors and lock them? Then none of you can get in and play at religion with this silly, empty-headed worship. I am not pleased. The GOD-of-the-Angel-Armies is not pleased. And I don't want any more of this so-called worship!
"I am honored all over the world. And there are people who know how to worship me all over the world, who honor me by bringing their best to me. They're saying it everywhere: 'God is greater, this GOD-of-the-Angel-Armies.'
"All except you. Instead of honoring me, you profane me. You profane me when you say, 'Worship is not important, and what we bring to worship is of no account,' and when you say, 'I'm bored—this doesn't do anything for me.' You act so superior, sticking your noses in the air—act superior to me, GOD-of-the-Angel-Armies! And when you do offer

something to me, it's a hand-me-down, or broken, or useless. Do you think I'm going to accept it? This is GOD speaking to you!
"A curse on the person who makes a big show of doing something great for me—an expensive sacrifice, say—and then at the last minute brings in something puny and worthless! I'm a great king, GOD-of-the-Angel-Armies, honored far and wide, and I'll not put up with it!"

Malachi is the final book of the Old Testament. From a historical stand point, this would be the last time that Israel would hear from God for several hundred years (approx. 400)..... the next time, would be a baby in a manger. It is similar to our wait for the rapture of the church. It does not mean God was hiding from Israel, surely individuals continue to have a relationships with the Lord. But the big picture, Malachi... this is it! God challenges Israel to put its best on the line, Put him first and honor him by offering the finest. I am reminded of when Jesus turns the water into wine. What he created was the best and the wedding host says most will bring the cheap stuff out at the end, but this wedding - the best was saved for the last. Don't wait, offer God the best you have - right NOW!

Supporting Scripture:
Deuteronomy 4:37

Read through the Bible a Chapter a day

Luke 5

Day 187

Revelation 1:17-18

When I saw him, I fell at his feet as though dead. Then he placed his right hand on me and said: "Do not be afraid. **I am the First and the Last. I am the Living One**; *I was dead, and now look, I am alive for ever and ever! And I hold the keys of death and Hades."*

Look at this promise: I am the First and the Last, I am The Living One (notice those caps!). Christ is God! Despite everything crazy thing going on in our world, you and I are told not to worry (easier said than done) God has this! As we have talked about before - He is in control! But even better, He overcame the Grave and is still with us. He holds the keys - all the keys!

Supporting Scripture:
Daniel 8:18

Read through the Bible a Chapter a day

Luke 6

Day 188

2 Kings 6:1-7

One day the group of prophets came to Elisha and told him, "As you can see, this place where we meet with you is too small. Let's go down to the Jordan River, where there are plenty of logs. There we can build a new place for us to meet."
"All right," he told them, "go ahead."
"Please come with us," someone suggested.
"I will," he said. So he went with them.
When they arrived at the Jordan, they began cutting down trees. But as one of them was cutting a tree, his ax head fell into the river. "Oh, sir!" he cried. "It was a borrowed ax!"
"Where did it fall?" the man of God asked. When he showed him the place, Elisha cut a stick and threw it into the water at that spot. Then the ax head floated to the surface.
"Grab it," Elisha said. And the man reached out and grabbed it.

Well if you want an example of how God is concerned over EVERY aspect of your life, here is a good one. At this point, an ax head would have been considered a very expensive item to own. Clearly this was borrowed and the prophet saw debtors prison in his future until he could work off the value of the ax head. Don't try and hide those items in your life you either don't want to address or you don't want to bother God with. If it concerns you - it concerns God! Take it to Him and leave it with Him. Remember Hezekiah (2 Kings 19:14-19: After Hezekiah received the letter from the messengers and read it, he went up to the LORD's Temple and spread it out before the LORD. And Hezekiah prayed this prayer before the LORD: "O LORD, God of Israel, you are enthroned between the mighty cherubim! You alone are God of all the kingdoms of the earth. You alone created the heavens and the earth. Bend down, O LORD, and listen! Open your eyes, O LORD, and see! Listen to Sennacherib's words of defiance against the living God.
"It is true, LORD, that the kings of Assyria have destroyed all these nations. And they have thrown the gods of these nations into the fire and burned them. But of course the Assyrians could destroy them! They were not gods at all—only idols of wood and stone shaped by human hands. Now, O LORD our God, rescue us from his power; then all the kingdoms of the earth will know that you alone, O LORD, are God.").

Have a conversation with your Heavenly Father today... He wants to have that conversation!

Read through the Bible a Chapter a day

Luke 7

Day 189

Psalm 110:4

The LORD has taken an oath and will not break his vow: "You are a priest forever in the order of Melchizedek."

Today we dig a bit deeper in the priesthood of Melchizedek and the connection to Christ, the new eternal Priest. King David reveals this truth in Psalms and the writer of Hebrews reiterates it here (Hebrews 7:23-25) "Now there have been many of those priests, since death prevented them from continuing in office; but because Jesus lives forever, he has a permanent priesthood. Therefore he **is** able to save **completely** those who come to God through him, because he **always** lives to intercede for them". Christ intercedes on our behalf whether we realize it or not.

Your faith is a powerful thing, believe this truth!

Supporting Scripture:
Hebrews 7:21-25

Read through the Bible a Chapter a day

Luke 8

Notes

Day 190

Matthew 28:17

When they saw him, they worshiped him; but some doubted.

Each of us has a comfort zone when it comes to belief in Jesus. Look back and see what Matthew states: When they saw him, they worshiped him; but some doubted. They all saw him at the same time, except for Thomas who remained unconvinced despite all of the witness reports. No, there may be a deeper meaning to this statement and I am convinced that the doubt erodes with the level of your commitment to Jesus. Our goal is to KNOW Christ on a deeper level and that happens when we dig into our Bibles and cry out to God. Then the doubt will begin to fade and your confidence in Jesus will take on new heights!

Supporting Scripture:
Luke 24:38
John 20:24-31
Mark 9:24

Read through the Bible a Chapter a day

Luke 9

Day 191

Isaiah 55:10-11

*"The rain and snow come down from the heavens
and stay on the ground to water the earth.
They cause the grain to grow,
producing seed for the farmer
and bread for the hungry.
It is the same with **my word.**
I send it out, and it **always** produces fruit.
It **will** accomplish all I want it to,
and it **will** prosper everywhere I send it.*

Here is a great big promise from God: Expect results when you are deep in Gods word or promises. God's word is really good by yourself, it is also meant to be shared. If you are sharing with someone or are pouring your heart out to God, expect God to move! As we have read on numerous occasions, you may have to wait for it - But God always respond to his word! He will never contradict His word!

How cool is that?

Supporting Scripture:
Leviticus 25:19
Deuteronomy 32:2

Read through the Bible a Chapter a day

Luke 10

Day 192

Judges 16:18-20

*Delilah realized he had finally told her the truth, so she sent for the Philistine rulers. "Come back one more time," she said, "for he has finally told me his secret." So the Philistine rulers returned with the money in their hands. Delilah lulled Samson to sleep with his head in her lap, and then she called in a man to shave off the seven locks of his hair. In this way she began to bring him down, and **his strength left him.**
Then she cried out, "Samson! The Philistines have come to capture you!"
When he woke up, he thought, "I will do as before and shake myself free." **But he didn't realize the LORD had left him.***

As we read about Samson and Delilah, we start the chapter with the realization that Samson had a problem. Really, the issue is sin, but he dabbled in it, he was teased by it, he taunted it and as sin always does, it finally trapped him. I don't care what the temptation is, it generally starts out teasing with you, it can be fun, it can be pleasurable but when it turns to down right sin - IT'S GOT YOU! It will happen to all of us, maybe multiple times. Don't play with fire, sooner or later you will get burnt.

Supporting Scripture:
Joshua 7:12

Read through the Bible a Chapter a day

Luke 11

Day 193

Acts 9:10-19

Now there was a believer in Damascus named Ananias. The Lord spoke to him in a vision, calling, "Ananias!"
"Yes, Lord!" he replied.
The Lord said, **"Go over to Straight Street, to the house of Judas. When you get there, ask for a man from Tarsus named Saul. He is praying to me right now. I have shown him a vision of a man named Ananias coming in and laying hands on him so he can see again."**
"But Lord," exclaimed Ananias, "I've heard many people talk about the terrible things this man has done to the believers in Jerusalem! And he is authorized by the leading priests to arrest everyone who calls upon your name."
But the Lord said, **"Go, for Saul is my chosen instrument to take my message to the Gentiles and to kings, as well as to the people of Israel. And I will show him how much he must suffer for my name's sake."**
So Ananias went and found Saul. He laid his hands on him and said, "Brother Saul, the Lord Jesus, who appeared to you on the road, has sent me so that you might regain your sight and be filled with the Holy Spirit." Instantly something like scales fell from Saul's eyes, and he regained his sight. Then he got up and was baptized. Afterward he ate some food and regained his strength.

Like Moses and Jonah and so many others, there are men and women who got the call to go and serve God. They made all sorts of excuses to not go, but fortunately they were persuaded to go. If Ananias had not gone to meet Paul (then Saul) many of us might have had a different outcomes in our lives. When we are called, we never really know how the outcome may end up - Like Ananias, we may not see the results of our efforts but God is still planting those seeds for future believers.

Supporting Scripture:
Ephesians 1:1

Read through the Bible a Chapter a day

Luke 12

Day 194

2 Kings 6:15-17

When the servant of the man of God got up and went out early the next morning, an army with horses and chariots had surrounded the city. "Oh no, my lord! What shall we do?" the servant asked.
"Don't be afraid," the prophet answered. "Those who are with us are more than those who are with them."
And Elisha prayed, "Open his eyes, LORD, so that he may see." Then the LORD opened the servant's eyes, and he looked and saw the hills full of horses and chariots of fire all around Elisha.

If we could see beyond our own limits and abilities we would realize the vastness of the kingdom of God. We are constantly surrounded by God and his angels. We can be aware simply by taking in all of God's creation and faith and of course His Word!

Supporting Scripture:
Genesis 15:1
Psalm 55:18

Read through the Bible a Chapter a day

Luke 13

Day 195

Psalm 100

Shout with joy to the LORD, all the earth!
Worship the LORD with gladness.
Come before him, singing with joy.
Acknowledge that the LORD is God!
He made us, and we are his.
We are his people, the sheep of his pasture.
Enter his gates with thanksgiving;
go into his courts with praise.
Give thanks to him and praise his name.
For the LORD is good.
His unfailing love continues forever,
and his faithfulness continues to each generation.

I think that I may have mentioned at some point that I am on a THANK YOU kick right now. Thanking those who have impacted my life and I am sharing this with my students. It really does all start with God. We need a big kick in the seat right now, and a good way to start is saying THANK YOU!

Supporting Scripture:
1 Kings 18:21

Read through the Bible a Chapter a day

Luke 14

Day 196

Isaiah 41:8-10

"But as for you, Israel my servant,
Jacob my chosen one,
descended from Abraham my friend,
*I have **called** you back from the ends of the earth,*
saying, 'You are my servant.'
*For I have **chosen** you*
and will not throw you away.
*Don't be afraid, for **I am with** you.*
*Don't be discouraged, for **I am** your God.*
*I **will** strengthen you and help you.*
*I **will** hold you up with my victorious right hand.*

Todays promise is filled with hope. Somehow, we walk around with the concept that we have chosen God, and yes, we decided to follow him. That is not how it started, God pursued us, he picked us. Once that happened, once we decided to follow the God of our lives, it is as Rocky Bolboa states it - The greatest day of the history of our life!

Supporting Scripture:
Isaiah 29:22

Read through the Bible a Chapter a day

Luke 15

Notes

Day 197

Proverbs 30:8-9

Keep falsehood and lies far from me;
give me neither poverty nor riches,
but give me only my daily bread.
Otherwise, I may have too much and disown you
and say, 'Who is the LORD?'
Or I may become poor and steal,
and so dishonor the name of my God.

God promises to take care of our needs if we will trust him to do so. The writer of Proverbs understands the fine line between trusting God and ignoring God and promoting self.

Supporting Scripture:
Matthew 6:11
Joshua 24:27

Read through the Bible a Chapter a day

Luke 16

Day 198

1 Thessalonians 2:13

*And we also thank God continually because, when you received the word of God, which you heard from us, you accepted it not as a human word, but as it actually is, **the word of God,** which is indeed at work in you who believe.*

If we are to truly understand the promises of God, then we must understand the power of the Bible. It is not merely written by human hands, it is written by writers who were inspired to reveal what God has said through the Holy Spirit. Think about this..... everything you have ever heard about Jesus has been passed down at some point and it all originated from the Bible. We do need to be careful, because there are things we have heard; slogans, phrases and sayings that are attributed to the words of God that are not in there at all. Pry it open and read it, you won't be sorry - I promise you! But the Bible also says that it's truth and power works for those who believe! So if you struggle to understand some scripture or stories or even parables, ask God for wisdom and then read James 1:5. He will never let you down, especially those who seek him!

Supporting Scripture:
Hebrews 4:12

Read through the Bible a Chapter a day

Luke 19

Day 199

James 4:1-8

What causes fights and quarrels among you? Don't they come from your desires that battle within you? You want something but don't get it. You kill and covet but you cannot have what you want. You quarrel and fight. You do not have, because you do not ask God. When you ask, you do not receive, because you ask with wrong motives, that you may spend what you get on your pleasures.
You adulterous people, don't you know that friendship with the world means hatred toward God? Anyone who chooses to be a friend of the world becomes an enemy of God. Or do you think Scripture says without reason that the spirit he has caused to live in us envies intensely? But he gives us more grace. That is why Scripture says:
"God opposes the proud but shows favor to the humble."
Submit yourselves, *then, to God.* **Resist the devil,** *and he* **will** *flee from you.* **Come near to God and he will come near to you**. *Wash your hands, you sinners, and purify your hearts, you double-minded.*

Today, we are yet reminded again to turn and lean into God. This passage from James is a stern reminder that evil is our enemy even though it might be dressed in a beautiful setting. It can cause us to turn to the world to seek our solution instead of turning to God. Resist the devil and he **will** flee from you. One thing Satan cannot stand is a Christian on their knees in obedience to God!

Supporting Scripture:
Matthew 5:21-22
Isaiah 54:5

Read through the Bible a Chapter a day

Luke 20

Day 200

Psalm 9:9-10

The LORD is a refuge for the oppressed,
a stronghold in times of trouble.
Those who know your name trust in you,
for you, LORD, have never forsaken those who seek you.

There are fantastic promises for you and I today. God is a refuge for the oppressed. I think of a castle with massive walls that protect the people inside - only better! Our relationship with God provides protection as a shelter. And God will never forget us! Ever! He will never forsake those who seek him. So I turned to the dictionary this morning to see what the word forsake means (I don't know about you, that is not a word I would use or have really heard recently outside the Bible): Forsake: **T**o renounce or turn away from entirely.
Isn't that something? We can never out pace, out race or hide from God. I know there are times we try, especially if there is something we may be ashamed of, but like it or not - we cannot hide from our God!

Isn't that incredible?

Supporting Scripture:
Deuteronomy 33:27

Read through the Bible a Chapter a day

Luke 21

Day 201

Galatians 6:7-10

Don't be misled—you cannot mock the justice of God. You will always harvest what you plant. Those who live only to satisfy their own sinful nature will harvest decay and death from that sinful nature. But those who live to please the Spirit will harvest everlasting life from the Spirit. So let's not get tired of doing what is good. At just the right time we will reap a harvest of blessing if we don't give up. Therefore, whenever we have the opportunity, we should do good to everyone—especially to those in the family of faith.

The past couple of days there has been a lot of talk about "God will not be mocked". Indeed he shall not be. Look, we live in evil times and we see events where we shake our heads in disgust and amazement of how low we can sink. Paul reminds us that we harvest what we plant and you and I should live to please the Spirit of God. Do good to everyone, especially to those in the family of faith.

Supporting Scripture:
Proverbs 22:8
1 Corinthians 6:9

Read through the Bible a Chapter a day

Luke 22

Day 202

1 John 4:18

*Such love has **no** fear, because perfect love expels **all** fear. If we are afraid, it is for fear of punishment, and this shows that we have not fully experienced his **perfect** love. We love each other because he loved us first.*

If we have learned anything, we learned that God is Love. And he has covered us with his love, it is everywhere around us, we cannot escape it (not that we would want to). When we commit our lives to Christ he comes and takes residence in our souls. This presence, is full and complete. We now have the reassurance of God in our lives. God's perfect love **DRIVES OUT** all our fears. No matter what it is, God's love conquers all. When we are fearful, the Bible says it is because we have not experienced his perfect love. Give it (your fear) to God. Let him deal with it - whatever it is, God is bigger, and we know we can trust him with it.

Supporting Scripture:
Romans 8:15
1 Corinthians 13

Read through the Bible a Chapter a day

Luke 23

Day 203

Revelation 3:14-22

Write this letter to the angel of the church in Laodicea. This is the message from the one who is the Amen—the faithful and true witness, the beginning of God's new creation:
"I know all the things you do, *that you are neither hot nor cold. I wish that you were one or the other! But since you are like lukewarm water, neither hot nor cold, I will spit you out of my mouth! You say, 'I am rich. I have everything I want. I don't need a thing!' And you don't realize that you are wretched and miserable and poor and blind and naked.* ***So I advise you to buy gold from me—gold that has been purified by fire. Then you will be rich. Also buy white garments from me so you will not be shamed by your nakedness, and ointment for your eyes so you will be able to see.*** *I correct and discipline everyone I love. So be diligent and turn from your indifference.*
"Look! ***I stand at the door and knock.*** *If you hear my voice and open the door, I* ***will*** *come in, and we* ***will*** *share a meal together* ***as friends****. Those who are victorious* ***will*** *sit with me on my throne, just as I was victorious and sat with my Father on his throne.*
"Anyone with ears to hear must listen to the Spirit and understand what he is saying to the churches."

Upon reading this today, I realized that Jesus is saying to me - Your efforts alone are not going to make it. We need to do business with Christ, relying on him for that very breath and life we have (Gold, white garments, and ointment). He wants a relationship with you and I and he is at the door right now! Open that door, invite him in and let him show you that what he offers is more precious than anything we can dream up!

Supporting Scripture:
Colossians 2:1-3

Read through the Bible a Chapter a day

Luke 24

Notes

Day 204

Psalm 33:6

The LORD merely spoke,
and the heavens were created.
He breathed the word,
and all the stars were born.

Here is the perfect example of the power of God's word; literally, His very breath is creating! He merely spoke and created the heavens. The stars; it seems, created almost by happenstance as the book of Genesis 1:16 tells us - oh yeah…. He also made the stars. With all that done, His most important creation, mankind, thats's right: You and I, were made in His image! And He breathed life in us as well!

Supporting Scripture:
Genesis 1:16
Genesis 2:7
Psalm 19:1-6

Read through the Bible a Chapter a day

Numbers 1

Day 205

2 Corinthians 4:16-18

That is why we never give up. Though our bodies are dying, our spirits are being renewed every day. For our present troubles are small and won't last very long. Yet they produce for us a glory that vastly outweighs them and will last forever! So we don't look at the troubles we can see now; rather, we fix our gaze on things that cannot be seen. For the things we see now will soon be gone, but the things we cannot see will last forever.

Seen in the perspective of eternity, the Christian's difficulties, whatever they may be - diminish in importance. The eternal glory is far greater than any suffering we may have in this life! Yes, God promises to help and protect us, we just need to remember that you and I are promised something far greater!

Supporting Scripture:
Psalm 18:45
Hebrews 11:1

Read through the Bible a Chapter a day

Numbers 2

Day 206

Psalm 2

Why are the nations so angry?
Why do they waste their time with futile plans?
The kings of the earth prepare for battle;
the rulers plot together
against the LORD
and against his anointed one.
"Let us break their chains," they cry,
"and free ourselves from slavery to God."
But the one who rules in heaven laughs.
The Lord scoffs at them.
Then in anger he rebukes them,
terrifying them with his fierce fury.
For the Lord declares, "I have placed my chosen king on the throne
in Jerusalem, on my holy mountain."
The king proclaims the LORD's decree:
"The LORD said to me, 'You are my son.
Today I have become your Father.
Only ask, and I will give you the nations as your inheritance,
the whole earth as your possession.
You will break them with an iron rod
and smash them like clay pots.'"
Now then, you kings, act wisely!
Be warned, you rulers of the earth!
Serve the LORD with reverent fear,
and rejoice with trembling.
Submit to God's royal son, or he will become angry,
and you will be destroyed in the midst of all your activities—
for his anger flares up in an instant.
But what joy for all who take refuge in him!

Psalm 2 does not have an official author although many believe it to be King David. Peter and John give the credit to David when they are quoted in part in Acts 4:24-26. We can relate to what is happening in our world today asking the very same questions. One more example to the relevance of the Bible in today's world.

Read through the Bible a Chapter a day

Numbers 3

Day 207

John 5:25-30

And I assure you that the time is coming, indeed it's here now, when the dead will hear my voice—the voice of the Son of God. And those who listen will live. The Father has life in himself, and he has granted that same life-giving power to his Son. And he has given him authority to judge everyone because he is the Son of Man. Don't be so surprised! Indeed, the time is coming when all the dead in their graves will hear the voice of God's Son, and they will rise again. Those who have done good will rise to experience eternal life, and those who have continued in evil will rise to experience judgment. I can do nothing on my own. I judge as God tells me. Therefore, my judgment is just, because I carry out the will of the one who sent me, not my own will.

When we look at the words of Jesus, we can see once again that His changes lives. We also witness that His words are eternal - They have always been and will always be. From Paul and his words about a time that is coming - Jesus will return for his family of believers and the dead will rise as well as those who are still alive! In the Book of Ezekiel, there is a different rising and that is of the gathering of dried bones in the desert. This is the rising of the nation Israel. Regeneration once again from a time long before Jesus. God has and is working.

Supporting Scripture:
1 Thessalonians 4:16-18
Ezekiel 37:11-14

Read through the Bible a Chapter a day

Numbers 4

Day 208

1 Peter 2:9-10

*But you are not like that, for you **are** a chosen people. You **are** royal priests, a holy nation, God's very own possession. As a result, you can show others the goodness of God, for he called you out of the darkness into his wonderful light.*
"Once you had no identity as a people;
*now you **are** God's people.*
Once you received no mercy;
*now you **have** received God's mercy."*

We have been changed! Just like we saw in John 1:12-13, 2 Corinthians 5:17 and Galatians 6:15-16, once we had no identity as a people, now we are recognized by God. There was a time when we received no mercy, now we receive God's mercy. You and I did not make that change, God did it! Just like James tells us: But don't just listen to God's word. You must do what it says (James 1:22) You and I are new creations as it states in the Holy Bible and that should motivate us to action. Let's go and be the people God has blessed us to be!

Supporting Scripture:
John 1:12-13
2 Corinthians 5:17
Galatians 6:15-16
James 1:22

Read through the Bible a Chapter a day

Numbers 5

Day 209

Luke 1:1-4

*Many people have set out to write accounts about the events that have been fulfilled among us. They used the eyewitness reports circulating among us from the early disciples. Having carefully investigated everything from the beginning, I also have decided to write an accurate account for you, most honorable Theophilus, so you can be **certain** of the truth of everything you were taught.*

The scriptures today goes back to the very basics about every word in scripture having meaning. As I was looking at the beginning of Luke, these words bounced off the page. It seems to me that there are times in our lives when scripture is reassuring. Another verse is John 20:31. I am not suggesting that anyone has lost their faith, but rather they need to be reminded about the realness of the word of God. Another scripture that reminds us of the certainty of scripture is 1 John 5:13 which reads: I have written this to you who believe in the name of the Son of God, so that you may **know** you have eternal life. These words we read this morning are there to bolster your faith, not leave you hanging. There is a huge difference between hoping and wondering about these words we read and knowing with certainty that they are real!

Supporting Scripture:
John 20:31
1 John 5:13

Read through the Bible a Chapter a day

Numbers 6

Day 210

Hebrews 12:1-4

*Therefore, since we are surrounded by such a **huge crowd of witnesses** to the life of faith, let us strip off every weight that slows us down, especially the sin that so easily trips us up. And let us run with endurance the race God has set before us. We do this by keeping our eyes on Jesus, the champion who initiates and perfects our faith. Because of the joy awaiting him, he endured the cross, disregarding its shame. Now he is seated in the place of honor beside God's throne. Think of all the hostility he endured from sinful people; then you won't become weary and give up. After all, you have not yet given your lives in your struggle against sin.*

I want to show you the shame and desperation of hell compared to Heaven. As I have read in the Bible, it may be a place of absolute isolation from God. That would be hell for sure, I also think it could just be a place of isolation where there is no one around you and all you have in your torment are the memories of the times you could have accepted Christ and didn't, leaving you in complete despair. Look at the number of times Jesus uses the phrase " Now throw this useless servant into outer darkness, where there will be weeping and gnashing of teeth.' (Matthew 25:30). Remember, this is forever - That would be utter despair and absolutely nothing you could about it. The good news is this is a place meant for Satan and his demons, if you are reading these words - **DROP WHAT YOU ARE DOING RIGHT NOW AND CRY OUT TO CHRIST TO SAVE YOU.** Now let's contrast that to Heaven. The Bible gives us a clear picture of that as well, starting with Hebrews 12:1-4. There is a huge crowd and they are cheering you on! I imagine a great arena watching you run , or maybe I should say THE race of life. You are always running to complete the race and those witnesses are on your side. There is no isolation in Heaven. There will also be no sun or moon because the Bible tells us God will provide all the light you will ever need (Revelation 21:22-27). You and I will have new bodies that will never age - "For we know that when this earthly tent we live in is taken down (that is, when we die and leave this earthly body), we will have a house in heaven, an eternal body made for us by God himself and not by human hands" (2 Corinthians 5:1). Finally, but certainly not the end of the description of Heaven - Jesus himself has been building us a residence: "Don't let your hearts be troubled. Trust in God, and trust also in me. There is more than enough room in my Father's home. If this were not so, would I have told you that **I am going to prepare a place for you**? When everything is ready, I will come and get you, so that you will always be with me where I am. And you know the way to where I am going" (John 14:1-4).

Supporting Scripture:
Luke 16:22-23

Read through the Bible a Chapter a day

Numbers 7

Notes

Day 211

1 Corinthians 1:18-25

*The message of the cross **is** foolish to those who are headed to destruction! But we who are being saved know **it is** the very power of God. As the scriptures say,*
*"I **will** destroy the wisdom of the wise*
*and **discard** the intelligence of the*
intelligent."
So where does this leave the philosophers, the scholars and the world's brilliant debaters?
*God **has** made the wisdom of this world look foolish. Since God in his wisdom saw to it that **the world would never know him through human wisdom**, he **has** used our foolish preaching to save those who believe. It is foolish to Jews who ask for signs from heaven. And it is foolish to the Greeks, who seek human wisdom. So when we preach that Christ was crucified, the Jews **are** offended and the Gentiles say it's all nonsense.*
*But to those called by God to salvation, both Jews and Gentiles, Christ **is** the power of God and the wisdom of God. This foolish plan of God **is** wiser than the wisest of human plans, and God's weakness **is** stronger than the greatest of human strength.*

Take a little time this morning and let this scripture soak in. Today, this generation is the most educated in history, yet we are also facing unprecedented division and turmoil. We need a Biblical worldview now more than ever. All the education in the world gains you nothing as you seek God. It provides no assurance of the promises of the scripture and worse, those who think they are somehow "saved" by their own human wisdom are doomed to destruction. God's plan is pretty basic: Jesus Christ!

Supporting Scripture:
Isaiah 29:14

Read through the Bible a Chapter a day

Numbers 8

Day 212

Psalm 73:21-28

Then I realized that my heart was bitter,
and I was all torn up inside.
I was so foolish and ignorant—
I must have seemed like a senseless animal to you.
***Yet** I still belong to you;*
you hold my right hand.
You guide me with your counsel,
leading me to a glorious destiny.
Whom have I in heaven but you?
I desire you more than anything on earth.
My health may fail, and my spirit may grow weak,
***but God** remains the strength of my heart;*
he is mine forever.
Those who desert him will perish,
for you destroy those who abandon you.
But as for me, how good it is to be near God!
I have made the Sovereign LORD my shelter,
and I will tell everyone about the wonderful things you do.

These verses speak volumes about the love, mercy and grace of God. On a few occasions in the past we have talked about the words "But God" and we see it here. Despite all the crap I pull in my life - God still saves me - he truly is the strength of my heart and my portion forever! He never leaves us - EVER!

Supporting Scripture:
Psalm 139:10

Read through the Bible a Chapter a day

Numbers 9

Day 213

Revelation 19:9-11

*And the angel said to me, "Write this: Blessed **are** those who are invited to the wedding feast of the lamb". And he added, "**These are the true words that come from God**". Then I fell down at his feet to worship him, but he said: "No, don't worship me. I am a servant of God, just like you and your brothers and sisters who **testify** about their faith in Jesus. Worship **only** God. For the essence of prophecy is to give clear witness for Jesus".*

John was clearly overwhelmed by what he witnessed in Heaven. What do we learn from this exchange with the angel:
God's word is true!
Worship only God!
Angels are servants of God, and we have the same objective - testify about your faith in Jesus.
Finally, the entire Bible is meant for one purpose - Glorify Christ!

Supporting Scripture:
Acts 10:25-26

Read through the Bible a Chapter a day

Numbers 10

Day 214

1 Corinthians 2:13

We don't have to rely on the world's guesses and opinions. We didn't learn this by reading books or going to school; we learned it from God, who taught us person-to-person through Jesus, and we're passing it on to you in the same firsthand, personal way.

Some time ago, we covered this. It is so powerful! You and I have the same opportunity as Paul to experience; first hand and with a direct connection, the realization of a true and perfect friendship with God through Jesus Christ! And that is available not by schooling or others, but only through God!

Let's live BIG!

Supporting Scripture:
Galatians 1:12
Galatians 1:15-16
John 1:12-13

Read through the Bible a Chapter a day

Numbers 11

Day 215

John 1:12-13

But to all who believed him and accepted him, he gave the right to become children of God. **They are reborn**—*not with a physical birth resulting from human passion or plan,* **but a birth that comes from God.**

We have discussed direct revelation with God in these past days. God is in the process of making everything "new". There is no better example than spring. New life comes to God's creation and as wonderful as that is - You and I have the opportunity for rebirth, the difference I find is: Ours is permanent! Ours is the result of what Jesus has done on our behalf and when we recognize and move on that action from Christ we become a new "creation", Born of God! This can only come from God, there is nothing we can do to earn it, it is a free gift for those who cry out and accept it.

Supporting Scripture:
Galatians 1:15-16

Read through the Bible a Chapter a day

Numbers 12

Day 216

Colossians 3:1-5

*Since, then, you **have** been raised with Christ, set your hearts on things above, where Christ **is**, seated at the right hand of God. Set your minds on things above, not on earthly things. For you died, and your life is **now** hidden with Christ in God. When Christ, who **is** your life, appears, then you also **will** appear with him in glory.*
Put to death, therefore, whatever belongs to your earthly nature: sexual immorality, impurity, lust, evil desires and greed, which is idolatry.

It is hard for people to keep looking up when there is so much going on around us. Here, Paul is telling us to do just that. How do we set our minds on things above, especially right now? Reach up on that shelf, dust off that Bible and crack it open. I would suggest a reading plan - perhaps a chapter a day. Not to put things in grizzly mode, we need to be sure we put to death those things which could become idols in our lives: homes, jobs, science, lifestyles, good grief, there are so many - I am not saying those things in themselves are bad, just don't let them become obsessions. They become idols. Remember our true source of freedom!

Supporting Scripture:
Philippians 3:19-20

Read through the Bible a Chapter a day

Numbers 13

Day 217

Isaiah 29:14

Because of this, I will once again astound these hypocrites with amazing wonders. The wisdom of the wise will pass away,
and the intelligence of the intelligent will disappear."

1 Corinthians 1:18-25

The message of the cross is foolish to those who are headed for destruction! But we who are being saved know it is the very power of God. As the Scriptures say, "I will destroy the wisdom of the wise
and discard the intelligence of the intelligent."
So where does this leave the philosophers, the scholars, and the world's brilliant debaters? God has made the wisdom of this world look foolish. Since God in his wisdom saw to it that the world would never know him through human wisdom, he has used our foolish preaching to save those who believe. It is foolish to the Jews, who ask for signs from heaven. And it is foolish to the Greeks, who seek human wisdom. So when we preach that Christ was crucified, the Jews are offended and the Gentiles say it's all nonsense.
But to those called by God to salvation, both Jews and Gentiles, Christ is the power of God and the wisdom of God. This foolish plan of God is wiser than the wisest of human plans, and God's weakness is stronger than the greatest of human strength.

If you can, take a little time this morning and let this scripture soak in. Today, this generation is the most educated in history, yet we are also facing unprecedented division and turmoil. We need a Biblical worldview now more than ever. All the education of the world offers you means nothing as you seek God. It provides no assurance of the promises of the scripture and worse, those who think they are somehow "saved" by their human wisdom are doomed to destruction. God's plan is pretty basic: Jesus Christ!

Read through the Bible a Chapter a day

Numbers 14

Notes

Day 218

Psalm 139:23-24

Search me, O God, and know my heart;
test me and know my anxious thoughts.
Point out anything in me that offends you,
and lead me along the path of everlasting life.

As I was reading my daily chapter in 1 Corinthians 5, I am reminded of what Paul says about associating with an immoral behavior, ours and others. So many in our society look at the Christian life as boring and no fun. They might say: too many rules and regulations, we are just a stuffy bunch.   However, freedom in Christ is a liberating experience!   We need to take inventory of our lives and just as David did in Psalm 139:23-24. It's a gutsy thing to ask God to search your heart and test your thoughts. He will show you what offends Him and that is what we need as we continue to trust and KNOW HIM!

Supporting Scripture:
1 Corinthians 5

Read through the Bible a Chapter a day

Numbers 15

Day 219

Hebrews 9:22

In fact, the law requires that nearly everything be cleansed with blood, and without the shedding of blood there is no forgiveness.

Concerning Good Friday and the death of our Lord. I wonder what happened on Saturday. The day in between. We don't know much about Saturday except that is was the Sabbath, and we know that the Disciples were probably hunkered down in a secret place. Then again, maybe not, Peter might have been alone struggling with himself over the denial of Jesus. The women may have been preparing their spices to anoint Jesus's body. One thing I am pretty sure of, they had not put two and two together about what Jesus said about that third day thing. But the Bible does say that the Chief priests and the Pharisees went to meet with Pilate about putting extra guards at the tomb because they knew what Jesus said about his resurrection. They said that it would be convenient for the disciples to come and steal the body. Interesting they remembered but the Disciples did not. I included Hebrews 9:22 because we need to remember what God says is the standard for forgiving sin. The price paid is severe, but in the case of Christ it was permanent and it was perfect.

Thank God for his perfect plan!

Supporting Scripture:
Exodus 29:21

Read through the Bible a Chapter a day

Numbers 16

Day 220

Exodus 33:11-17

*Inside the Tent of Meeting, the LORD would speak to Moses face to face, **as one speaks to a friend**. Afterward Moses would return to the camp, but the young man who assisted him, Joshua son of Nun, would remain behind in the Tent of Meeting.*
One day Moses said to the LORD, "You have been telling me, 'Take these people up to the Promised Land.' But you haven't told me whom you will send with me. You have told me, 'I know you by name, and I look favorably on you.' If it is true that you look favorably on me, let me know your ways so I may understand you more fully and continue to enjoy your favor. And remember that this nation is your very own people."
The LORD replied, "I will personally go with you, Moses, and I will give you rest—everything will be fine for you."
Then Moses said, "If you don't personally go with us, don't make us leave this place. How will anyone know that you look favorably on me—on me and on your people—if you don't go with us? For your presence among us sets your people and me apart from all other people on the earth."
*The LORD replied to Moses, "I will indeed do what you have asked, for I look favorably on you, and **I know you by name.**"*

God spoke to Moses face to face, as one speaks to a friend. I want that! The truth is: I have that and so do you, if we would just realize that we can speak to God who is our friend through prayer and worship!. When Jesus died on the cross, He opened the path directly to God that our sin blocked! How about we say to God: Teach us your ways. I want that too! As we have read in other verses, we can know God and learn from him. Now wait a minute, we have that as well.... we have the Bible which is God's story and can read all about God and His story. We also have the promise of God's active participation in our lives - his presence goes with us always. Finally and what a way to cap this morning - God KNOWS your name! That is not to say he only knows your name, he knows every aspect of your life. In fact, God tells us in Isaiah 49:16 that our names are engraved in the palms of His hands! Your personality, your nature, your fear, your hopes and dreams, and yes, your sin. God knows your name, and wants to spend time with you as a friend. Isn't that awesome?

Supporting Scripture:
Isaiah 49:16

Read through the Bible a Chapter a day

Numbers 17

Day 221

Psalm 130

Out of the depths I cry to you, O LORD;
O Lord, hear my voice.
Let your ears be attentive
to my cry for mercy.
If you, O LORD, kept a record of sins,
O Lord, who could stand?
*But with you **there is** forgiveness,*
therefore you are feared.
*I **wait** for the LORD, my soul **waits**,*
*and in his **word** I put my hope.*
*My soul **waits** for the Lord*
more than watchmen wait for the morning,
more than watchmen wait for the morning.
O Israel, put your hope in the LORD,
*for **with** the LORD is unfailing love*
*and **with** him is full redemption.*
*He himself **will** redeem Israel*
*from **all** their sins.*

This is a reminder from Psalm 46:10. There are hundreds of references in the Bible about waiting for God, something that rubs wrong on our society today. Waiting for God is trusting in God. How we all need to be reminded of these promises. How our nation needs to hear this word. It is perfect at Christmas time, this is the reason Jesus came - to save us.

Supporting Scripture:
Psalm 46:10

Read through the Bible a Chapter a day

Numbers 18

Day 222

Jeremiah 33:1-3

*While Jeremiah was still confined in the courtyard of the guard, the LORD gave him this second message: "This is what the LORD says—the LORD who **made** the earth, who **formed** and **established i**t, whose name is the LORD: Ask me and I **will** tell you remarkable secrets you do not know about things to come.*

Do I firmly grasp the reality that God is with me all the time? Here is Jeremiah, in prison when God comes to him and encourages him to call on God (Pray). Not only should we pray to God, we need to listen because he will answer your prayer. We see the same thing happen to Paul while he is prison (Acts 18:9, 23:11). What an incredible time to be alive. You and I have the ability to call out to God - the Creator and Establisher of all creation who **promises** a response. Notice also that Jeremiah mentions who created all this around us and the word "establishes" it. You want to affect our world for the good? Pray to the Creator and the Establisher of the earth, not some false religion so many around us are trying to create. Mankind cannot solve these issues, only God can! The question really is: are we calling out boldly to God?

Supporting Scripture:
Acts 18:9

Read through the Bible a Chapter a day

Numbers 19

Day 223

John 5:17-18

*So the Jewish leaders began harassing Jesus for breaking the Sabbath rules. But Jesus replied, **"My Father is always working, and so am I."** So the Jewish leaders tried all the harder to find a way to kill him. For he not only broke the Sabbath, he called God his Father, thereby making himself equal with God.*

Take a few minutes and look back at your year. It's an opportunity to look back at it and see a blessing or two or maybe lots of them. Here is the important thing to remember, God is still here, working, God is still in control! Jesus is still preparing a place for us, he is still our mediator!
Nothing has changed, except that we are a little closer to the day when he finally says - enough! But I want you to see the response to Jesus and his statement - they hated him - they tried to kill him. His message was not received well, is it any wonder why our message brings the response it does?

Supporting Scripture:
John 9:4

Read through the Bible a Chapter a day

Numbers 20

Day 224

Hosea 14:9

*Let those who **are** wise understand these things.*
*Let those **with** discernment listen carefully.*
*The paths of the LORD **are** true and right,*
and righteous people live by walking in them.
But in those paths sinners stumble and fall.

We know God's ways are not our ways, those who follow God and read his word will contemplate the ways of God, when we are serious about listening to his ways. The world does not see this, and it becomes a stumbling block to it. God's word is the standard by which everything else is measured. It's that Biblical worldview we follow.

Supporting Scripture:
Psalm 107:43

Read through the Bible a Chapter a day

Numbers 21

Notes

Day 225

Daniel 2:47

The king said to Daniel, "Surely your God is the God of gods and the Lord of kings and a revealer of mysteries, for you were able to reveal this mystery."

By all accounts King Nebuchadnezzar was a bad dude. If you looked at him wrong he could have you killed. He was evil. Yet, God had a plan for him. It did not happen over night, but gradually, Nebuchadnezzar would soften towards God. There are numerous references throughout the Bible that Kings and all leaders are placed where they are by God's directions. In fact, Jeremiah 27:6 calls him "my servant" (Now I will give all your countries into the hands of my servant Nebuchadnezzar king of Babylon; I will make even the wild animals subject to him) so he was a key part of God's plan. But even the King recognized that God was the God of gods and the Lord of kings and the revealer of mysteries.
Look what **Psalm 19:1-4** says:
The heavens declare the glory of God;
the skies proclaim the work of his hands.
Day after day they pour forth speech;
night after night they reveal knowledge.
They have no speech, they use no words;
no sound is heard from them.
Yet their voice goes out into all the earth,
their words to the ends of the world.

There are no words needed for evidence of God and his greatness..... Even the heavens declare it.

Supporting Scripture:
Deuteronomy 10:17
1 Timothy 6:15-16

Read through the Bible a Chapter a day

Numbers 22

Day 226

Daniel 6:35

*His rule **is** everlasting, and his kingdom **is** eternal. All the people of the earth are nothing compared to him. He does **as** he pleases among the angels of heaven and among the people of the earth. No one can stop him or say to him, 'What do you mean by doing these things?'*

This quote was not by an Apostle, or a Prophet or follower of Christ.
This quote is from King Nebuchadnezzar. To see the full context of his statement look at **verse 34**: After this time had passed, I, Nebuchadnezzar, looked up to heaven. My sanity returned, and I praised and worshiped the Most High who lives forever. Nebuchadnezzar was one bad dude. Yet he is described by God in the Bible as his servant (**Jeremiah 27:6** - With my great power and outstretched arm I made the earth and its people and the animals that are on it, and I give it to anyone I please. Now I will give all your countries into the hands of **my servant** Nebuchadnezzar king of Babylon; I will make even the wild animals subject to him.). Kings, Presidents, Prime Ministers - all leaders are under the control of God. While we may not understand God's movements or motives, he is working all things out towards his conclusion. In the case of Nebuchadnezzar, he would finally recognized the control of God in his life and ended up worshiping God. May our leaders understand God's control in our world and universe and worship him, the only true God!.

Supporting Scripture:
Daniel 6:34
Jeremiah 27:6

Read through the Bible a Chapter a day

Numbers 23

Day 227

Ezekiel 36:27

*And I **will** put my Spirit in you so that you will follow my decrees and be careful to obey my regulations.*

God promised us his Holy Spirit, and he gives him freely to all who choose to follow him. In the Old and new Testament He is the third person of the Trinity. And make no mistake, he is God! We should always be aware of him and listen to his quiet voice and not grieve him. **Ephesians 4:30** tells us: *And do not bring sorrow to God's Holy Spirit by the way you live. Remember, he has identified you as his own, guaranteeing that you will be saved on the day of redemption.*
You have been sealed by the Spirit of God! **Psalm 51:10-11** says: *Create in me a clean heart, O God. Renew a loyal spirit within me. Do not banish me from your presence, and don't take your Holy Spirit from me.*

Supporting Scripture:
Ephesians 4:30
Psalm 51:10-11

Read through the Bible a Chapter a day

Numbers 24

Day 228

Luke 11:28

Jesus replied, "But even more blessed are all who hear the word of God and put it into practice."

Well there it is, more practical advice from Jesus. Do what it says. But this is not the only place we are reminded to read the words of God and do what it says. Check out **Joshua 1:8:** *Study this Book of Instruction continually. Meditate on it day and night so you will be sure to obey everything written in it. Only then will you prosper and succeed in all you do.* In addition **James 1:22** offers this: *But don't just listen to God's word. You must do what it says. Otherwise, you are only fooling yourselves.* I want to succeed in all I do, how about you? God's words include blessing and success and these words are hard to find on our world today!

Supporting Scripture:
Joshua 1:8
James 1:22

Read through the Bible a Chapter a day

Numbers 25

Day 229

1 Corinthians 8:3

But the person who loves God is the one whom God recognizes.

Do you have the ability to love God without fully knowing Him? Throughout the Bible we see men and women who walked and knew God. There is Enoch, Abraham, Elijah, Moses, Esther, David, Mary and the other Marys, Peter, Paul... the list goes on and on. For those of us who are married, we loved our spouses before we got married, fully knowing them has been a lifetime of experiences. Paul is saying that God knows who truly loves Him. Back in Isaiah, God reveals that He is our husband (54:5). When we committed our lives to Him, we did not know Him fully and we may never know Him as fully as we can, here is the really important part - God recognizes us! We are engraved in the palm of His hand (Isaiah 49:16)

Supporting Scripture:
Isaiah 49:16
Isaiah 54.5

Read through the Bible a Chapter a day

Numbers 26

Day 230

Job 1:9-12

Satan replied to the LORD, "Yes, but Job has good reason to fear God. You have always put a wall of protection around him and his home and his property. You have made him prosper in everything he does. Look how rich he is! But reach out and take away everything he has, and he will surely curse you to your face!"
"All right, you may test him," the LORD said to Satan. "Do whatever you want with everything he possesses, but don't harm him physically." So Satan left the LORD's presence.

Have you ever wondered about God's promise of protection? There is an exchange between God and Satan at the beginning of the book of Job that describes the unseen protection around Job. If you read that exchange, you understand that nothing happens to us unless God allows it. Now, please understand that is no guarantee that we will understand why God would allow something to happen, sometimes that is revealed through time or maybe not. I don't know the answer to that; however, that should not stop us from realizing that we are indeed protected by God and NOTHING can penetrate that wall of promise!

Supporting Scripture:
2 Kings 6:15-17

Read through the Bible a Chapter a day

Numbers 27

Day 231

John 14:25-26

*I am telling you these things now while I am still with you. But when the Father sends the Advocate as my representative—that is, the Holy Spirit—he **will t**each you everything and **will** remind you of everything I have told you.*

You and I have the Holy Spirit of God to teach us everything and to remind us of the words Jesus Christ has said. That is something new that the prophets of the Old Testament did not have. Does that mean He will teach you everything? Yes, that is what Jesus is saying. The Holy Spirit will reveal everything we need to know to live this life He guides us through. He also reminds us of the words Jesus has spoken in our Bibles. It is interesting to me that Jesus reminds us immediately after his promise of the Holy Spirit that He is giving us a gift. Verse 27 tells us: "I am leaving you with a gift—peace of mind and heart. And the peace I give is a gift the world cannot give. So don't be troubled or afraid. Don't take my word for it.... Read it yourselves!

Supporting Scripture:
Acts 2:33
Numbers 6:26

Read through the Bible a Chapter a day

Numbers 28

Notes

Day 232

1 Corinthians 10:13

***No** test or temptation that comes your way is beyond the course of what others have had to face. All you need to remember is that **God will never let you down**; he'll **never** let you be pushed past your limit; he'll **always** be there to help you come through it.*

It is very easy for us to think that whatever we are going through, no one else has gone through. The Bible says something different, saying no matter what it is - someone else has gone through it as well. That is not the important thing for us here. God is faithful, he will never forget about you or let you down. We go through these trials with God at our side. Don't depend on what your emotions tell you, KNOW that the word of God (Jesus)(John 1:1-2) never lets us down!

Supporting Scripture:
2 Peter 2:9

Read through the Bible a Chapter a day

Numbers 29

Day 233

Proverbs 1:7

Fear of the LORD is the foundation of true knowledge, but fools despise wisdom and discipline.

There are numerous scriptures in the Bible about the "Fear of the Lord" Proverbs 1:7 is one of them. What exactly is the Fear of the Lord? We think of fear as a negative for the most part. We fear, we are scared, we worry; we have anxiety: all conditions God tells us we should not do in the Bible. To have the Fear the Lord is a positive: Awesome, respect, to truly look upon God and realize who He is - To truly know God and worship Him is to Fear the Lord. That is not to say that God, as Jesus states in Luke 12:4-5 should not be feared. He is the only one, after we die who can allow us to be thrown into hell and suffer the second death. If you have not accepted Jesus Christ, you should fear that. Even that fear can drive you to Christ which is a positive.

Supporting Scripture:
Exodus 20:20
James 1:5

Read through the Bible a Chapter a day

Numbers 30

Day 234

Luke 17:12-19

As he was going into a village, ten men who had leprosy met him. They stood at a distance and called out in a loud voice, "Jesus, Master, have pity on us!"
*When he saw them, he said, "**Go**, show yourselves to the priests." And as they went, **they were cleansed.***
One of them, when he saw he was healed, came back, praising God in a loud voice. He threw himself at Jesus' feet and thanked him—and he was a Samaritan.
*Jesus asked, "Were not all ten cleansed? Where are the other nine? Has no one returned to give praise to God except this foreigner?" Then he said to him, "**Rise and go; your faith has made you well.**"*

I always wonder if I could be the one who comes back or one of the nine who does not. To be sure, all ten showed faith and their physical healing was assured. However, it was the one who came back and praised God to Jesus. He was not only healed, he was Saved! I am not sure if I had mentioned this or not, but I am on a personal quest. I want to give a heart filled thank you to those who impacted my life. It has been an interesting experience thus far.... I'm not done yet, not by a long shot.

Thank God today for him saving you!

Supporting Scripture:
Matthew 9:22
James1:22

Read through the Bible a Chapter a day

Numbers 31

Day 235

Psalm 67

May God be merciful and bless us.
May his face smile with favor on us.
May your ways be known throughout the earth,
your saving power among people everywhere.
May the nations praise you, O God.
Yes, may all the nations praise you.
Let the whole world sing for joy,
because you govern the nations with justice
and guide the people of the whole world.
May the nations praise you, O God.
Yes, may all the nations praise you.
Then the earth will yield its harvests,
*and God, our God, **will** richly bless us.*
*Yes, God **will** bless us,*
*and people all over the world **will** fear him.*

May we always see the love God has laid before us. Not just us, may the world around us open their eyes and souls to see what God has done and what he is going to do!

Supporting Scripture:
Numbers 6:24-26

Read through the Bible a Chapter a day

Numbers 32

Day 236

2 Samuel 6:6-7

*When they came to the threshing floor of Nacon, Uzzah reached out and **took hold of the ark of God**, because the oxen stumbled. The LORD's anger burned against Uzzah because of his irreverent act; therefore God struck him down, and he died there beside the ark of God.*

We all know that our bodies are the temple of God's Spirit. Maybe we all don't know this. We should celebrate this and be thankful that this is a direct response from God when we entrusted ourselves to Christ. That happened immediately after you opened the door to your Savior. God defends his temple and there are examples in the old testament such as 2 Samuel 6:6-7 and Paul tells us 1 Corinthians 3: 16-17 that if anyone destroys the temple he will be destroyed. You are in the ownership of God, you were bought with a price (1 Corinthians 6:19-20). Don't look to the world to understand this, it will not. In fact, when David was bringing God's ark into Jerusalem he was dancing and singing before the ark with all his might. But look what Michal did when she saw David in celebration - she resented him and the Bible says she despised him (2 Samuel 6:14-16). You are made for communion with God, he has taken residence in your heart. The world does not understand this, you are not to conform to the ways of the world (**Romans 12:1-2**)! Take care of that Temple! You do not own it, look at **Ecclesiastes 12:6-7** (Yes, remember your Creator now while you are young, before the silver cord of life snaps and the golden bowl is broken. Don't wait until the water jar is smashed at the spring and the pulley is broken at the well. For then the dust will return to the earth, and the spirit will return to God who gave it).

Supporting Scripture:
2 Samuel 6:14-16
Romans 12:1-2
1 Corinthians 3:16-17
1 Corinthians 6:19-20

Read through the Bible a Chapter a day

Numbers 33

Day 237

John 21:24-25

This is the same disciple who was eyewitness to all these things and wrote them down. And we all know that his eyewitness account is reliable and accurate.
There are so many other things Jesus did. If they were all written down, each of them, one by one, I can't imagine a world big enough to hold such a library of books.

There are are many references in the Book of John that describes the Disciple "The Disciple whom Jesus loved." We now see by his own admission that it was John. We can trust the eyewitness accounts in this book as reliable and accurate. John continued: What he describes in this book is just a few of the works of Jesus. He goes on to explain if everything was written down, there would not be enough space in this world to hold all the documented cases. While we may not have all of the stories, we have been given all we need to know!

Supporting Scripture:
Mark 13:31

Read through the Bible a Chapter a day

Numbers 34

Day 238

Proverbs 28:26

Those who trust their own insight are foolish, but anyone who walks in wisdom is safe.

As we go day by day, living our lives the best we we can, we at some point will come to the point of realizing that God is calling you to dive deeper in your relationship with him. Your salvation is the most important event that will ever take place in your life, but that is not the end of your walk with God. Sanctification (which if I can define it is the process during which God begins to transform you into the image of Christ) begins and really at that point you have a couple of choices, stay or play. What I mean by this is you can stay yourself, going towards the process of sanctification dragging your heels into the ground and not wanting to give up your life: or, you can play and follow God, allowing him to transform you into who he created you to be. Proverbs 28:26 says: Those who trust in themselves are fools, but those who walk in wisdom are kept safe.

The cool part of this process is that once you "Go All In" it is no longer yours to fight, It is God who fights your battle   We see this over and over again: **Exodus 14:13**, **1 Samuel 12:16 and 2 Chronicles 20:15**. I am certainly not saying this is easy, there is a very good chance you will suffer loss and certainly some pain along the way. But look what **2 Corinthians 1:9** says: "Indeed, we felt we had received the sentence of death. But this happened that we **might not rely on ourselves but on God,** who raises the dead".

So, at some point we have to answer the following question: *You trusted God for your salvation the most precious thing you will ever give, do you trust him for everything else in your life?*

Supporting Scripture:
Exodus 14:13
1 Samuel 12:16
2 Chronicles 20:15
2 Corinthians 1:9

Read through the Bible a Chapter a day

Numbers 35

Notes

Day 239

Ecclesiastes 12:6-7

*Remember him—before the silver cord is severed,
and the golden bowl is broken;
before the pitcher is shattered at the spring,
and the wheel broken at the well,
and the dust returns to the ground it came from,
and the* **spirit returns to God who gave it.**

Time is short, make sure you are right with God. The only way to do that is through Jesus Christ! (John 14:1-9) "Don't let your hearts be troubled. Trust in God, and trust also in me. There is more than enough room in my Father's home. If this were not so, would I have told you that I am going to prepare a place for you? When everything is ready, I will come and get you, so that you will always be with me where I am. And you know the way to where I am going."
"No, we don't know, Lord," Thomas said. "We have no idea where you are going, so how can we know the way?"
Jesus told him, **"I am the way, the truth, and the life. No one can come to the Father except through me.** If you had really known me, you would know who my Father is. From now on, you do know him and have seen him!"
Philip said, "Lord, show us the Father, and we will be satisfied."
Jesus replied, "Have I been with you all this time, Philip, and yet you still don't know who I am? **Anyone who has seen me has seen the Father!** So why are you asking me to show him to you?

Supporting Scripture:
Job 20:8

Read through the Bible a Chapter a day

Numbers 36

Day 240

Acts 1:9-11

*"After saying this, he was taken up into a cloud while they were watching, and they could no longer see him. As they strained to see him rising into heaven, two white-robed men suddenly stood among them. Men of Galilee," they said, "why are you standing here staring into heaven? Jesus has been taken from you into heaven, but someday he **will** return from heaven in the same way you saw him go!"*

In the past we talked about the odds of the fulfillment of every promise of Jesus in the Old Testament, One in 10157 (uh, that is 157 zeroes) and that is just based on 48 promises. The Old testament holds over 300! Here in Acts 1, we have the promise of the return of the Lord in the future. The angels spoke to the apostles as Jesus was taken up and they reminded them - HE'S COMING BACK! And that promise is the culmination of all the promises in the Bible! Our world today is really in a mess and I have made the prediction that there is no answer (man-made, that is). Truly the only solution to this is the return of Jesus Christ and The Bible tells us that IS going to happen!

Lean into God, keep reading and looking up - He is coming back!

Supporting Scripture:
Matthew 16:27

Read through the Bible a Chapter a day

Acts 1

Day 241

1 Corinthians 13:4-8

Love suffers long and is kind; love does not envy; love does not parade itself, is not puffed up; does not behave rudely, does not seek its own, is not provoked, thinks no evil; does not rejoice in iniquity, but rejoices in the truth; bears all things, believes all things, hopes all things, endures all things.
Love never fails. But whether there are prophecies, they will fail; whether there are tongues, they will cease; whether there is knowledge, it will vanish away.

Love never fails! I like the way that sounds. Some day, everything we know will be gone, burned up, washed away - just gone. Love remains. As we journey together, let us remember love. We have to come together or we fall divided and I think God's plan is far better - don't you?

Supporting Scripture:
1 Thessalonians 5:14

Read through the Bible a Chapter a day

Acts 2

Day 242

Psalm 80:3

Restore us, O God;
make your face shine on us,
that we may be saved.

As I read Psalm 80, I am reminded of **2 Chronicle 7:14**
If my people, *who are called by my name, will humble themselves and pray and seek my face and turn from their wicked ways, then I will hear from heaven, and **I will** forgive their sin and will heal their land.* We need to CRY out to God for our country. There is a reason God directs His command to you and I. There is division in our country right now (and it has been there for a while) and no matter which side you fall, this division falls at the feet of Christ. Jesus himself said, "Father, forgive them, they know not what they are doing." This is a spiritual battle and it falls right into the difference between right and wrong, good and evil and life or death.

You and I can cry out to God for forgiveness and to heal our nation.

Supporting Scripture:
2 Chronicles 7:14

Read through the Bible a Chapter a day

Acts 3

Day 243

Exodus 16:35-36

And the children of Israel did eat manna forty years, until they came to a land inhabited; they did eat manna, until they came unto the borders of the land of Canaan.

I picked up on something I had never seen before. It was in Exodus 16. The children of Israel ate manna everyday until they passed over into Canaan - or The land filled with milk and honey. God provided for them every meal for 40 years. Then he delivered them into "A land filled with Milk and Honey" just as he promised (Exodus 3:8). This is similar to the story of the widow and oil (2 Kings 4:1-7) For those who make a decision of following God, He provides His grace and provision. Lean into Him and depend upon Him and you too will see how God will move in your life. I don't believe in a "prosperity" gospel, but I do believe God will supply us with everything we need in our lives just as Paul tells us in **2 Corinthians 9:10** *"For God is the one who provides seed for the farmer and then bread to eat. In the same way, he will provide and increase your resources and then produce a great harvest of generosity in you."*   Lean into Him, you will never be sorry!

Supporting Scripture:
Joshua 5:10-12
2 Kings 4:1-7
Exodus 3:8
2 Corinthians 9:10

Read through the Bible a Chapter a day

Acts 4

Day 244

Amos 1:1

*This message was **given** to Amos, a **shepherd** from the town of Tekoa in Judah. He received this message in visions two years before the earthquake, when Uzziah was king of Judah and Jeroboam, was king of Israel.*

The promise of this short scripture is that God can and will use anyone he wants to bring his message to his people. Amos was a farmer and shepherd, not a prophet, priest, movie star, politician etc.... God is not looking for the person with the most qualifications by the worlds standard. He is looking for the person who is willing to stand up against hypocrisy and faithfully share the truth with those around them. God is not looking for ability, he is looking for **availability**. He doesn't call the qualified, he **qualifies the called!**
That could be you and I, look around you, people are screaming for help! No, they may not come to you and tell you that, the evidence is overwhelming!

Supporting Scripture:
Zechariah 14:5

Read through the Bible a Chapter a day

Acts 5

Day 245

Genesis 12:1-3

Now the LORD had said to Abram:
"Get out of your country,
From your family
And from your father's house,
*To a land that I **will** show you.*
*I **will** make you a great nation;*
*I **will** bless you*
And make your name great;
*And you **shall** be a blessing.*
*I **will** bless those who bless you,*
*And I **will** curse him who curses you;*
*And in you all the families of the earth **shall** be blessed."*

Look at the promises in this scripture. God is saying to Abram: Get away from here, you can't focus on me when you are distracted with the world around you. Focus on me and I will bless you without measure... Granted, Abraham would be the father of all, and through him the nation Israel was born and God's plan to save humanity. And what if Abram said no? The same answer Mordecai gave Esther: "If you remain silent at this time, relief and deliverance for the Jews **will arise from another place**, but you and your fathers family will perish. And who knows but that you have come to royal position for such a time as this?"
You and I have the same promise. We also can say no. But what might you miss by saying no to that calling?
There is life in saying YES!

Supporting Scripture:
Esther 4:14

Read through the Bible a Chapter a day

Acts 6

Notes

Day 246

Matthew 14:27

But Jesus immediately said to them: ***"Take courage! It is I. Don't be afraid."***

This verse occurs when the Disciples saw Jesus walking on the water. It's a ghost - they said as they cried out in fear. They were with Jesus every day, they saw all the miracles yet they were still shocked to see Jesus as God, especially when he shows up at a time they least expected. Don't we do the same thing? We go along and then when God does something extraordinary we are shocked because he shows up when we least expect. Yet the message is exactly the same: Take courage, it is I. Don't be afraid. We have a God who see us in and through everything, we should always expect him - then there is no fear because we are depending upon him!

Another awesome promise!

Supporting Scripture:
Daniel 10:12

Read through the Bible a Chapter a day

Acts 7

Day 247

1 Corinthians 15:3-9

*I passed on to you what was **most important** and what had also been passed on to me. Christ died for our sins, **just as the Scriptures said**. He was buried, and he was raised from the dead on the third day, j**ust as the Scriptures said.** He was **seen** by Peter and then by the Twelve. After that, he was **seen** by more than 500 of his followers at one time, most of whom are still alive, though some have died. Then he was **seen** by James and later by all the apostles. Last of all, as though I had been born at the wrong time, I also **saw** him. For I am the least of all the apostles. In fact, I'm not even worthy to be called an apostle after the way I persecuted God's church.*

Here it is, what may be the culmination of the whole Bible. Everything points to Christ! Here we see that it is all **JUST AS THE SCRIPTURE SAYS!** We can believe it! If it was false, then talk about fake news, it would be the greatest sham ever pulled on all creation. Billions would have been mislead. But it is true! Every word of God's story is TRUE! Nothing in all creation is more important than what we read here!

Supporting Scripture:
1 Peter 1:3
Acts 26:23

Read through the Bible a Chapter a day

Acts 8

Day 248

Ephesians 5:18-20

Don't be drunk with wine, because that will ruin your life. Instead, be filled with the Holy Spirit, singing psalms and hymns and spiritual songs among yourselves, and making music to the Lord in your hearts. And give thanks for everything to God the Father in the name of our Lord Jesus Christ.

Paul *is* telling you and I not to be drunk with wine or anything else for that matter, because it **will** ruin your life. Be filled with the Holy Spirit that has been given to you by God! Some think of this as an emotional experience; it is not, it is physical and we receive the Holy Spirit directly from God. He is God, living in us. God's will for our lives is to live in Him and just as we would "fill up" our cars with energy (gas or electric) God will "fill us up with His Spirit! But you gotta ask and accept Him!

And one more thing: Give thanks for *EVERYTHING* to God the Father in the name of our Lord Jesus Christ!

Supporting Scripture:
Proverbs 20:1

Read through the Bible a Chapter a day

Acts 9

Day 249

1 Samuel 5:1-4

After the Philistines captured the Ark of God, they took it from the battleground at Ebenezer to the town of Ashdod. They carried the Ark of God into the temple of Dagon and placed it beside an idol of Dagon. But when the citizens of Ashdod went to see it the next morning, Dagon had fallen with his face to the ground in front of the Ark of the LORD! So they took Dagon and put him in his place again. But the next morning the same thing happened - Dagon had fallen face down before the Ark of the LORD again. This time His head and hands had broken off and were lying in the doorway; only the trunk of his body was left intact.

We have discussed idol worship before. Here is an excellent example of how a jealous God deals with idol worship. We should not look at images, people, structures, careers, lifestyles or anything else as a replacement for worship of Almighty God.

Supporting Scripture:
Isaiah 40:18-20

Read through the Bible a Chapter a day

Acts 10

Day 250

2 Corinthians 5:1-5

For we know that if the earthly tent we live in is destroyed, we have a building from God, an eternal house in heaven, not built by human hands. Meanwhile we groan, longing to be clothed instead with our heavenly dwelling, because when we are clothed, we will not be found naked. For while we are in this tent, we groan and are burdened, because we do not wish to be unclothed but to be clothed instead with our heavenly dwelling, so that what is mortal may be swallowed up by life. Now the one who has fashioned us for this very purpose is God, who has given us the Spirit as a deposit, guaranteeing what is to come.

The word Tent always brings a spirited conversation in our house. Camping is not a favorite topic. To be sure, years ago sleeping in a tent sounded like fun, but it seemed every time the tent was set up, rain would fall and you guessed it - leaky tent! Yet, there is adventure in a tent, it is portable, fairly quick to set up and does provide some relief from the elements until that storm arrives. In a way, that sets up the model for this morning's promise. Our earthly bodies are thought of as those tents. Our bodies provide shelter for the most precious pearl.... our souls. These bodies begin wearing out and as much as we would love them to continue, inevitably they will give up. God has a better structure for us however, one that is permanent and perfect! You and I have already been given the promise and that is the Holy Spirit who is the deposit on what we can expect to come!
There is no house hunting, God has built the perfect structure for us!

Supporting Scripture:
2 Peter 1:13-14

Read through the Bible a Chapter a day

Acts 11

Day 251

Psalm 140

Rescue me, Lord, from evildoers;
protect me from the violent,
who devise evil plans in their hearts
and stir up war every day.
They make their tongues as sharp as a serpent's;
the poison of vipers is on their lips.
Keep me safe, Lord, from the hands of the wicked;
protect me from the violent,
who devise ways to trip my feet.
The arrogant have hidden a snare for me;
they have spread out the cords of their net
and have set traps for me along my path.
I say to the Lord, "You are my God."S
Hear, Lord, my cry for mercy
Sovereign Lord, my strong deliverer,
you shield my head in the day of battle.
Do not grant the wicked their desires, Lord;
do not let their plans succeed.
Those who surround me proudly rear their heads;
may the mischief of their lips engulf them.
May burning coals fall on them;
may they be thrown into the fire,
into miry pits, never to rise.
May slanderers not be established in the land;
may disaster hunt down the violent.
I know that the Lord secures justice for the poor
and upholds the cause of the needy.
Surely the righteous will praise your name,
and the upright will live in your presence.

David was no stranger to difficulty and enemies. Starting with jealousy from his own brothers to Saul wanting to kill him to his own son trying to remove him, he had ample opportunity to cry out to God. The Word of God assures us that our Father hears our cries and responds. In Psalm 3:4, for example, David wrote, "To the Lord, I cry aloud, and he answers me His holy hill." When we call aloud for help in Jesus' name, we invite His power into the situation. Remember that there is strength in just speaking His name. When we cry out to God, He may remove the problem immediately, yet we often have to wait for His perfect timing. Harsh circumstances might even be allowed to remain for His good purposes. But we can always count on His comfort and presence, which enable us to live with joy and hope. I say to the Lord, You are my God!

Lean into him today!

Supporting Scripture:
Psalm 3:4

Read through the Bible a Chapter a day

Acts 12

Day 252

Ruth 4:13-22

So Boaz took Ruth into his home, and she became his wife. When he slept with her, the LORD enabled her to become pregnant, and she gave birth to a son. Then the women of the town said to Naomi, "Praise the LORD, who has now provided a redeemer for your family! May this child be famous in Israel. May he restore your youth and care for you in your old age. For he is the son of your daughter-in-law who loves you and has been better to you than seven sons!"

Naomi took the baby and cuddled him to her breast. And she cared for him as if he were her own. The neighbor women said, "Now at last Naomi has a son again!" And they named him Obed. He became the father of Jesse and the grandfather of David.

This is the genealogical record of their ancestor Perez:
Perez was the father of Hezron.
Hezron was the father of Ram.
Ram was the father of Amminadab.
Amminadab was the father of Nahshon.
Nahshon was the father of Salmon.
Salmon was the father of Boaz.
Boaz was the father of Obed.
Obed was the father of Jesse.
Jesse was the father of David.

Now we see in the little book of Ruth, how God planned everything out as we watch for the birth of Jesus. To show you how important this Bible we read is, Ruth was the daughter-in-law to Naomi whose husband and sons had died. Ruth refused to leave Naomi. These were not royalty, they were a widow and her daughter-in-law. Yet God saw a reason to not only have her story as a book of the Bible, but she was the mother of David's grandfather Obed, a vital part of the linage to Christ. There is a reason she is included, and just like the vast universe with all the stars at night - it is there to guide us to one conclusion - God. He is in control and he wants us to trust him in everything. He truly is all we need.

Read through the Bible a Chapter a day

Acts 13

Notes

Day 253

1 Corinthians 16:13-14

Be on guard. Stand firm in the faith. Be courageous. Be strong. ¹⁴ And do everything with love.

These two versus may be some of the shortest in the Bible, yet they pack a lot of power in them. This advice from Paul is needed so badly today. We do need to stand firm in our faith these days. We do need to be courageous and strong! Verse fourteen may be the most important of all, do everything in love! I don't think it is necessary to push back, I do think we need to stand up for our faith and if we get knocked down, get back up, be resilient. Remember Paul's definition of love from **1 Corinthians 13:** *Love is patient and kind. Love is not jealous or boastful or proud or rude. It does not demand its own way. It is not irritable, and it keeps no record of being wronged. It does not rejoice about injustice but rejoices whenever the truth wins out. Love never gives up, never loses faith, is always hopeful, and endures through every circumstance.*

Supporting Scripture:
1 Corinthians 13:4-8
1 Corinthians 1:8
Titus 1:9
Joshua 1:5-9

Read through the Bible a Chapter a day

Acts 14

Day 254

Psalm 32:2-5

*Yes, what joy for those whose record the LORD has **cleared** of guilt, whose lives are lived in complete honesty! When I refused to confess my sin, my body wasted away, and I groaned all day long. Day and night your hand of discipline was heavy on me. My strength evaporated like water in the summer heat. Finally, I confessed **all** my sins to you and stopped trying to hide my guilt. I said to myself, "I will confess my rebellion to the LORD." **And you forgave me! All my guilt is gone.***

I wish we could remember these words. We live in a constant battle of guilt and anxiety. Somehow we have forgotten God's promise of being washed white as snow. Cleaned permanently, God has forgotten our sin and we should do the same!

Supporting Scripture:
Romans 4:7-8
2 Corinthians 5:19

Read through the Bible a Chapter a day

Acts 15

Day 255

John 14:8-10

Philip said, "Lord, show us the Father and that will be enough for us." Jesus answered: "Don't you know me, Philip, even after I have been among you such a long time? **Anyone who has seen me has seen the Father.** *How can you say, 'Show us the Father'? Don't you believe that I am in the Father, and that the Father is in me? The words I say to you I do not speak on my own authority. Rather, it is the Father, living in me, who is doing his work.*

A couple of days ago, I had an encounter while I was subbing in a class. A group of students was talking (loudly, I might add) and I walked over to them to ask them to quiet down. "God dammit" one student said and I ask him not to swear in class - his response was that he was not swearing. My comment was he does not know what he is saying - with that another student said out loud "Jesus Christ" and I said to him, don't blame him. I asked them both not to use God's name in vain. The student who said "Jesus Christ" said: I said Jesus, not God.... OOPS, wrong thing to say and I said Jesus is God. His response was: "no he isn't, he is God's son". Now I always keep a small bible in my book bag and I asked him to come up to the teachers desk. I explained to him why I said what I said and then I showed him this scripture. He was to put it mildly, blown away. I said what you are saying is not wrong, you just have not gone deep enough into it. The Bible is very clear who God is and you and I need to be patient when we are speaking to people about our living and loving God. Unfortunately, not all churches read scripture or even study it, and partly because of that; there are a large number of Christians who have not or do not know what's in the Bible. I should know.... I was one.
Patience, my friends.

Supporting Scripture:
Isaiah 9:6

Read through the Bible a Chapter a day

Acts 16

Day 256

2 Thessalonians 1

Paul, Silas and Timothy,
To the church of the Thessalonians in God our Father and the Lord Jesus Christ:
Grace and peace to you from God the Father and the Lord Jesus Christ.
We ought always to thank God for you, brothers, and rightly so, because your faith is growing more and more, and the love all of you have for one another is increasing. Therefore, among God's churches we boast about your perseverance and faith in all the persecutions and trials you are enduring.
*All this is evidence that God's judgment **is** right, and as a result you **will** be counted worthy of the kingdom of God, for which you are suffering. God **is** just: He **will** pay back trouble to those who trouble you and give relief to you who are troubled, and to us as well. This **will** happen when the Lord Jesus **is** revealed from heaven in blazing fire with his powerful angels. He **will** punish those who do not know God and do not obey the gospel of our Lord Jesus. They **will** be punished with everlasting destruction and shut out from the presence of the Lord and from the majesty of his power on the day he comes to be glorified in his holy people and to be marveled at among all those who have believed. This includes you, because you believed our testimony to you.*
With this in mind, we constantly pray for you, that our God may make you worthy of his calling, and that by his power he may fulfill every good purpose of yours and every act prompted by your faith. We pray this so that the name of our Lord Jesus may be glorified in you, and you in him, according to the grace of our God and the Lord Jesus Christ.

Two items resonated with me today. Paul's confidence and authority to speak and offering promises we should be aware of. The fact is: Jesus is coming back! And when he does, every eye will see him. Every tongue will confess his name and every knee will bow to him. Then those who have not believed and those who are evil (the Bible does not separate them, if you do not believe and do not obey the gospel of Jesus - there is eternal punishment awaiting them, and separation from God. However, there will be many who will believe and those will marvel and be filled with an eternity of joy. This is Paul's word and promise to the church in Thessalonica, they apply to us as well!

Supporting Scripture:
Romans 8:28

Read through the Bible a Chapter a day

Acts 17

Day 257

Exodus 3:13-14

Moses said to God, "Suppose I go to the Israelites and say to them, 'The God of your fathers has sent me to you,' and they ask me, 'What is his name?' Then what shall I tell them?"
*God said to Moses, **"I AM WHO I AM.** This is what you are to say to the Israelites: 'I AM has sent me to you.'"*

"I AM" has sent me to you. That was the response God gave Moses. In the entire Bible the phrase "I AM" has been spoken over 700 times. Over 500 in the Old Testament and over 200 times in the New Testament. Jesus used the term many times. here is a short list:

I AM the bread of life
I AM the living bread
I AM the light of the world
I AM the one I claim to be
I AM the gate
I AM the good shepherd
I AM the resurrection
I AM the way, the truth and the life
I AM in the Father, and the Father is in me
I AM in you
I AM the true vine
I AM the Alpha and Omega
I AM the first and the last

I love these, but they all remind us of the final I AM:

I AM coming soon!

These are not just for Moses and the Disciples, they are for us as well!

Supporting Scripture:
Genesis 32:29

Read through the Bible a Chapter a day

Acts 18

Day 258

Matthew 15:16-20

Are you still so dull?" Jesus asked them. "Don't you see that whatever enters the mouth goes into the stomach and then out of the body? ***But the things that come out of a person's mouth come from the heart, and these defile them****. For out of the heart come evil thoughts—murder, adultery, sexual immorality, theft, false testimony, slander. These are what defile a person; but eating with unwashed hands does not defile them."*

These days, these words really sting. We as a society have become very, as Jesus states "dull" to the sting of what comes out of our mouths. These days it is even worse, because we can sit down and tear out a persons soul with an email or text or post on some social media site. We speak first and discover the ramifications later. Our spite and vindictiveness is uniquely ours. This is personal to each one of us and we need to address it with God personally. But it is even worse than we think it is. Jesus is saying here that if we even think the things we may say or write - that's just as bad as saying or writing them. Take a step back before you attack and think through what is getting ready to come out. Very difficult, but somehow if there is a way to think before we react perhaps we can change how we think and respond - Maybe Love?

Supporting Scripture:
Matthew 5:22

Read through the Bible a Chapter a day

Acts 19

Day 259

Haggai 2:4-5

But now the LORD says: **Be strong***, Zerubbabel.* **Be strong,** *Jeshua son of Jehozadak, the high priest.* **Be strong,** *all you people still left in the land. And now* **get to work,** *for* **I am with you,** *says the LORD of Heaven's Armies.* **My Spirit remains** *among you, just as I* **promised** *when you came out of Egypt. So* **do not be afraid.'**

Need some encouragement today? God's promised word is timeless. The Exodus occurred sometime around 1500 BC and it is estimated that this book of Haggai was written in the vicinity of 450 BC. The point is that God was still encouraging His people. We see similar words in Joshua 1. Be strong and get busy doing doing the work I have given to you. God is still with us just as he has promised!

Supporting Scripture:
1 Chronicles 28:20
Exodus 33:14

Read through the Bible a Chapter a day

Acts 20

Notes

Day 260

Mark 16:6-7

*But the angel said, "**Don't be alarmed**. You are looking for Jesus of Nazareth, who was crucified. He isn't here! He is risen from the dead! Look, this is where they laid his body. Now go and tell his disciples, **including Peter**, that Jesus is going ahead of you to Galilee. You will see him there, **just as he told you** before he died."*

Stay calm!
God knows your name!
The words of Jesus are true!
There is power in knowing these attributes of these scriptures. Yes, these words have been told over and over at Easter. Yet for me, as I dig a little deeper I see words of wisdom that are true throughout my life, and can be used to help you through each day!

Supporting Scripture:
Mark 14:28
John 21:1-23

Read through the Bible a Chapter a day

Acts 21

Day 261

Genesis 5:21-24

*When Enoch was 65 years old, he became the father of Methuselah. After the birth of Methuselah, Enoch lived in **close fellowship** with God for another 300 years, and he had other sons and daughters. Enoch lived 365 years, walking in **close fellowship** with God. Then one day he disappeared, because God took him.*

Lately, I have been thinking about Enoch. One of two individuals who were taken by God without dying (The other was Elijah). I find myself wanting that closer relationship with God much like Abraham who God referred to as His friend (James 2:23). I am also reminded of Micah when I read this verse this morning. In Micah 6, we are reminded that there is not enough to give away or good you can be to earn God's favor. He simply wants a relationship with you and for you to lean in and depend upon God (6-8). That is in sharp contrast to what this world view is telling us. If you desire that relationship with God, cry out to Him and then wait on God to move and surely he will!

Supporting Scripture:
James 2:23
Micah 6:6-8

Read through the Bible a Chapter a day

Acts 22

Day 262

James 5:17-18

Elijah was a man just like us. *He prayed earnestly that it would not rain, and it did not rain on the land for three and a half years. Again he prayed, and the heavens gave rain, and the earth produced its crops.*

Did you see that? Elijah was a regular dude. A human being, just like you and I. Yet, he made it stop raining (well, he didn't but the Bible says he prayed earnestly). He also prayed earnestly for the rain. If you recall the story, Elijah was one who went to heaven without dying. He and Enoch were pulled from this life without dying. So one might ask: What do they have that we don't have to get such a privilege? They had a deep personal relationship with God. Enoch walked with God. Look at the wonderful promise we have from Jesus in John 11:25-26: J*esus said to her, "I am the resurrection and the life. The one who believes in me will live, even though they die; and whoever lives by believing in me will never die. Do you believe this?"* We have a promise from the mouth of Jesus that by belief in him, we will never die. Now please read this carefully: We have a relationship with Jesus Christ who **is** God. We don't receive this promise any other way. Not by the things we have done, or by going to church, or being religious - IT IS BY BELIEVING IN CHRIST!

DO YOU BELIEVE THIS?

Supporting Scripture:
John 11:25-26
2 Kings 2:11

Read through the Bible a Chapter a day

Acts 23

Day 263

Mark 6:37-38

But he answered, "You give them something to eat."
They said to him, "That would take more than half a year's wages! Are we to go and spend that much on bread and give it to them to eat?"
"How many loaves do you have?" he asked. "Go and see."

We can be pretty resourceful right? Given an opportunity to fix some dilemma, or we face some overwhelming problem, we get to work knowing it is on us to make things right. The Disciples were faced with such an issue when the gang, along with Jesus is faced with how to feed 5000 (now the Bible tells us that was the men in the group, add families to the mix and we might be in excess of 10,000). Jesus, begins our scripture today with a statement: "You give them something to eat". He was testing them, how creative are you? There was no way they had the resources, even if they could raise the money needed to buy the bread, by the time they put that together, went and bought enough bread, time would have run out. No, this was a test, how much do you trust God in your circumstance. They discovered that their provision amounted to 5 loaves of bread and two fish (and that was not even their own). We know the rest of the story, when faced with overwhelming circumstances, beyond our ability to resolve - we need to drop our hands to our sides and ask God to step in. He has the solution, more than likely it is completely different that anything we can even begin to comprehend. God wants us to depend on him!

Supporting Scripture:
2 Kings 4:42-44

Read through the Bible a Chapter a day

Acts 24

Day 264

Amos 5:8

It is the LORD who created the stars,
the Pleiades and Orion.
He turns darkness into morning
and day into night.
He draws up water from the oceans
and pours it down as rain on the land.
The LORD is his name!

It is not often, but certainly one of my favorites is a night sky that is simply breathtaking. To see the Milky Way and it's starry host. What a sight! This morning I see this in Amos: He made the Pleiades and Orion. These constellations pre-date man and were made and named by God himself. We know that in a day long before GPS and other navigation aids the stars were used (and still are) to navigate. But their purpose is even more than that, look what Psalm 19 says:
The heavens declare the glory of God;
the skies proclaim the work of his hands.
Day after day they pour forth speech;
night after night they reveal knowledge.
They have no speech, they use no words;
no sound is heard from them.
Yet their voice goes out into all the earth,
their words to the ends of the world.
The sky above us pours forth an understanding that God is the creator and we are to marvel (not worship, that worship belongs to God alone) at its existence. If you want an amazing experience, take some time to find a dark field or yard and simply look up. You will be glad you did.

Supporting Scripture:
Job 38:31

Read through the Bible a Chapter a day

Acts 25

Day 265

Ezekiel 1:18

Their rims were high and awesome, and all four rims were full of eyes all around.

Ezekiel's vision in chapter one is full of symbolism. God presented himself to Ezekiel and a vision of heaven, I hope you can take a look at that if you have an opportunity to read it. Soon after Ezekiel sees the cherubim, he sees wheels and those wheels were full of eyes. The way the wheels moved allowed then to move in any direction and up and down. It is thought that these wheels were symbolic for the Omnipresence of God. Then we see that the wheels are full of eyes - this is the promise for today - God's view and he sees everything, don't try too hard to reason it out - **KNOW IT!** He knows what is going on in and around your life and mine - We are never out of his view! There is nothing he does not know about when it comes to his children - he sees it all!

Supporting Scripture:
Revelation 4:6

Read through the Bible a Chapter a day

Acts 26

Day 266

Jeremiah 6:16

This is what the Lord says:
"Stand at the crossroads and look;
ask for the ancient paths,
ask where the good way is, and walk in it,
*and you **will** find rest for your souls.*
But you said, 'We will not walk in it.'

What a promise this is and believe me folks, a lot of people need to be reminded that there is indeed rest for our souls if we will just look to God's word and the promises within.
Look what Jesus says in Matthew 11:28-30 "Come to me, all you who are weary and burdened, and I **will** give you rest. Take my yoke upon you and learn from me, for I am gentle and humble in heart, and you **will** find rest for your souls. For my yoke is easy and my burden is light." I would imagine the heartbreak God would have watching his children suffer under the fear and worry. Cast your cares on God, he can handle everything you give him - I Promise you. Remember we have very small problems when we understand we worship a very big God!!

Supporting Scripture:
Matthew 11:28-30

Read through the Bible a Chapter a day

Acts 27

Notes

Day 267

Acts 2:24

***But God** raised him from the dead, freeing him from the agony of death, because it was impossible for death to keep its hold on him.*
*You killed the author of life, **but God** raised him from the dead. We **are** witnesses of this. Acts 3:15*
***But God** demonstrates his own love for us in this: While we were still sinners, Christ died for us. Romans 5:8*

Words are important and as we have already discussed, every word of the Bible has meaning! These three verses have something in common: **BUT GOD!** God has acted and changed the course of human misery. In fact, if we look carefully at these three verses we can see a progression. Peter mentions in Acts 2:24 - **But God** raised him from the agony of death. In Acts 3:15 he again says **But God** raised him from death - AND we are witnesses of this. And finally, Paul tells us in Romans 5:8 tells why this all happened - God was demonstrating his love for us, that while we are sinners - Christ died for us! **But God** is God putting a stamp on what he has done, and he did it for one reason - To save us!

Supporting Scripture:
Acts 3:15
Romans 5:8

Read through the Bible a Chapter a day

Acts 27

Day 268

Deuteronomy 1:29-31

Then I said to you, "Do not be terrified; do not be afraid of them. The LORD your God, who is going before you, will fight for you, as he did for you in Egypt, before your very eyes, and in the wilderness. There you saw how the LORD your God carried you, as a father carries his son, all the way you went until you reached this place."

Think a minute about Good Friday. I suppose if we knew what God knew it would be a Good day, it would be the only day God would need to demonstrate His love for us. Thousands of years were taken to prepare for this. Of course, we have the benefit of having the Bible in our hands to know how this turns out, and as Moses tells us in the first chapter of Deuteronomy, God went before us and and fought for us and really created the pathway for us in the wilderness. He promised all this long ago and He continues to save even after thousands of years and millions of lives - He carries us to this point.

So, what do **you** do about Jesus? It's a decision each of us must make.

Supporting Scripture:
Nehemiah 4:14

Read through the Bible a Chapter a day

Deuteronomy 1

Day 269

Psalm 8

LORD, our Lord,
how majestic is your name in all the earth!
You have set your glory
in the heavens.
Through the praise of children and infants
you have established a stronghold against your enemies,
to silence the foe and the avenger.
When I consider your heavens,
the work of your fingers,
the moon and the stars,
which you have set in place,
what is mankind that you are mindful of them,
human beings that you care for them?
You have made them a little lower than the angels
and crowned them with glory and honor.
You made them rulers over the works of your hands;
you put everything under their feet:
all flocks and herds,
and the animals of the wild,
the birds in the sky,
and the fish in the sea,
all that swim the paths of the seas.
LORD, our Lord,
how majestic is your name in all the earth!

I love this Psalm. Make no mistake, it is God who created this universe and everything in it. What is interesting to me is where you and I fit into the equation. God created us, gave us souls when we were conceived and we have the choice to make, honor God and all he has made or not. We have the choice to follow him or not, we have choice to become friends with God or not.

Supporting Scripture:
Genesis 15:5

Read through the Bible a Chapter a day

Deuteronomy 2

Day 270

2 Chronicles 32:7-8

"Be strong and courageous. Do not be afraid or discouraged because of the king of Assyria and the vast army with him, for there is a greater power with us than with him. With him is only the arm of flesh, but with us is the LORD our God to help us and to fight our battles." And the people gained confidence from what Hezekiah the king of Judah said.

I want to encourage you today!
This story comes from the King Hezekiah and the land was being invaded by the Assyrians and Sennacherib. If you take the time to read the entire chapter, the enemy was trying to fill the minds of the people to doubt God and Hezekiah. Then Hezekiah spoke to the people.....
Hezekiah and the Prophet Isaiah cried out to God in prayer and the entire Assyrian army was routed. You may not have a Sennacherib taunting you today, you may have some other assailant nipping at you. Hezekiah's words speak for all who follow, seek and lean into God. Be comforted today that God will help us and fight our battles!

Supporting Scripture:
2 Kings 14-19

Read through the Bible a Chapter a day

Deuteronomy 3

Day 271

Isaiah 45:1-7

This is what the LORD says to Cyrus, **his anointed one,**
whose right hand he will empower.
Before him, mighty kings will be paralyzed with fear.
Their fortress gates will be opened,
never to shut again.
This is what the LORD says:
"I will go before you, Cyrus,
and level the mountains.
I will smash down gates of bronze
and cut through bars of iron.
And I will give you treasures hidden in the darkness—
secret riches.
I will do this so you may know that I am the LORD,
the God of Israel, the one who calls you by name.
"And why have I called you for this work?
Why did I call you by name when you did not know me?
It is for the sake of Jacob my servant,
Israel my chosen one.
I am the LORD;
there is no other God.
I have equipped you for battle,
though you don't even know me,
so all the world from east to west
will know there is no other God.
I am the LORD, and there is no other.
I create the light and make the darkness.
I send good times and bad times.
I, the LORD, am the one who does these things.

King Cyrus of Persia played a critical role in the history of Israel. He was the one who allowed the people of Israel to return to their homeland and rebuild the Jewish temple. Cyrus did not know of God. Yet the Bible says God chose him by name. Not only did God call him by name, He also promised that He will remove all the barriers around Cyrus, all for the sake of Israel. This is a wonderful promise made not only to Cyrus and Israel, it is also for us today. God knows you and I by name, and if you will allow him, He will remove the barriers around us as well.
Cry out to your savior and trust His response!

Supporting Scripture:
Jeremiah 25:9

Read through the Bible a Chapter a day

Deuteronomy 4

Day 272

John 19:30

*When he had received the drink, Jesus said, "**It is finished.**" With that, he bowed his head and gave up his spirit.*

"It is finished". The final words of Jesus before he died on the cross. God had completed a major chapter in his story. Jesus came as a man for a reason, a purpose and he had completed his work. Now He has left us with a decision to make. God has done everything to clear the path between us and him and now it is our choice: To follow him or not, to pass the good news on to others or not. The Bible is clear on our path forward yet we also have the choice to follow God's word. But make no mistake, God has done for us what we cannot do for ourselves.
Salvation is found in no one else, for there is no other name under heaven given to mankind by which we must be saved.

Supporting Scripture:
Acts 4:12

Read through the Bible a Chapter a day

Deuteronomy 5

The Boxer and the Prison

For I was in prison and you came and visited me. (Matt 25:36 – paraphrase)
Then the righteous will answer him, Lord, when did we see you in prison and visit you? The King will reply, I tell you the truth, whatever you did to one of the least of these my brothers of mine, you did for me.

I have gotten to know Alphonso "Glory" Bailey who founded the Down, But Not Out Ministry. This organization reaches out to men incarcerated in local Indiana Correctional Facilities as well as Boys and Girls Clubs and the Juvenile Detention Centers teaching character and integrity. Alphonso and I and Dr. Johnnie Blount who is a Pastor and heads up Bridging the Gap Ministry in North Carolina went to make a presentation to the Plainfield, Indiana Correctional Facility. Before I get to carried away, I should explain that I had been talking to Alphonso for several weeks about this visit and I was really unsure of my desire to go. The week prior to going to the prison we had scheduled to go in. It was one of those moments when you have your conscience on both shoulders….. One side saying forget it, you don't want to go there and the other side saying: you committed to go – go! The side with the I don't want to go won and I reasoned that I would just tell Alphonso that I had something come up and I would not make it. I never made that call, but decided to go!! 10 minutes before I was to meet Alphonso and 5 minutes into the ride, he called me and the prison had cancelled due to a power outage. We agreed to meet for lunch anyway and had a good laugh about the good and bad little conscience sitting on my shoulder. God rewarded me that day for the right decision!

Anyway, fast forward one week. As we walked into the facility, Alphonso asked me if I would be like to say anything to which I said: "No, I am just an observer". So of course after the initial opening and 4 great music videos Alphonso says Glory! I have a couple of guests with me today - Dr. Johnnie Blount (who has been here before) and Brother Jeff and he preceded to stick the microphone in my face! LOL. Well, I have never before in my life stood before 114 prison inmates all listening to me and I have absolutely nothing to say. So, I said the first thing on my mind - "I am scared to death of being here in front of you today".

Fortunately, God had a better idea and filled my mouth with the following: "I am scared to death to be standing here right now. But I have even a greater fear: THE FEAR OF THE LORD! What does that mean? If I believe God is with us here in this prison, He is sitting between you, around you. I believe that if God is in here with us then He is outside this prison as well, he is in your cells and in fact he is everywhere - all at the same time! Now if that is the case, and I believe it to be so - then God is watching everything you and I have to say and do, every word and every thought - So, to me the Fear of The Lord is that I better watch and correct every thought I have, every word I say because I am in fact saying and thinking such things in front of a HOLY GOD, The Creator! Dr. Johnnie Blount then gave an excellent presentation about 2 Corinthians 6 teaching the fact that God is not only your God but is also your eternal "Father" and "Daddy" to us all!

To my amazement I watched 52 out of 114 men and 2 prison guards make commitments of faith to Christ! It was a powerful time and I realized once again: You do not have to look far at all to realize the pain and hurt in this world. God IS AMAZING and I hope you all will realize this in your own lives. The harvest is full, the workers are few!

Just a quick mention of Down, But not Out….. Alphonso Bailey is an ex Professional boxer and was on the US Amateur Boxing team. As a ranked fighter he had a wonderful opportunity to make the big time! I would like to say that it was fairy tale life for him, but the reality is that he himself spent 2 years in prison in Kentucky which prepared him for God's calling. He has been in this Prison Ministry for several years and loves to share the message.

Alphonso Bailey is an inductee in the New Jersey Boxing Hall of Fame - 11/2024

Here is a short YouTube video about the ministry: **Down But Not Out - Alphonso Bailey**

Day 273

Ecclesiastes 3:11

Yet God has made everything beautiful for its own time. He has planted eternity in the human heart, but even so, people cannot see the whole scope of God's work from beginning to end.

You might read all of Ecclesiastes 3; in it, you will find what may be the oldest lyrics of all time by the band the Byrds in the 1965 tune: Turn, Turn, Turn. The song was written by Pete Seeger and does fully acknowledge the Bible as its origin. Wow, 3000 years and we still see God's word at work!

Supporting Scripture:
Ecclesiastes 3

Read through the Bible a Chapter a day

Deuteronomy 6

Notes

Day 274

Revelation 11:8

*And their bodies will lie in the main street of Jerusalem, the city that is **figuratively** called "Sodom" and "Egypt," the city where their Lord was crucified.*

I am reading through the book of Revelation, and stumbled on to a scripture that caught my attention (well, the entire book gets my attention, but this stood out to me). In chapter 11, the Bible tells of two messengers from Heaven who will prophesy 1260 days or 3 and a half years. They will cause all kinds of trouble for those who are left behind and have still not caught on to the message that God continues to call all people to himself. After the period of 3 and half years, these two messengers will be killed by the antichrist. Here is what caught my attention: Their bodies will be left in the street of Jerusalem, the city that is **figuratively** called "Sodom and Egypt". Of course we know Jesus was crucified in Jerusalem. Here is the thing, Sodom was destroyed because of its lack of morals and frankly had descended into a place of perversion and wickedness. For it's part, Egypt represent bondage and slavery for God's people. Yet here we see John's vision: Jerusalem has become just like those two places. Is it possible for us to see this as the condition that the world finds itself before the return of Jesus Christ? A two second sweep of the news and we see the perversion all around us and while physical slavery still exists around the world in various locations, slavery to sin and self absorption and idol worship is everywhere including within you and I.

Here is what I believe, I will not see these events and if you are a Christian you won't either. But it is a reminder that we are living in the season of the return of Jesus. Keep reading that word of God, listen for the trumpet sound and keep looking up because the rapture is the next event!

Supporting Scripture:
Ecclesiastes 3:15

Read through the Bible a Chapter a day

Deuteronomy 7

Day 275

Ephesians 1:16-17

*I have not stopped giving thanks for you, remembering you in my prayers. I keep asking that the God of our Lord Jesus Christ, the glorious Father, may give you the Spirit of wisdom and revelation, so that **you may know him better.***

From Paul to the Ephesians, he reminds us that wisdom and revelation come directly from God. And it is God who gives this wisdom so that we may know Him better. I love that, it takes us back to that theme of actually knowing God. God is not a stranger and He longs for a relationship with you and I.

Supporting Scripture:
Galatians 1:12
Galatians 1:15

Read through the Bible a Chapter a day

Deuteronomy 8

Day 276

Colossians 2:8-10

See to it that no one takes you captive through hollow and deceptive philosophy, which depends on human tradition and the elemental spiritual forces of this world rather than on Christ.
For in Christ all the fullness of the Deity lives in bodily form, *and* ***in Christ you have been brought to fullness****. **He is the head over every power and authority.***

I hope you are staying and keeping busy. Not sure about you, but I can only watch about 20 seconds from the news these days. It is very important that we maintain other outlets. Study God's word because just as it says about the world being dependent on human tradition and elemental spiritual forces, they are not focused on Christ! But listen to this - Jesus is God - in person! You and I have been brought to fullness - IT'S OVER. CASE CLOSED! We are sealed. Finally, we see this little gem - He is the head over every power and authority. Nothing gets by Christ, our God knows it all and you are here for a reason! There are no accidents, or surprises! God's hand is upon us!

Supporting Scripture:
Galatians 4:4-7

Read through the Bible a Chapter a day

Deuteronomy 9

Day 277

Psalm 121

*I look up to the mountains—
does my help come from there?
My help comes from the LORD,
who made heaven and earth!
He will not let you stumble;
the one who watches over you will not slumber.
Indeed, he who watches over Israel
never slumbers or sleeps.
The LORD himself watches over you!
The LORD stands beside you as your protective shade.
The sun will not harm you by day,
nor the moon at night.
The LORD keeps you from all harm
and watches over your life.
The LORD keeps watch over you as you come and go,
both now and forever.*

We have discussed fear. It's very easy to get caught up in fear, especially these days. The sad truth for many of us, fear has become so common, we no longer consider it fear, we adapt to it and it can be used it stop things we might use to serve God and others. Hate to do this to you, but I am a perfect example. A good friend of mine has a prison ministry and he invited me to go and minister to a local correctional facility with him. I did everything I could to not go, but finally I said - yes! While I was driving to meet him, it was literally like what you see in the movies, One angel sitting on my right shoulder and the enemy on my left shoulder arguing their points. Until I said OUT LOUD - STOP, we're doing this! It turned out to be a wonderful blessing and it helped me to understand and know, fear is nothing when trusting God. God's word says to us that he protects us, he surrounds us, in fact; nothing can come to us without going through God first. What an incredible promise he has given to us with his continual care!

Supporting Scripture:
Psalm 1:6

Read through the Bible a Chapter a day

Deuteronomy 10

Day 278

John 10:9

*Yes, **I am** the gate. Those who come in through me **will** be saved. They **will** come and go freely and **will** find good pastures.*

A few years ago while Brytni (our grand daughter) was here, we took her for a riding lesson at a local stable. After the lesson, we were walking through the stable towards the exit, several of the instructors asked us to make sure we were out of the walkway: "Because when the horses are released from the stable they go to pasture". You did not want to be in the way, the horses are so excited to get to the pasture we would have been trampled!
That to me is freedom! They don't mind being in the stable because that is protection and shelter to them, yet being able to come and go to the pasture was obviously a delight for them. That's what I thought of when I read this this morning. First off, we are SAVED by I AM!! Upon closer examination, this is also a vision for us what life will be like when we are in the presence of Jesus.

More wonderful promises from God!

Supporting Scripture:
Isaiah 58:11

Read through the Bible a Chapter a day

Deuteronomy 11

Day 279

Genesis 17:1-8

When Abram was ninety-nine years old, the LORD appeared to him and said, ***"I am God Almighty; walk before me faithfully and be blameless. Then I will make my covenant between me and you and will greatly increase your numbers."***
*Abram fell facedown, and God said to him, "As for me, this is my covenant with you: You will be the father of many nations. No longer will you be called Abram; your name will be Abraham, for **I have** made you a father of many nations. **I will** make you very fruitful; **I will** make nations of you, and kings will come from you. **I will** establish my covenant as an everlasting covenant between me and you and your descendants after you for the generations to come, **to be your God** and **the God of your descendants after you**. The whole land of Canaan, where you now reside as a foreigner, **I will** give as an everlasting possession to you and your descendants after you; and **I will be their God**.*

If we look back just a few chapters, we see Enoch and Noah both of whom the Bible says walked before God or walked with God. Now we see Abram who now is called Abraham being told to walk before God and be blameless. This is an amazing few verses - look at the promises of God Almighty (El-Shaddai)! I am reminded what Micah 6:8 says: No, O people, the LORD has told you what is good, and this is what he requires of you: to do what is right, to love mercy, and to **walk humbly** with your God. I cannot state this enough, God wants and longs for a relationship with you and I. This makes what Jesus Christ did on the cross even more amazing... There is nothing that stands before you to block your way to God except that sin thing. If you have not accepted Jesus Christ into your heart, you should consider that a priority! Walk before God faithfully, and be blameless!

Supporting Scripture:
Micah 6:8

Read through the Bible a Chapter a day

Deuteronomy 12

Day 280

Jeremiah 39:17-18

*But I **will** rescue you from those you fear so much. Because you trusted me, I **will** give you your life as a reward. I **will** rescue you and keep you safe. I, the LORD, have spoken!'"*

Look at all those "will's"! It's a done deal, God has your back! Trust in God! Again, don't rely on your own devices - if for no other reason, (as a wise man once said to me) you have no idea what you may be missing by not trusting how God will work out your circumstances!

Supporting Scripture:
Psalm 34:22
Romans 10:11

Read through the Bible a Chapter a day

Deuteronomy 13

Notes

Day 281

Psalm 145:13

*For your kingdom is an everlasting kingdom.
You rule throughout all generations.
The LORD **always** keeps his promises;
he is gracious in all he does.*

Talk about a word this morning! The Lord always keeps His promises. Tie that together with **2 Corinthians 1:18-20** (*As surely as God is faithful, our word to you does not waver between "Yes" and "No." For Jesus Christ, the Son of God, does not waver between "Yes" and "No." He is the one whom Silas, Timothy, and I preached to you, and as God's ultimate "Yes," he always does what he says. For all of God's promises have been fulfilled in Christ with a resounding "Yes!" And through Christ, our "Amen" (which means "Yes") ascends to God for his glory.*) and we have an amazing glance at the grace and perfection of God towards His children. What a fantastic word for us in this Bible, what an awesome God we love and depend upon!

Supporting Scripture:
2 Corinthians 1:17-22

Read through the Bible a Chapter a day

Deuteronomy 14

Day 282

Psalm 91:4

He will cover you with his feathers. He will shelter you with his wings. His faithful promises are your armor and protection.

Carrying over from yesterday's scripture, there are hundreds if not thousands of promises that are contained in the Bible for the child of God (by the way, they are all - EVERY ONE confirmed through Christ! 2 Corinthians 1:20). Psalm 91 is loaded with promises from God. Rest in him, trust him and he will watch and keep you. Interesting also, if this looks familiar, this is the scripture Satan used against Jesus during the temptation of Christ in Matthew 4. Satan was attempting to use Scripture to trap Christ. So be warned, Satan knows scripture and he will; if he can, twist scripture as part of his deception. What was Christ response? "Do not put the Lord your God to the test." That is great advice, we cannot expect God's protection if we are living like hell.

Supporting Scripture:
Matthew 4:6-7

Read through the Bible a Chapter a day

Deuteronomy 15

Day 283

Joshua 18:3

So Joshua said to the Israelites: "How long will you wait before you begin to take possession of the land that the Lord, the God of your fathers, has given you?

Today's promise from God is not a future promise but one he has already brought too fruition. In this case, the land was promised to the nation of Israel. But it is more than just land, it's all the promises of God. It is up to us to move and pray on those promises in faith. God has given us the power to move the mountains of our lives if we will just have the faith to do so.

Supporting Scripture:
Matthew 17:20

Read through the Bible a Chapter a day

Deuteronomy 16

Day 284

Matthew 10:34-39

*Do not suppose that **I have** come to bring peace to the earth. **I did not** come to bring peace, but a sword. For **I have** come to turn "'a man **against** his father,*
*a daughter **against** her mother,*
*a daughter-in-law **against** her mother-in-law —*
*a man's enemies **will be** the members of his own household.'*
*"Anyone who loves their father or mother more than me is not worthy of me; anyone who loves their son or daughter more than me is not worthy of me. Whoever does not take up their cross and follow me is not worthy of me. **Whoever finds their life will lose it, and whoever loses their life for my sake will find it.***

Not every promise in the Bible promises comfort. There are many that make us uncomfortable, this is a good thing. The Word of God is at war with our souls. For many of us, I think the current difficulties in our society reminds us that time may very well be short and we need to be sure we are in the right place spiritually. Re-read these words of Jesus and let them penetrate our souls.

Supporting Scripture:
Luke 14:26

Read through the Bible a Chapter a day

Deuteronomy 17

Day 285

Isaiah 43:1-3

But now, this is what the Lord says -
*he who **created** you, O Jacob,*
*he who **formed** you, O Israel:*
"Fear not, for I have redeemed you;
*I have summoned you by **name**; you are mine.*
When you pass through the waters,
I will be with you;
and when you pass through the rivers,
they will not sweep over you.
When you walk through the fire,
you will not be burned;
the flames will not set you ablaze.
For I am the Lord your God,
the Holy One of Israel, your Savior;
I give Egypt for your ransom,
Cush and Seba in your stead.

In case you have ever wondered where you came from, God has given you an answer:
But now, this is what the Lord says—
he who created you, Jacob,
he who formed you, Israel:
"Do not fear, for I have redeemed you;
I have summoned you by name; you are mine.
God recalls the history of the Israelites and the exodus out of Egypt.
What a promise we have from God: I **will be with you!** (emphasis added) No matter where we go, what we have done, God is with us!
I will be with you;
and when you pass through the rivers,
they will not sweep over you.
When you walk through the fire,
you will not be burned;
the flames will not set you ablaze.
For I am the Lord your God,
the Holy One of Israel, your Savior;
He loves us, he does not say I have loved you or I will love you - HE LOVES US - Now, forever and it will never end!
He is God, there is no other, you are loved and cared for by God himself:
Before me no god was formed,

nor will there be one after me.
I, even I, am the Lord,
I am left with these words this morning after reading this,

WOW!!!

Read through the Bible a Chapter a day

Deuteronomy 18

Day 286

John 16:33

*I have told you these things, so that in me you **may** have peace. In this world you **will** have trouble. But take heart! I **have** overcome the world.*

Say this out loud today - God is in control! Jesus has overcome the world!
You have read the number of times I have said every word of the Bible has meaning..... here I am going beyond that and saying even punctuation has meaning. Note the exclamation point after - But take heart - Jesus is making an important point here - Don't lose hope, keep your wits - God is in control of everything! Keep in mind when this was happening, after the last supper and Jesus has told the Disciples what was getting ready to happen. I'm sure they were despondent, confused and scared.
No matter what is happening in our world today, Jesus has overcome the world and nothing happens that God does not allow to happen.

What a promise we have from God himself!

Supporting Scripture:
Revelation 2:7

Read through the Bible a Chapter a day

Deuteronomy 19

Day 287

Exodus 20:1-6

*And God **spoke** all these words:*
*"I **am** the Lord your God, who brought you out of Egypt, out of the land of slavery.*
*"You shall have **no** other gods before me.*
*"You **shall not** make for yourself an idol in the form of **anything** in heaven above or on the earth beneath or in the waters below. You **shall not** bow down to them or worship them; for I, the Lord your God, **am a jealous God**, punishing the children for the sin of the fathers to the third and fourth generation of those who hate me, but showing love to a thousand generations of those who love me and keep my commandments.*

God makes clear in the Ten Commandments what we can and cannot do. We have to be careful these days, idols come in all kinds of sizes and shapes. It could be a career, hobby, spouses, children, lifestyle, government, science, money, there are so many you could probably put yours in this blank_____. Pick your battles wisely, but cast your cares to God who loves you. With all that is happening these days remember that knowledge of the Trinity of God and of his word, the Bible gives you a Biblical worldview. We can understand how others might have a standard worldview, but as believers in Jesus Christ, we must remember God expects us to rely on him, and in return we can trust him - no matter what!

Supporting Scripture:
Deuteronomy 7:9

Read through the Bible a Chapter a day

Deuteronomy 20

Notes

Day 288

Luke 12:22-26

Then Jesus said to his disciples: "Therefore I tell you, do not worry about your life, what you will eat; or about your body, what you will wear. Life is more than food, and the body more than clothes. Consider the ravens: They do not sow or reap, they have no storeroom or barn; yet God feeds them. ***And how much more valuable you are than birds!*** *Who of you by worrying can add a single hour to your life? Since you cannot do this very little thing, why do you worry about the rest?*

I love this, probably because I am so guilty of it. Worry: it is like it is built into our being. To me, Jesus is not saying - Don't be concerned. He is saying don't obsess over it. You are a child of God and if God takes care of the smallest part of creation, he will surely watch over you!

Supporting Scripture:
Psalm 147:9

Read through the Bible a Chapter a day

Deuteronomy 21

Day 289

Psalm 117

Praise the LORD, all you nations.
Praise him, all you people of the earth.
*For his **unfailing** love for us is powerful;*
*the LORD's faithfulness **endures** forever.*
Praise the Lord.

Even though this is the shortest chapter of the Bible, it has a lasting punch. Short or long, the words of God **are** true and powerful! Here is something we should always be mindful of:

God is crazy about you!

Supporting Scripture:
Romans 15:11

Read through the Bible a Chapter a day

Deuteronomy 22

Day 290

Jude 24-25

*To him who **is** able to keep you from stumbling and to **present** you before his glorious presence without fault and with great joy— to the **only** God our Savior be glory, majesty, power and authority, through Jesus Christ our Lord, before all ages, now and forevermore!*
Amen.

The book of Jude has only one chapter and it is the last book of the New Testament before Revelation. When we read this book it is a reminder of where we are in our society. We are constantly being bombarded with a worldly world view philosophy that promotes an everything goes mentality. Hopefully, 'you can now see that a Biblical worldview is the track we want to be on. Jude is rather emphatic about two views of sexuality. He mentions the results of homosexuality- we ourselves know the results - it does not end well. Remember, the Bible is the only authority on God's Word. No politician, Minister, self help book or celebrity is a replacement for the word of God!
You and I hold in our hands, heads and our hearts the true words of God!

Supporting Scripture:
Colossians 1:22

Read through the Bible a Chapter a day

Deuteronomy 23

Day 291

Daniel 7:13-14

*As my vision continued that night, I saw someone like a son of man coming with the clouds of heaven. He approached the Ancient One and was led into his presence. He was given authority, honor, and sovereignty over all the nations of the world, so that people of every race and nation and language would obey him. His rule is **eternal**—it will **never** end. His kingdom will never be destroyed.*

This vision of Daniel is the first reference of The Messiah being the Son of Man, a reference that Jesus would claim about himself. He is enthroned as the leader of everything and this will never be taken from him and the promise to you and I is he is trustworthy and true.

He is God!

Supporting Scripture:
Revelation 1:13

Read through the Bible a Chapter a day

Deuteronomy 24

Day 292

2 Thessalonians 2:13

As for us, we can't help but thank God for you, dear brothers and sisters loved by the Lord. We are always thankful that God chose you to be among the first to experience salvation—a salvation that came through the Spirit who makes you holy and through your belief in the truth.

Here is a promise from God to us that deserves your attention. From the very beginning of his creation, the Bible tells us that you and I were chosen for salvation. This is very hard to grasp, it is something so big I cannot put my mind around, so I have to just believe and Praise God! To think that over the thousands of years and the billions of people who have walked this earth.... God picked us.

Now that we know this, what are we gonna do about it?

Supporting Scripture:
Jeremiah 1:4-5

Read through the Bible a Chapter a day

Deuteronomy 25

Day 293

Psalm 18:30

*God's way **is** perfect.*
***All** the LORD's promises prove true.*
*He is a shield for **all** who look to him for protection.*

I never get tired of reading about God's promises or his protection of our lives. It never gets old, but is always refreshing. In our cycle of news these days there is not much to cheer about. It is truly the only good news we can read about everyday.

Keep reading that Bible...

Supporting Scripture:
2 Samuel 22:31
1 Thessalonians 2:13
Proverbs 30:5
2 Peter 1:21
2 Timothy 3:16-17
Psalm 119:160

Read through the Bible a Chapter a day

Deuteronomy 28

Day 294

James 1:16-18

*So don't be misled, my dear brothers and sisters. Whatever is good and perfect **is** a gift coming down to us from God our Father, who created **all** the lights in the heavens. He **never** changes or casts a shifting shadow. He chose to give birth to us by giving us his **true** word. And we, out of all creation, became his prized possession.*

You might be getting tired of my constant reference to the words of God. I hope not, because it is the source of everything we believe. Think about how you received the Good News as a child - someone read the Bible. Think about your Pastor and the messages he gives - someone read the Bible. You see, every time we hear the promises of God - it originated in the Bible, and my contention is that we can't get enough. Our soul, our being - thrives on more. I think the goal is to fill ourselves with so much God, that the junk around us no longer carries weight. I am not talking about the God gifts, I am talking about the lies, the divisiveness, the lying media and politicians and the junk we get caught up in. God's word keeps us focused!
And it keeps coming our way, keep reading that word!

Supporting Scripture:
2 Corinthians 5:17

Read through the Bible a Chapter a day

Deuteronomy 27

Notes

Day 295

Genesis 6:8-9

*But Noah **found favor** in the eyes of the LORD.*

This is the account of Noah and his family.
*Noah **was** a righteous man, blameless among the people of his time, and he **walked faithfully** with God.*

Notice, Noah was not a righteous man because because of his works, the money he gave, whether he went to church or not (not that these things are bad) he was righteous because **he walked with God**. Day in and out, he thought, prayed, worshipped and walked with God. **Hosea 6:6** says "I'm after love that lasts, not more religion.
I want you to know GOD, not go to more prayer meetings." (The Message). One more thought, just a reminder: the words that are bolded may be small and in our normal conversation may be inconsequential, but in the Bible every word has significance **Proverbs 30:5** - "Every word of God is flawless; he is a shield to those who take refuge in him.

Supporting Scripture:
Genesis 5:21-22
Hebrews 11:7
Hosea 6:6

Read through the Bible a Chapter a day

Deuteronomy 28

Day 296

2 Corinthians 6:14-18

Don't team up with those who are unbelievers. How can righteousness be a partner with wickedness? How can light live with darkness? What harmony can there be between Christ and the devil? How can a believer be a partner with an unbeliever? And what union can there be between God's temple and idols? For we are the temple of the living God. As God said:
"I will live in them
and walk among them.
I will be their God,
and they will be my people.
Therefore, come out from among unbelievers,
and separate yourselves from them, says the LORD.
Don't touch their filthy things,
and I will welcome you.
*And **I will be your Father**,*
*and **you will be my sons and daughters**,*
says the LORD Almighty."

This is the scripture God has given us that says: Don't be yoked with unbelievers. Don't get sucked into situations where you are listening and taking part with those who practice antichrist practices. Instead, we are to be looking to God as our heavenly Father, depending on Him as we did our parents who provided what we needed when we were unable to provide for ourselves. God is our Abba - our "Heavenly Daddy"!

Supporting Scripture:
Exodus 4:22
Romans 12:1-2

Read through the Bible a Chapter a day

Deuteronomy 29

Day 297

Ezekiel 37:5-6

*This is what the Sovereign LORD says: Look! I **am** going to put breath into you and **make** you live again! I **will** put flesh and muscles on you and cover you with skin. I **will** put breath into you, and you **will** come to life. Then you **will** know that **I am** the LORD."*

There are scriptures that are so to the point, so critical to our study that we want to examine and expound upon them. Yet many of these scriptures are so obvious, little needs to be added to understand. Life springs up in us when God breaths his life giving breath into us. Ezekiel 37 is yet one more example of God's willingness to demonstrate His awesome love and power to provide you and I an opportunity to live, love and lean into Him for all we need both spiritually and physically. It all starts with acknowledging HIM, You CAN know God! Cry out to HIM today!

Supporting Scripture:
Genesis 2:7
Job 33:4

Read through the Bible a Chapter a day

Deuteronomy 30

Day 298

1 Samuel 10:6-7

*The Spirit of the LORD **will** come powerfully upon you, and you **will** prophesy with them; and you **will be changed into a different person**. Once these signs are fulfilled, do whatever your hand finds to do, **for God is with you**.*

I will grant you that 1 Samuel 10 may not be a hot spot for reassuring words from God, it does though - as this whole beautiful collection of books does: Spring with life! These are words from Samuel to Saul when he becomes Israel's first king. There are promises and similar words for us from 2 Corinthians 5:17 (Therefore, if anyone is in Christ, the new creation has come: The old has gone, the new is here!). You and I also have the reassurance of God's presence in our lives.

Supporting Scripture:
2 Corinthians 5:17

Read through the Bible a Chapter a day

Deuteronomy 31

Day 299

Joshua 1:2

He said, "Moses my servant is dead. Therefore, the time has come for you to lead these people, the Israelites, across the Jordan River into the land **I am giving them**.

Back on Day 39 we talked about the promise of God to the Israelites as they crossed the Jordan into the promise land. With verse two we see a new beginning; however, it began with the death of Moses. These people, the Israelites had the need for a leader, that was always the case. God recognized that the people would not follow God on their own. What we see with this verse is that they were not going to take the land God was giving them on their own, it was God's grace that would accomplish this. The same is true for you and I and we need to both see it and acknowledge it. It is God's grace that you and I live and breath and succeed. Yes, we must stand and be courageous. Yes, we must overcome our fear, that is also the gift of God's grace!

Supporting Scripture:
Psalm 45:2

Read through the Bible a Chapter a day

Deuteronomy 32

Day 300

Psalm 50:7

*"O my people, listen as I speak.
Here are my charges against you, O Israel:
I am God, your God!*

Don't be discouraged, this scripture is not condemning. It is correcting. It is not about God destroying, it is Him bringing His children through the fire. How do we know this? He reaffirms who He is to us and for us - He is God - our God! If you continue to read this psalm, you see that He wants to be our worship, our sacrifice. He wants us to understand that God made it all and we can go directly to Him for everything! Look how he finishes the thought:
*Make thankfulness your sacrifice to God,
and keep the vows you made to the Most High.
Then call on me when you are in trouble,
and I will rescue you, and you will give me glory."* (Psalm 50:14-15)

Supporting Scripture:
Psalm 50

Read through the Bible a Chapter a day

Deuteronomy 33

Day 301

Acts 1:23-26

So they nominated two men: Joseph called Barsabbas (also known as Justus) and Matthias. Then they all prayed, "O Lord, you know every heart. Show us which of these men you have chosen as an apostle to replace Judas in this ministry, for he has deserted us and gone where he belongs." Then they cast lots, and Matthias was selected to become an apostle with the other eleven.

The Apostles drew lots to see who would replace Judas. I find this interesting because in our day of technology and social media we can find out about someone simply by a "Google" search or Linkedin or other social media. These guys made a decision as important as who would be one of the twelve by casting lots. This is like drawing straws, spinning a bottle or throwing dice. My Bible reference on why they cast lots for Judas's replacement was to give God the choice. Some say they believed in luck or coincidence, but this is an illustration that they trusted that God is in control at all times. By the way, this is the last time "casting lots" is referred to in the Bible.

Supporting Scripture:
Revelation 2:23
1 Samuel 14:41

Read through the Bible a Chapter a day

Deuteronomy 34

Notes

Day 302

Romans 1:18-32

*But God **shows** his anger from heaven against all sinful, wicked people who suppress the truth by their wickedness. They **know** the truth about God because **he has made it obvious** to them. For ever since the world was created, people have seen the earth and sky. **Through everything God made, they can clearly see his invisible qualities**—his eternal power and divine nature. So **they have no excuse** for not knowing God. Yes, they knew God, but they wouldn't worship him as God or even give him thanks. And they began to think up foolish ideas of what God was like. As a result, their minds became dark and confused. **Claiming to be wise, they instead became utter fools.** And instead of worshiping the glorious, ever-living God, they worshiped idols made to look like mere people and birds and animals and reptiles.*

*So God abandoned them to do whatever shameful things their hearts desired. As a result, they did vile and degrading things with each other's bodies. **They traded the truth about God for a lie.** So they **worshiped and served the things God created instead of the Creator himself, who is worthy of eternal praise!** Amen. That is why God abandoned them to their shameful desires. Even the women turned against the natural way to have sex and instead indulged in sex with each other. And the men, instead of having normal sexual relations with women, burned with lust for each other. Men did shameful things with other men, and as a result of this sin, they suffered within themselves the penalty they deserved.*

Since they thought it foolish to acknowledge God, he abandoned them to their foolish thinking and let them do things that should never be done. Their lives became full of every kind of wickedness, sin, greed, hate, envy, murder, quarreling, deception, malicious behavior, and gossip. They are backstabbers, haters of God, insolent, proud, and boastful. They invent new ways of sinning, and they disobey their parents. They refuse to understand, break their promises, are heartless, and have no mercy. They know God's justice requires that those who do these things deserve to die, yet they do them anyway. Worse yet, they encourage others to do them, too.

As much as I would love to say to you this morning that this passage was meant for a long, long time ago.. it is not. It applies as much to today as any time in the past, perhaps even more so today. Maybe this is why Paul says flee from sexual promiscuity, run from it and don't turn back. The same can be said about any idol worship. The good news in all this is this: The truth of God is evident for all to see, even now! He desires all people to come to Him and repent. He never changes - He loves his creation and mankind IS His greatest pleasure! Remember John 3:16?

Read through the Bible a Chapter a day

Romans 1
Day 303

2 Corinthians 6:14-7:1

Do not be yoked together with unbelievers. For what do righteousness and wickedness have in common? Or what fellowship can light have with darkness? What harmony is there between Christ and Belial? Or what does a believer have in common with an unbeliever? What agreement is there between the temple of God and idols? For we are the temple of the living God. As God has said:
"I will live with them
and walk among them,
and I will be their God,
and they will be my people." *(Promise)*
Therefore,
"Come out from them
and be separate,
says the Lord.
Touch no unclean thing,
and **I will receive you."** *(Promise)*
And,
"I will be a Father to you,
and you will be my sons and daughters,
says the Lord Almighty." *(Promise)*
(7:1) Therefore, **since we have these promises,** *dear friends, let us purify ourselves from everything that contaminates body and spirit, perfecting holiness out of reverence for God.*

Here is some social distancing for you... A fews day ago we discussed 2 Corinthians 6:14-18. I have added some context here and verse 7:1. God wants us to be examples of holy. We clearly have to live in this world but do not have to follow the ways of this world (2 Corinthians 10:3). What we need to remember are the promises God has already made to us, just as Paul reminds us in verse 7:1. We have these promises, they have already been delivered upon, let's live like it.

Supporting Scripture:
2 Corinthians 10:3

Read through the Bible a Chapter a day

Romans 2

Day 304

Job 38:1-7

Then the LORD answered Job from the whirlwind: "Who is this that questions my wisdom with such ignorant words? Brace yourself like a man, because I have some questions for you, and you must answer them. "Where were you when I laid the foundations of the earth? Tell me, if you know so much. Who determined its dimensions and stretched out the surveying line? What supports its foundations, and who laid its cornerstone as the morning stars sang together and all the angels shouted for joy?

Doesn't this address so many issues we have going on right now? Look, God runs the universe, and everything in it. We are wise to read these words and place the care back in God's hands were it belongs. When we consider the creation and all that it entails, God has this covered to the finest detail.

Our job is to marvel at the splendor of our creator!

Supporting Scripture:
Job 38
1 Kings 19:10-13

Read through the Bible a Chapter a day

Romans 3

Day 305

Psalm 138:1-3

I give you thanks, O LORD, with all my heart;
I will sing your praises before the gods.
I bow before your holy Temple as I worship.
I praise your name for your unfailing love and faithfulness;
for your promises are backed
by all the honor of your name.
As soon as I pray, you answer me;
you encourage me by giving me strength.

I would like to offer a little advice to you today.
Many times, all we can say to God is Thank You! Thank You for your love and your faithfulness! Your very name is HOLY! Your Word is Holy! THANK YOU! Here is that advice: Find a quiet spot and show your love and thanksgiving to Jesus. Don't do this for anyone else, do it for God. Do it for yourself! You will have time for worship in Church and with others, this is YOUR time with your God!

Supporting Scripture:
Matthew 6:6
Lamentations 2:18

Read through the Bible a Chapter a day

Romans 4

Day 306

1 Samuel 16:7

*But the **LORD*** *said to Samuel, "Don't judge by his appearance or height, for I have rejected him. The LORD doesn't see things the way you see them. People judge by outward appearance, but the **LORD looks at the heart.***

When David was selected to be king, no one suspected it would be David. He had seven brothers and all passed before Samuel but the Lord kept saying no; that was until David. Look what the Lord says to Samuel: "But the Lord". Whenever you see "But the Lord" or "But God", hang on, because He is preparing to do something we usually don't see happening - in this case, the anointing of David. We all can understand judging by outward appearance, we do it every day. Fortunately, for all of us... The Lord looks at the heart! He knows when we are serious and when we are giving lip service or stepping into action when we think people might notice, thinking we are saying or doing the right things at the right time instead of crying out from our hearts - and He does not hold it against us. Always remember this: God wants your attention and a relationship with the real you... He knows who you are, He is your Creator, your God and your Friend and your Savior. He knows your heart!

Supporting Scripture:
Isaiah 49:16

Read through the Bible a Chapter a day

Romans 5

Day 307

Proverbs 20:22

Do not say, "I'll pay you back for this wrong!"
*Wait for the LORD, and he **will** deliver you.*

Whew, this easier said than done. There are volumes of Biblical references to waiting on God to move. It is easy for us to say "these days" are more difficult and there is more craziness happening around us, and that may be true. But taking matters on our own, is basically demonstrating our lack of faith or patience that God will move. The Bible says clearly that he **WILL** deliver you. Our part in this is **WAITING** for God. That displays faith and patience and godly resolve!

Lean into the loving hands of your Heavenly Father.

Supporting Scripture:
Psalm 46:10
Joshua 23:10
Romans 12:19

Read through the Bible a Chapter a day

Romans 6

Day 308

Proverbs 20:27

The LORD's light penetrates the human spirit,
exposing every hidden motive.

Here, we are witnesses to more promises of God's divine nature, which never leaves us. He knows every deed and exposes every motive, even impure, self gratifying ones we can conjure up. Cool thing though, he will point them out and help you with godly interaction to bring us back to his purpose.

Supporting Scripture:
Psalm 119:105
1 Samuel 16:7
Psalm 139:23-24

Read through the Bible a Chapter a day

Romans 7

Notes

Day 309

John 16:26-28

***Then** you will ask in my name. I'm not saying I will ask the Father on your behalf, for the **Father himself loves you dearly** because you love me and believe that I came from God. Yes, I came from the Father into the world, and now I will leave the world and return to the Father."*

That day is now! When we speak and ask in Jesus' name. Pay attention to this: It's not so much the words "in Jesus name", it's that we are in tune with what Jesus wants us to do. It's that we know Him and love Him. It's that relationship we have! God will answer because we are living in God's will. God loves you and I - it says it right there in the Bible.

What an incredible promise... From the mouth of God!

Supporting Scripture:
Romans 8:34

Read through the Bible a Chapter a day

Romans 8

Day 310

Nehemiah 9:3-8

*They stood where they were and read from the **Book of the Law of the Lord their God for a quarter of the day, and spent another quarter in confession and in worshiping the Lord their God.** Standing on the stairs of the Levites were Jeshua, Bani, Kadmiel, Shebaniah, Bunni, Sherebiah, Bani and Kenani. **They cried out with loud voices to the Lord their God.** And the Levites—Jeshua, Kadmiel, Bani, Hashabneiah, Sherebiah, Hodiah, Shebaniah and Pethahiah—said: "**Stand up and praise the Lord your God**, who is from **everlasting to everlasting**."*

*"Blessed be your glorious name, and may it be exalted above all blessing and praise. **You alone are the Lord. You made the heavens, even the highest heavens, and all their starry host, the earth and all that is on it, the seas and all that is in them. You give life to everything, and the multitudes of heaven worship you.***

*"**You are the Lord God,** who chose Abram and brought him out of Ur of the Chaldeans and named him Abraham. You found his heart faithful to you, and you made a covenant with him to give to his descendants the land of the Canaanites, Hittites, Amorites, Perizzites, Jebusites and Girgashites. **You have kept your promise because you are righteous.***

Here is my question to you: Has anything changed? Is he still from everlasting to everlasting? Look up, and see - are the heavens still filled with the starry host? Look around you, is there still life all around you? Is God still righteous?

Again I ask, has anything changed? No my friends...... God keeps his promises and we will all be witnesses to this - He promised!

Supporting Scripture:
Genesis 15:4-6

Read through the Bible a Chapter a day

Romans 9

Day 311

Malachi 3:1

*See, I **will** send my messenger, who **will** prepare the way before me. Then suddenly the Lord you are seeking **will** come to his temple; the messenger of the covenant, whom you desire, **will** come," says the LORD Almighty.*

Not sure about you, but I get tired of the rollercoaster we are riding. We go from one extreme to another, and there is no indication that it will subside any time in our near future.
You see, in this temporary environment we are in, we seek the short term. Almost never are we seeking the longer term solutions. This is not necessarily about politics, but it does prove to be a good example. When a new administration steps into power we have the 100 day plan - truth is, they are just trying to get ready for the next election. Now let's compare that to THE GOD WHO NEVER CHANGES. His covenants with his people NEVER CHANGE. God's covenant will never be broken! That is exciting, and that is what our hope is. God's new covenant is a promise of an eternal inheritance. Because of Jesus's sacrifice on the cross - you and I are heirs to all of heaven.

We can count on that promise!

Supporting Scripture:
Hebrews 9:15

Read through the Bible a Chapter a day

Romans 10

Day 312

1 Samuel 2:1-10

Then Hannah prayed:
"My heart rejoices in the LORD!
The LORD has made me strong.
Now I have an answer for my enemies;
I rejoice because you rescued me.
No one is holy like the LORD!
There is no one besides you;
there is no Rock like our God.
"Stop acting so proud and haughty!
Don't speak with such arrogance!
For the LORD is a God who knows what you have done;
he will judge your actions.
The bow of the mighty is now broken,
and those who stumbled are now strong.
Those who were well fed are now starving,
and those who were starving are now full.
The childless woman now has seven children,
and the woman with many children wastes away.
The LORD gives both death and life;
he brings some down to the grave but raises others up.
The LORD makes some poor and others rich;
he brings some down and lifts others up.
He lifts the poor from the dust
and the needy from the garbage dump.
He sets them among princes,
placing them in seats of honor.
For all the earth is the LORD's,
and he has set the world in order.
"He will protect his faithful ones,
but the wicked will disappear in darkness.
No one will succeed by strength alone.
Those who fight against the LORD will be shattered.
He thunders against them from heaven;
the LORD judges throughout the earth.
He gives power to his king;
he increases the strength of his anointed one."

The Bible has some beautiful prayers in it including this one from Hannah. She was married to a man that had two wives and his name was Elkanah. The thing was, he loved Hannah. She was barren and she prayed fervently for a child. She even offered up her child to service to God - in other words she would happily give God what he gave her. She did conceive and she gave the child back to God as she promised and she was blessed. This prayer is a response.

Supporting Scripture:
1 Chronicles 29:10-20

Read through the Bible a Chapter a day

Romans 11

Day 313

Matthew 13:44-45

The Kingdom of Heaven is like a treasure that a man discovered hidden in a field. In his excitement, he hid it again and sold everything he owned to get enough money to buy the field. "Again, the Kingdom of Heaven is like a merchant on the lookout for choice pearls. When he discovered a pearl of great value, he sold everything he owned and bought it!

Clearly, Jesus is describing for you and I what our response to finding God SHOULD be. We should be so excited that we are willing to throw everything aside and pursue our relationship with God. I don't know about you, it has taken me years and I am just beginning to understand what this means. I don't think Jesus is saying to toss away everything, rather what things are a hinderance to your worship and friendship with God. Figure that out, and you might be on your way.

Supporting Scripture:
Isaiah 55:1

Read through the Bible a Chapter a day

Romans 11

Day 314

2 Corinthians 9:6-15

*Remember this: Whoever sows sparingly **will** also reap sparingly, and whoever sows generously will also reap generously. Each of you should give what you have decided in your heart to give, not reluctantly or under compulsion, for **God loves a cheerful giver.** And God is able to bless you abundantly, so that in all things at all times, having all that you need, you **will** abound in every good work. As it is written:*
"They have freely scattered their gifts to the poor;
their righteousness endures forever."
*Now he who supplies seed to the sower and bread for food **will** also supply and increase your store of seed and **will** enlarge the harvest of your righteousness. You **will** be enriched in every way so that you can be generous on every occasion, and through us your generosity will result in thanksgiving to God. This service that you perform is not only supplying the needs of the Lord's people but is also overflowing in many expressions of thanks to God. Because of the service by which you have proved yourselves, others will praise God for the obedience that accompanies your confession of the gospel of Christ, and for your generosity in sharing with them and with everyone else. And in their prayers for you their hearts will go out to you, because of the surpassing grace God has given you. **Thanks be to God for his indescribable gift!***

God has given each of us everything we will ever need to accomplish his objective for our lives. Nothing is left out. Everything you do is watched by God, so you can give with all your pleasure, resources, time - all of it! Have fun as you give it away!

Supporting Scripture:
Isaiah 55:10

Read through the Bible a Chapter a day

Romans 11

Day 315

Isaiah 25:1

O LORD, I will honor and praise your name,
for you are my God.
You do such wonderful things!
You planned them long ago,
and now you have accomplished them.

As we face times like we live right now, it is helpful to remember that God planned all this a long, long time ago. You and I were known by God at the very beginning, there are no surprises to God in his creation. We may respond with questions - God however, does not.

Have a great day!

Supporting Scripture:
Psalm 145:2

Read through the Bible a Chapter a day

Romans 14

Notes

Day 316

Acts 9:5

Who are you, lord?" Saul asked.

I have become fascinated by this question of Paul. There are other times in the Bible that a man or woman has asked God his name, Jacob wrestled with God, Gideon, and Samson's parents. All asked His name and the answer was the same: Why do you need to know my name? In Mark, Jesus even asks the disciples: Who do people think I am? Even though he persecuted Christians, Paul knew who God was, he was a Jew and they claim to worship God. All that being the case, this encounter with the risen Jesus would change Paul forever. This leaves the obvious observation, are we asking today: Who are you, Lord? Keep reading, the answer may be just a page away!

Supporting Scripture:
Genesis 32:22-30
Judges 6:11-22
Judges 13:17
Mark 8:27-29

Read through the Bible a Chapter a day

Romans 15

Day 317

Ecclesiastes 11:5

Just as you cannot understand the path of the wind or the mystery of a tiny baby growing in its mother's womb, so you cannot understand the activity of God, who does all things.

What if:
We could fully understand all of God's secrets?
We could understand all that God has made?
We could understand God's omnipresence around us?
We could fully understand God's grace?
We could fully understand God's mercy?
We could fully understand God's love?
We could fully understand God's patience?
We could fully understand God's faithfulness?
We could understand God's forgiveness?
We could fully understand his plan for our souls?
We could fully understand: The Father, The Son and The Holy Spirit?

Would that change anything?

Supporting Scripture:
Psalm 139:14-16

Read through the Bible a Chapter a day

Romans 16

Day 318

Acts 2:21

*But **everyone** who calls on the name of the LORD **will** be saved.*

This is the scripture that Peter quotes in Acts, and Paul uses in Romans 10:13, proving yet again that God's promises are true and that the whole Bible is true! Today, we hear some say that only the New Testament is valid today - all Scripture speaks to us: old and new! Look at Joel 2:32. As craziness seems to be popping up everywhere these days, this scripture reminds us that you and I may be the only person to speak to others about God's love through Jesus they may ever hear. Many are not church goers and many still are not going back to church. Remember God's promise: **Everyone** who calls on the name of the Lord **will** be saved!

Supporting Scripture:
Joel 2:32
Romans 10:13

Read through the Bible a Chapter a day

Joshua 1

Day 319

Revelation 4:8-11

Each of these living beings had six wings, and their wings were covered all over with eyes, inside and out. Day after day and night after night they keep on saying,
"Holy, holy, holy is the Lord God, the Almighty—
the one who always was, who is, and who is still to come."
Whenever the living beings give glory and honor and thanks to the one sitting on the throne (the one who lives forever and ever), the twenty-four elders fall down and worship the one sitting on the throne (the one who lives forever and ever). And they lay their crowns before the throne and say,
"You are worthy, O Lord our God,
to receive glory and honor and power.
For you created all things,
and they exist because you created what you pleased."

Today we read that **God is holy**.
We have already discussed God's holiness over these past months. Here we see that they celebrate God's holiness in heaven! Every creature here on earth or in heaven (and under the earth - namely the demons) all understand who God is. Even the demons saw Jesus as who he was (Mark 1: 23-24). You and I have an image of holy and that does not even come close to the reality of our Holy Heavenly Father! God is utterly and supremely untainted and His holiness is completely unique and incomprehensible.

Supporting Scripture:
Isaiah 6:2

Read through the Bible a Chapter a day

Joshua 2

Day 320

Exodus 15:22-26

Then Moses led the people of Israel away from the Red Sea, and they moved out into the desert of Shur. They traveled in this desert for three days without finding any water. When they came to the oasis of Marah, the water was too bitter to drink. So they called the place Marah (which means "bitter").
Then the people complained and turned against Moses. "What are we going to drink?" they demanded. So Moses cried out to the LORD for help, and the LORD showed him a piece of wood. Moses threw it into the water, and this made the water good to drink.
It was there at Marah that the LORD set before them the following decree as a standard to test their faithfulness to him. He said, "If you will listen carefully to the voice of the LORD your God and do what is right in his sight, obeying his commands and keeping all his decrees, then I will not make you suffer any of the diseases I sent on the Egyptians; for I am the LORD who **heals you.**"

It is fitting that we continue to study the names and attributes for our Holy God today, we see Jehovah-rophe or "Jehovah heals". God alone provides the remedy for mankind's brokenness through His son, Jesus Christ. The Gospel is the physical, moral and spiritual remedy for all people!

Supporting Scripture:
Numbers 33:8

Read through the Bible a Chapter a day

Joshua 3

Day 321

Leviticus 20:7-8

*So set yourselves apart to be holy, for **I am** the LORD your God. Keep all my decrees by putting them into practice, for **I am** the LORD who **makes** you holy.*

The phrase "I am" is listed hundreds of time in the Bible. Old or New Testaments, it's there! Here God is displaying one of his holy names **Jehovah-M'Kaddish** or "the God who sanctifies". He reminds us it is THE LORD who sanctifies! The day you accepted Jesus Christ as Lord and Savior that was instant - you are saved. Sanctification however, that takes the rest of your life here on earth.

That's a team effort with God!

Supporting Scripture:
John 17:19

Read through the Bible a Chapter a day

Joshua 4

Day 322

Isaiah 46:4-5

*I **will** be your God throughout your lifetime—*
until your hair is white with age.
*I made you, and I **will** care for you.*
*I **will** carry you along and save you.*
"To whom will you compare me?
Who is my equal?

Take a few minutes and read this through, several times if needed. God's promises are real, and what we have discussed during your read of this book reaffirms God's standing love for each of us. It is consistent, I dare you to read deeper!

Supporting Scripture:
Psalm 71:18

Read through the Bible a Chapter a day

Joshua 5

Notes

Day 323

2 Peter 1:3-13

*By his divine power, God has given us **everything** we need for living a godly life. We have received all of this by coming to know him, the one who called us to himself by means of his marvelous glory and excellence. And because of his glory and excellence, he has given us **great and precious promises**. These are the **promises** that **enable** you to share his divine nature and **escape** the **world's corruption** caused by human desires. In view of all this, make every effort to **respond to God's promises**. **Supplement** your faith with a **generous provision** of **moral excellence**, and moral excellence with **knowledge**, and knowledge with **self-control**, and self-control with **patient endurance**, and patient endurance with **godliness**, and godliness with **brotherly affection**, and brotherly affection with **love** for everyone. The more you grow like this, the more productive and useful you will be in your knowledge of our Lord Jesus Christ. But those who fail to develop in this way are shortsighted or blind, forgetting that they have been cleansed from their old sins. So, dear brothers and sisters, **work hard** to prove that you really are among those God has called and chosen. Do these things, and you will never fall away. Then God will give you a grand entrance into the eternal Kingdom of our Lord and Savior Jesus Christ.*

Talk about Promises - Here is Peter promising all the promises of the Bible! These promises from God are not just for us to claim and hope, they are there to bring us through this life successfully. But according to this, they don't just happen, we have to work at it. We have to wrestle with it. It starts with coming to know him and that starts with reading his word. Then, as we learned the other day - is the maturing process leading us through the 2 P's - Perseverance and Patience and finally godly love. Then as we grow in these qualities - we become more productive and useful in our knowledge of Jesus Christ. Maybe another way of saying this is - God can use us! He is shaping and molding us into the image of the Lord.

Read through the Bible a Chapter a day

Joshua 6

Day 324

Acts 1:4

*On one occasion, while he was eating with them, he gave them this command: "Do not leave Jerusalem. but **wait** for the gift my Father **promised**, which you have heard me speak about.*

Here we have two amazing truths:
- God has made you promises that you will receive. Especially the promise of His Holy Spirit.
- Waiting is a blessing.

Now to be fair, we may or may not appreciate the promise and I am sure we don't want to wait for it, but God knows the perfect time for the promises and the waiting and when you see them you know it is from God..... and there is nothing better than that.

Supporting Scripture:
Psalm 46:10

Read through the Bible a Chapter a day

Joshua 7

Day 325

3 John:11

Dear friend, don't let this bad example influence you. Follow only what is good. Remember that those who do good prove that they are God's children, and those who do evil prove that they do not know God.

You and I are reminded that we should always be seeking what is good. I know it seems pretty basic and self explained. John is reminding us that we should always be seeking what is right, even though these days (at least to me), things seem backwards, And as Christians following the word of God, the word of God should be the preference to that of the world which seems confused, tired and frankly: stinks.

Supporting Scripture:
Psalm 34:14

Read through the Bible a Chapter a day

Joshua 8

Day 326

Proverbs 21:30

No human wisdom or understanding or plan can stand against the LORD.

Good Morning! It's hard to believe we are already at Day 326. It is for me anyway. I have included a Proverb this today - it is another wisdom scripture! All around us we are subjected to a worldly viewpoint. And frankly, that viewpoint is full of untruths and misguided philosophies. Everywhere we look we see it and it's frustrating. I need to remind myself that there is no human wisdom or understanding or plan that can stand up to God - NONE!

Whew, I feel better, how about you?

Supporting Scripture:
Job 12:13
2 Chronicles 13:12
Isaiah 8:10

Read through the Bible a Chapter a day

Joshua 9

Day 327

Deuteronomy 32:39

"See now that I myself am He!
There is no god besides me.
I put to death and I bring to life,
I have wounded and I will heal,
and no one can deliver out of my hand.

It helps to see the authority of God. To be reminded that all things are under the control of God. God has given each of us time on this earth. It is all up to Him. Even pathetic politicians and others like them who serve themselves don't get it.
Lean into God, he is the only answer!

Supporting Scripture:
Isaiah 41:4

Read through the Bible a Chapter a day

Joshua 10

Day 328

Matthew 19:4-6

"Haven't you read the Scriptures?" Jesus replied. "They record that from the beginning 'God made them male and female.'" And he said, "'This explains why a man leaves his father and mother and is joined to his wife, and the two are united into one.' Since they are no longer two but one, let no one split apart what God has joined together."

Take a good look at this verse, there is a great deal of very important information. Jesus is confronted by some Pharisees who were there to test him. Look at the first thing he asks them: What does the Bible say? He is speaking about the foundation of marriage. God created marriage. He did so with the intention of preserving generation after generation. For many, marriage has become an idol, that is for a different day. Here in Matthew 19 Jesus discusses divorce and makes it very clear that marriage is between one man and one woman. That's it. The sanctity of marriage was ordained by God himself and relates to us as much today as it ever has.

Supporting Scripture:
Genesis 1:27
Genesis 5:1-2
Ephesians 5:30-32

Read through the Bible a Chapter a day

Joshua 11

Day 329

2 Timothy 1:8-14

So never be ashamed to tell others about our Lord. And don't be ashamed of me, either, even though I'm in prison for him. With the strength God gives you, be ready to suffer with me for the sake of the Good News. For God saved us and called us to live a holy life. He did this, not because we deserved it, but because that was his plan from before the beginning of time—to show us his grace through Christ Jesus. And now he has made all of this plain to us by the appearing of Christ Jesus, our Savior. He broke the power of death and illuminated the way to life and immortality through the Good News. And God chose me to be a preacher, an apostle, and a teacher of this Good News.

That is why I am suffering here in prison. But I am not ashamed of it, for I know the one in whom I trust, and I am sure that he is able to guard what I have entrusted to him until the day of his return.

Hold on to the pattern of wholesome teaching you learned from me—a pattern shaped by the faith and love that you have in Christ Jesus. Through the power of the Holy Spirit who lives within us, carefully guard the precious truth that has been entrusted to you.

We usually think of influential people as those who have authority, position, or power in the world, but in reality, we all have influence to one degree or another. The term describes the capacity to have an effect on someone else's character, development, or behavior. This is exactly what Christ has called believers to do by proclaiming the gospel and encouraging one another in the faith. However, in order to have a godly impact on others, we must first be convinced that the Bible is true. Then as we grow in knowledge of the truth, we can help others know Jesus, understand scriptural principles, and live obediently by them. Paul advised Timothy to "retain the standard of sound words" in the faith (2 Timothy 1:13), and these same truths have been delivered to us: **1. *The Bible is the inspired, infallible Word of God.*** There are no mistakes in it, and it is wholly true (2 Timothy 3:16; John 17:17). **2. *There is one God, and He exists in three persons.*** The Father, the Son, and the Holy Spirit are all members of the triune Godhead (Matthew 28:19). **3. *Eternal life is received only through faith in Jesus.*** Salvation cannot be earned by good works (John 14:6; Ephesians 2:8-9). **4. *Jesus will one day return for those who believe in Him,*** and He'll take them to heaven (John 14:2-3). But unbelievers will remain under divine wrath. As the culture around us becomes more resistant to Christian influence, holding to these convictions will require solid commitment and steady courage. So determine not to let compromise steal away what you know to be true.

Read through the Bible a Chapter a day

Joshua 12

Notes

Day 330

Genesis 18:14

*Is anything too hard for the Lord? **I will return** to you at the appointed time next year, and Sarah will have a son."*

Even Sarah laughed when she heard this one! There are said to be some seven thousand, five hundred of promises in God's Bible. Many of these promises are impossible on our own, but ALL things are possible through God. Our job is believe that my friends!

Supporting Scripture:
Jeremiah 32:17
Matthew 19:26

Read through the Bible a Chapter a day

Joshua 13

Day 331

Job 28:20

Where then does wisdom come from?
Where does understanding dwell?
It is hidden from the eyes of every living thing,
concealed even from the birds of the air.
Destruction and Death say,
"Only a rumor of it has reached our ears."
*God **understands** the way to it*
*and he **alone** knows where it dwells,*
for he views the ends of the earth
and sees everything under the heavens.
When he established the force of the wind
and measured out the waters,
*when he **made** a decree for the rain*
and a path for the thunderstorm,
then he looked at wisdom and appraised it;
*he **confirmed** it and **tested** it.*
And he said to man,
*"The **fear** of the Lord—that **is** wisdom,*
and to shun evil is understanding."

I wonder about a lot of things…. Does God sometimes looks at the futile attempts of man and says: "your close" or maybe he laughs and says: "your not even close". Man finds wisdom from God. A quick look at James 1:5 (If any of you lacks wisdom, you should ask God, who gives generously to **all** without finding fault, and it will be given to you. But when you ask, you must believe and not doubt, because the one who doubts is like a wave of the sea, blown and tossed by the wind. That person should not expect to receive anything from the Lord. Such a person is double-minded and unstable in all they do.) So in both instances we see that wisdom comes from God. These days, these are "fightin" words because the world has its own version of wisdom - how can we know the difference? The answer may lie in James verse - God will give generously to all who ask, but the world's wisdom is generally self serving and conditional. That is not say that all worldly wisdom is bad, it's that God's is much better!

Supporting Scripture:
James 1:5

Read through the Bible a Chapter a day

Joshua 14

Day 332

Acts 4:18-20

*Then they called them in again and commanded them not to speak or teach at all in the name of Jesus. But Peter and John replied, "Judge for yourselves whether it is right in God's sight to obey you rather then God. For we **cannot help** speaking about what we have seen and heard."*

The early church was persecuted severely. Peter and John were threatened to never speak or teach in the name of Jesus. Yet their response was: "we can't help but talk about what we have seen and heard" (this came after Peter healed the crippled beggar). This is not just about the beggar, this is their testimony. They then prayed (Acts 4:24-31) to God for a voice that was loud and bold. The answer to the threats they were receiving was to boldly proclaim the gospel. The place were they were meeting shook and the Holy Spirit came upon them and they spoke the word of God boldly. God answered their prayer exactly the way they asked. How do we respond when pressed? Do we ask God for that bold voice? For myself, the answer is no..... but I am going to begin the pray for boldness. I hope you will join me!

Supporting Scripture:
Acts 4:24-31

Read through the Bible a Chapter a day

Joshua 15

Day 333

Luke 18:1-8

*Then Jesus told his disciples a parable to show them that they should **always** pray and **not** give up. He said: "In a certain town there was a judge who neither feared God nor cared about men. And there was a widow in that town who kept coming to him with the plea, 'Grant me justice against my adversary.'*

"For some time he refused. But finally he said to himself, 'Even though I don't fear God or care what about men, yet because this widow keeps bothering me, I will see that she gets justice, so that she won't eventually wear me out with her coming!'"

*And the Lord said, "Listen to what the unjust judge says. And **will** not God bring about justice for his chosen ones, who cry out to him day and night? **Will** he keep putting them off? I tell you, he **will** see that they get justice, and quickly. **However, when the Son of Man comes, will he find faith on the earth?"***

This is the story of the persistent widow. When Jesus is telling this story, he does so to remind his disciples that they should be persistent with prayer and never give up. This judge was a powerful man, and as the Bible tells us, he did not care about anything but his own self. But the widow was persistent, to the degree that this judge was tired of her persistence. Despite what he could have done to her, she never gave up. Christ then uses this story as a vision about persistent prayer to God. Jesus also reminds us that some day, he will return - and he asks the question: Will he find a people who are persistent in prayer? I think we would all agree that we are living in a particularly fascinating time. I choose these words because no matter what is going on, God is still on the throne! Maybe what this nation needs right now is persistent Christ followers who are driven to prayer and committed to seeking Godly wisdom and results only God can bring. A little later in the chapter Jesus tells a crowd: "What is impossible with men is possible with God. "

Supporting Scripture:
Isaiah 40:31

Read through the Bible a Chapter a day

Joshua 16

Day 334

Jeremiah 32:17

"O Sovereign LORD! You made the heavens and earth by your strong hand and powerful arm. Nothing is too hard for you!

Today I have much to say about today's scripture. After all, we have read together so much this year: I am not going to say anything!
This is for you, Over on the right, there is a place for you to write you thoughts, prayers, whatever you need **after** prayerful consideration. Here is what I would ask you - In your Bible, write "Thank You" next to Jeremiah 32:17

Supporting Scripture:
Jeremiah 1:4-8
Genesis 1:1
Deuteronomy 9:29
2 Kings 19:15
Psalm 102:25
Matthew 19:26

Read through the Bible a Chapter a day

Joshua 17

Day 335

Isaiah 41:4

Who has done this and carried it through,
calling forth the generations from the beginning?
I, the LORD—with the first of them
and with the last —I am he.

What a mighty word this is! It is God who wakes us up in the morning, carries us along and has done so generation after generation. He was on the scene at the beginning and he will be on the scene until the end, always has been, and will always be!

Only God!

Supporting Scripture:
Genesis 1:1
Isaiah 46:10

Read through the Bible a Chapter a day

Joshua 18

Day 336

1 Samuel 1:19

Early in the morning they arose and worshiped before the Lord and then went back to their home in Ramah. Elkanah lay with Hannah his wife, and **the Lord remembered her**. *In the course of time Hannah conceived and gave birth to a son. She named him Samuel, saying, "Because I asked the Lord for him".*

Today's scripture takes us to Hannah, the mother of Samuel. As with others, she was married to a man with at least two wives, she was barren, and her husband loved her. She was in misery, weeping and praying to God - even offering to give the child back to God if he would just grant this request. God remembered Hannah and she praised him for it. Like others we have discussed in the past, Hannah is important in that she gave birth to the last judge of Israel and the first prophet after Moses. It was Samuel who would usher in the Kingship's of Saul and David. We see the importance of God using godly women to shape the path as we continue to roll towards the Birth of Jesus.

Supporting Scripture:
Genesis 21:1

Read through the Bible a Chapter a day

Joshua 19

Notes

Day 337

Psalm 103:13-17

As a father has compassion on his children,
so the LORD has compassion on those who fear him;
*for **he knows** how we are formed,*
*he **remembers** that we are dust.*
The life of mortals is like grass,
they flourish like a flower of the field;
the wind blows over it and it is gone,
and its place remembers it no more.
But from everlasting to everlasting
*the LORD's love **is** with those who fear him,*

God knows the things we forget. How we live our lives, many thinking of immortality (We live as though we will never perish). The truth is everyone ultimately will pass through the door of death. Fortunately, God has compassion and understands our days. His love is with those who fear him. Surely he has put in place a permanent solution to bridge the gap between God and mankind.

Thank you Lord:
- For your caring
- For your compassion
- For your mercy and grace.
- For remembering that we are dust.
- And finally, that when we expire here in this life, our soul is returned to you!

Praise God!

Supporting Scripture:
Ecclesiastes 12:7

Read through the Bible a Chapter a day

Joshua 20

Day 338

Genesis 1:31

God saw all that he had made and it was very good. And there was evening and there was morning - the Sixth day

As with everything we read in the Bible, there is meaning. This morning we peek at God's creation. I have really never considered the phrase "and there was evening and there was morning". Let's look at it this way:

Darkness = obscurity and chaos

Morning = order and calm

Though Genesis is a literal account of creation, there is another layer of understanding and depth. On day one, God took creation and brought order from the chaos. On the second day, He continued His work and brought about more order. This continued through day six until creation was complete and therefore the obscurity and chaos of creation was brought into order. Why didn't day seven have an evening and morning? In a literal sense it did, it had a sunrise and a sunset. But there is more to the story than daylight. Creation was finished and it was whole, in order, and "very good". **And that is our promise for today - God brings order, not chaos** All this from the mouth of God. He whispered and created.

How cool is that?

Supporting Scripture:
Psalm 104:24
Jeremiah 10:12

Read through the Bible a Chapter a day

Joshua 21

Day 339

Psalm 12:6

And the words of the LORD are flawless,
like silver purified in a crucible,
like gold refined seven times.

Here is a great example of The Bible and it's perfect word. There are numerous times we read such words, like Proverbs 30:5. I believe it is also a word many cannot stomach, they know the truth and the light shines in the darkness exposing evil deeds. Some don't want that exposure, they are more than happy to stay in the dark. If you read the Bible, you will be exposed to the LIGHT! What you do with it is the decision we all have to make.

Supporting Scripture:
Proverbs 30:5
Deuteronomy 29:29

Read through the Bible a Chapter a day

Joshua 22

Day 340

John 6:51

*"I am the living bread that came down from heaven. Whoever eats this bread **will** live forever. This bread is my flesh, which I **will** give for the life of the world."*

Throughout his earthly ministry, Jesus knew who he was. He was God, but explaining this to the devout Jews at the time was not really a simple message. They had blinders on and they could not see past their past as a people. It is a reality he would face his entire ministry. Yet for those who would listen and follow him he makes a beautiful promise: Eternal Life! He even predicts that his death will open a passage to all the world (a promise made for you and I). I think I shared an experience that I had a few months ago with a student who had learned in Church (this is how he perceived it) that Jesus was the Son of God, but that Mary, his Mother was to be worshipped as well and that Jesus was just a good guy. We had an interesting conversation, but he freaked out when I explained that Jesus is God. Anyway, he stopped me in the hallway and apologized for his scene. He had a long chat with his mother who explained who Jesus Christ is. My suggestion: Keep reading that Bible, God will direct you if your heart is in it.

Supporting Scripture:
Hebrews 10:10

Read through the Bible a Chapter a day

Joshua 23

Day 341

1 Thessalonians 4:16-18

For the Lord himself will come down from heaven with a commanding shout, with the voice of the archangel, and with the trumpet call of God. First, the believers who have died will rise from their graves. Then, together with them, we who are still alive and remain on the earth will be caught up in the clouds to meet the Lord in the air. Then we will be with the Lord forever. So encourage each other with these words.

There are about 7.3 billion people in the world today, with approximately 31% professing Christianity. And we think the time between 2020 to now has been a tough time, what do you suppose will happen when 1/3 of the entire population just vanishes? The rapture of the church is the next "big" event to take place in terms of prophetic timing and every piece of the puzzle has now been put in place, in other words it could happen at any time. Now is the time to prepare, now is the time to make sure your relationship with God is secure. Now is the time for us to warn others. What is coming is far more chaotic than a virus, a distant war, and a crumbling society around us. This has been just a small taste of what will happen. No one will know when it is going to happen, but I would suggest thinking about this in terms of the next day. It could be sooner than any of us realizes.

Supporting Scripture:
Matthew 24:31

Read through the Bible a Chapter a day

Joshua 24

Day 342

Isaiah 57:1-2

Good people pass away;
the godly often die before their time.
But no one seems to care or wonder why.
No one seems to understand
that God is protecting them from the evil to come.
For those who follow godly paths
will rest in peace when they die.

One of the greatest mysteries of life is that of death. Especially the death of good people, young people - ones who in our view died before their time. The Bible has an answer for what you and I call premature death and as many times as I have read through this book, I never saw this, Isaiah 57:1-2. Having said that, Moses as we have seen in the past - died. He was healthy and as "strong as ever". Yet His time had come. It is God who has determined our days here on earth. God never intended us to die. The original plan for us was to live with God eternally, death is the result of the sin of Adam and Eve. This of course cannot ease the pain of the death of a loved one, especially a child. We grieve because of death. We can however, gain wisdom by realizing that life is fully under the control of God.

Lets not waste another moment wandering....

Supporting Scripture:
Deuteronomy 34:6-7
Job 14:5
Psalm 90:12

Read through the Bible a Chapter a day

1 Corinthians 1

Day 343

Matthew 22:23-33

That same day Jesus was approached by some Sadducees—religious leaders who say there is no resurrection from the dead. They posed this question: "Teacher, Moses said, 'If a man dies without children, his brother should marry the widow and have a child who will carry on the brother's name.' Well, suppose there were seven brothers. The oldest one married and then died without children, so his brother married the widow. But the second brother also died, and the third brother married her. This continued with all seven of them. Last of all, the woman also died. So tell us, whose wife will she be in the resurrection? For all seven were married to her."
*Jesus replied, "Your mistake is that **you don't know the Scriptures, and you don't know the power of God.** For when the dead rise, they will neither marry nor be given in marriage. In this respect they will be like the angels in heaven. "But now, as to whether there will be a resurrection of the dead—haven't you ever read about this in the Scriptures? Long after Abraham, Isaac, and Jacob had died, God said, **'I am the God of Abraham, the God of Isaac, and the God of Jacob.' So he is the God of the living, not the dead."***

John 11:25-26
Jesus told her, "I am the resurrection and the life. Anyone who believes in me will live, even after dying. Everyone who lives in me and believes in me will never ever die. Do you believe this, Martha?"

Here is a promise for us about death. First up, Jesus reminds us that God is the God of the living, not the dead. Yet even though Abraham, Isaac and Jacob had died long before he speaks these words he reminds the Sadducees that they are still under the care of God. Jesus also reminds us who He is in John 11, He is the resurrection and the life. Even after dying, we still live. We will never die. I do not proclaim to fully understand this, I just know it's true!

Supporting Scripture:
John 11:25-26

Read through the Bible a Chapter a day

1 Corinthians 2

Notes

Day 344

Nahum 1:7

The Lord is good,
a refuge in times of trouble.
He cares for those who trust in him,

There are times when we can read a verse in this beloved Bible and apply that verse which means so much. This is a great description of God and His love for each of us. Break it down, spell it out: God is good! God is great, who are we kidding! He is a refuge for his children. Finally, He cares for those who trust Him. So that may be a starting point for us. Do we trust Him? After 344 days, I hope the answer is a resounding YES! If you are struggling, I have a secret for you, CRY out to God. We have learned that God will answer prayer that is in His will, and He wants you to trust Him. He will respond, you'll see....

Supporting Scripture:
Jeremiah 33:11

Read through the Bible a Chapter a day

1 Corinthians 3

Day 345

Ezra 6:22

Then they celebrated the Festival of Unleavened Bread for seven days. There was great joy throughout the land because the LORD had caused the king of Assyria to be favorable to them, so that he helped them to rebuild the Temple of God, the God of Israel.

I wonder how many have gone to this little verse for some inspiration?
Think about that, the nation Israel had been in captivity for 70 years, and King Cyrus has opened the flood gates to let them return to Jerusalem to rebuild their temple. After a brief time when detractors tried to stop the building, a decree was found by then King Darius. Not only did they open the opportunity, they paid for it and as the Bible states they even supported what they needed - all because God changed the attitude of a king! No one is safe from God (wink, wink)! He can change anyone.... Let's pray for our leaders, even if we stand absolutely opposite of what they do, Our God can change minds and attitudes.

Supporting Scripture:
Exodus 12:17

Read through the Bible a Chapter a day

1 Corinthians 4

Day 346

Titus 1:1-3

Paul, a servant of God and an apostle of Jesus Christ to further the faith of God's elect and their knowledge of the truth that leads to godliness — **in the hope of eternal life, which God, who does not lie, promised before the beginning of time**, *and which now at his appointed season he has brought to light through the preaching entrusted to me by the command of God our Savior,*

Did you catch this little gem in the book of Titus? Eternal life is God promise from the beginning of time. And God does not lie! With this you and I should be living as Paul and the other Apostles - preaching and teaching others (and by preaching, I mean we profess our faith when we have the opportunity). What is there to fear, we have his promise!

Supporting Scripture:
Numbers 23:19
2 Timothy 1:1

Read through the Bible a Chapter a day

1 Corinthians 5

Day 347

Psalm 40:6-8

*Sacrifice and offering you did not desire—
but my ears you have opened—
burnt offerings and sin offerings you did not require.
Then I said, "Here I am, I have come—
it is written about me in the scroll.
I desire to do your will, my God;
your law is within my heart."*

Hebrews 10:5-10
*Therefore, when Christ came into the world, he said:
"Sacrifice and offering you did not desire,
but a body you prepared for me;
with burnt offerings and sin offerings
you were not pleased.
Then I said, 'Here I am—it is written about me in the scroll —
I have come to do your will, my God.'"
First he said, "Sacrifices and offerings, burnt offerings and sin offerings you did not desire, nor were you pleased with them" —though they were offered in accordance with the law. Then he said, "Here I am, I have come to do your will." He sets aside the first to establish the second. And by that will, we* **have been** *made holy through the sacrifice of the body of Jesus Christ once for all.*

No, you are not seeing double. David wrote Psalm 40 about Jesus. Paul writes that those words became true with Jesus and because of the sacrifice of Jesus's body on the cross, you and I have been made holy - Once for all! Case closed! This is another case of Jesus being described in the Old Testament, hundreds of years before he was born.

Read through the Bible a Chapter a day

1 Corinthians 6

Day 348

John 14:15-17

If you love me, obey my commandments. And I will ask the Father, and he will give you another Advocate, who will never leave you. He is the Holy Spirit, who leads into all truth. The world cannot receive him, because it isn't looking for him and doesn't recognize him. But you know him, because he lives with you now and later will be in you.

Check out this promise from Jesus. He promises to talk to God the Father on our behalf, who in turn, promises God's Holy Spirit and look how he is described: Our friend! This friend will never leave us and not only is he with is - HE IS IN US! Knowing this, doesn't it make sense that we live like God is with us, we have something few people have: The God of the Universe, the creator of everything - living in us!

O' Lord, don't let us abuse what you have provided. Let us use this for good, recognizing the opportunities you have uniquely set aside for each of us. Open our eyes and ears and our minds O' God, to see the world as you see it.

Supporting Scripture:
Acts 1:8

Read through the Bible a Chapter a day

1 Corinthians 7

Day 349

Zechariah 1:3-4

Therefore tell the people: This is what the LORD Almighty says: 'Return to me,' declares the LORD Almighty, 'and I will return to you,' says the LORD Almighty. Do not be like your ancestors, to whom the earlier prophets proclaimed: This is what the LORD Almighty says: 'Turn from your evil ways and your evil practices.' But they would not listen or pay attention to me, declares the LORD.

Forgive me if I am wrong, but it seems to me that this is an important message for us today. Everywhere we turn we see mixed messages, and many of these from folks who claim to be Christians. If we turn to God, he will turn towards us. It's that simple, it's another glorious promise from our God!

Supporting Scripture:
Job 22:23
2 Chronicles 7:14

Read through the Bible a Chapter a day

1 Corinthians 8

Day 350

1 Thessalonians 3:11-13

Now may our God and Father himself and our Lord Jesus clear the way for us to come to you. May the Lord make your love increase and overflow for each other and for everyone else, just as ours does for you. May he strengthen your hearts so that you will be blameless and holy in the presence of our God and Father when our **Lord Jesus comes with all his holy ones.**

It seems Paul was obsessed with the return of Jesus. He mentions it several times in his letters including here in 1 Thessalonians. Many believe that the next big reveal is the rapture of the church and the way it is laid out in the Bible is that it could occur at any moment. Paul lived with the expectation that Jesus could return at any time and so should we. Here is that thing, it is inevitable that we will meet our God face to face someday. Whether that happens at the end of our lives or the rapture - that appointment is guaranteed. Ecclesiastes 12:7 says: and the dust returns to the ground it came from, and the spirit returns to God who gave it. It always amazes me how people think these words refer to someone else but not themselves. Make sure we have resolved our relationship with God through Jesus Christ, that day may be today!

Supporting Scripture:
Matthew 25:31

Read through the Bible a Chapter a day

1 Corinthians 9

Notes

Day 351

Colossians 1:15-20

He is the image of the invisible God, the firstborn of all creation. For by him all things were created, in heaven and on earth, visible and invisible, whether thrones or dominions or rulers or authorities—all things were created through him and for him. And he is before all things, and in him all things hold together. And he is the head of the body, the church. He is the beginning, the firstborn from the dead, that in everything he might be preeminent. For in him all the fullness of God was pleased to dwell, and through him to reconcile to himself all things, whether on earth or in heaven, making peace by the blood of his cross.

Christ was there at the beginning! He is fully God and fully man. His perfect plan included him coming as a baby, to grow in example and live a perfect life. Not perfect by our standards, but by God's standard.

Supporting Scripture:
John 1:18
Hebrews 11:27

Read through the Bible a Chapter a day

1 Corinthians 10

Day 352

Job 1:20-22

Job stood up and tore his robe in grief. Then he shaved his head and fell to the ground to worship. He said,
"I came naked from my mother's womb,
and I will be naked when I leave.
The LORD gave me what I had,
and the LORD has taken it away.
Praise the name of the LORD!"
In all of this, Job did not sin by blaming God.

I could probably never fully understand all that Job experienced in chapter one of the book of Job. I am thankful for that. Having said that; some of us have, and I am reminded of this pain as we continue to look around us at recent events. Our country is experiencing some really horrifying realities. And yes, many of us are angry, frustrated and many have emotions that have not been touched in a long time. Here is the thing: God is still on the throne of Heaven. He is still in control. Never look past this reality. Job was in anguish when he fell to his knees and worshipped God - Did you catch that? With all that he went through - He worshipped God!
Cry out to God with your pain, with your understanding or lack of it - worship God!

Supporting Scripture:
Psalm 39:1

Read through the Bible a Chapter a day

1 Corinthians 11

Day 353

Habakkuk 1:1-5

This is the message that the prophet Habakkuk received in a vision.
Habakkuk's Complaint
How long, O LORD, must I call for help?
But you do not listen!
"Violence is everywhere!" I cry,
but you do not come to save.
Must I forever see these evil deeds?
Why must I watch all this misery?
Wherever I look,
I see destruction and violence.
I am surrounded by people
who love to argue and fight.
The law has become paralyzed,
and there is no justice in the courts.
The wicked far outnumber the righteous,
so that justice has become perverted.
The LORD replied,
"Look around at the nations;
look and be amazed!
For I am doing something in your own day,
something you wouldn't believe
even if someone told you about it.

Tucked away in the middle of the Minor prophets is the book of Habakkuk, who is given an oracle and we might do well to pay attention. He has his complaint and it is as if he is crying out to God and to his surprise, God answers! If you continue reading this, God breaks the news to him that the Babylonians are coming. This to me sounds very much the way our society is going today. We are wondering where God is, why doesn't he move to fix this mess. Well the answer is, he is moving! He is getting ready and we need to brace ourselves - it's going to an awesome answer. With awesome I mean it is going to be an overwhelming response. Look, God holds you and I accountable for this mess... he is expecting us who know better to pray and seek him out. Remember 2 Chronicles 7:14 (if my people, who are called by my name, will humble themselves and pray and seek my face and turn from their wicked ways, then I will hear from heaven, and I will forgive their sin and will heal their land)? There is nothing we can do to solve the problems we have. Hate, envy, sin, climate change, pride, violence - there is no human solution. Regardless of the garbage you hear from the media and power seeking politicians who just throw money around to say they tried - the only answer is God and it is up to you and I to drop to our knees and cry out to God for his answer. He has one, I can assure you of that.

Let's get busy!

Supporting Scripture:
2 Chronicles 7:14

Read through the Bible a Chapter a day

1 Corinthians 12

Day 354

James 3:13-18

If you are wise and understand God's ways, prove it by living an honorable life, doing good works with the humility that comes from wisdom. But if you are bitterly jealous and there is selfish ambition in your heart, don't cover up the truth with boasting and lying. For jealousy and selfishness are not God's kind of wisdom. Such things are earthly, unspiritual, and demonic. For wherever there is jealousy and selfish ambition, there you will find disorder and evil of every kind.
But the wisdom from above is first of all pure. It is also peace loving, gentle at all times, and willing to yield to others. It is full of mercy and the fruit of good deeds. It shows no favoritism and is always sincere. And those who are peacemakers will plant seeds of peace and reap a harvest of righteousness.

The Bible tells us that there are two kinds of wisdom. One from the devil and one from God. Basically, if it's all about me - there's a problem. Godly wisdom on the other hand begins with living a holy life. It is gentle and compassionate - filled with mercy and blessings for others. Living right can actually build a healthy community! What a sharp contrast to the message we hear these days.

Supporting Scripture:
1 Peter 2:12
Proverbs 11:18

Read through the Bible a Chapter a day

1 Corinthians 13

Day 355

Luke 2:19-20

*But Mary **treasured** up all these things and pondered them in her heart. The shepherds returned, **glorifying and praising** God for all the things they had heard and seen, which were just as they had been told.*

Being told about the Gospel leaves us with a response: Yes or No.
Along with this response, the Gospel also brings us an emotional reaction. This morning we see two different type of responses. Mary with her quiet reaction, taking in all she was witnessing and wondering what it all means and the shepherds who went away praising and glorifying God because everything happened to them just as they had been told. This was because they had witnessed a babe in the manger. I wonder what they thought as time went along and they followed a baby turned child, child turned teenager, teenager turned young man, young man turned Savior, Savior turned God.
They, just like us are witnesses to the greatest story ever told... The response is still:
Yes or No, even after 2000+ years!

Supporting Scripture:
2 Corinthians 1:17-22

Read through the Bible a Chapter a day

1 Corinthians 14

Day 356

Proverbs 6:16-19

There are six things the LORD hates,
seven that are detestable to him:
haughty eyes,
a **lying tongue***,*
hands that shed innocent blood,
a **heart that devises wicked schemes***,*
feet that are quick to rush into evil,
a **false witness who pours out lies**
and **a person who stirs up dissension among brothers***.*

We see here a list of don'ts. We are surrounded by these items all day, no matter where you look, read, or watch we are overrun with these things. My suggestion: Look elsewhere, study the truth. Turn off the TV (especially at news time). Be very careful with social media. We must be sure we are not contributing to these items.

Supporting Scripture:
Deuteronomy 19:10
Zechariah 8:17

Read through the Bible a Chapter a day

1 Corinthians 15

Day 357

Matthew 5:13

"You are the salt of the earth. But if the salt loses its saltiness, how can it be made salty again? It is no longer good for anything, except to be thrown out and trampled underfoot."

Think today about salt. Once it loses its saltiness it is basically useless. Jesus reminds us that we are the salt of the earth. In the days of Jesus, salt was used as a preservative. Salt was highly regarded as a commodity. But that was in its primary use. Once it was used it was discarded. You and I are compared to salt. We are different from those around us, if we lower our standards we become basically useless because we no longer stand out in the crowd. But nowadays it's not just us, but churches that stand to lose their saltiness. Many churches are no longer focused on the Bible, but current affairs and social justice issues and are no longer preaching God's word but whatever is accepted in the society we live in. - they lose their saltiness and are no longer useful.

Stay in the Bible, be the salt of the earth!

Supporting Scripture:
Luke 14:34-35

Read through the Bible a Chapter a day

1 Corinthians 16

Notes

Day 358

Acts 8:31

"How can I," he said, "unless someone explains it to me?" So he invited Philip to come up and sit with him.

The story of Phillip and the Eunuch is a very basic lesson for us. The question is: Are we ready to share our story? It does not have to be fancy with all the big words we hear from some, just share what your relationship with Jesus is.

The Bible is the sword of the Spirit, which is the only part of our armor used for offense. We should be ready to share with anyone at anytime.

Supporting Scripture:
Ephesians 6:17

Read through the Bible a Chapter a day

Judges 1

Day 359

Isaiah 26:9

In the night I search for you;
in the morning I earnestly seek you.
For only when you come to judge the earth
will people learn what is right.

You and I need to be determined and purposeful as we seek and praise God. Being determined (this is probably a poor example, it's what happens when you baby sit a pup) is like a pup out strolling through the grass. With every odor, every sniff, that pup keeps its attention. At every turn, we should be seeking and praising God!

Supporting Scripture:
Isaiah 55:6
Matthew 6:33
Hebrews 11:6

Read through the Bible a Chapter a day

Judges 2

Day 360

Matthew 12:38-41

Today and tomorrow we will look at a couple of Biblical stories that we can be sure of simply because Jesus tells us so. Today is Jonah...

One day some teachers of religious law and Pharisees came to Jesus and said, "Teacher, we want you to show us a miraculous sign to prove your authority."
But Jesus replied, "Only an evil, adulterous generation would demand a miraculous sign; but the only sign I will give them is the sign of the prophet Jonah. For as Jonah was in the belly of the great fish for three days and three nights, so will the Son of Man be in the heart of the earth for three days and three nights.
"The people of Nineveh will stand up against this generation on judgment day and condemn it, for they repented of their sins at the preaching of Jonah. Now someone greater than Jonah is here—but you refuse to repent.

We can be sure of the story of Jonah because Jesus himself verifies that it is real.

Supporting Scripture:
Jonah 1:14-17

Read through the Bible a Chapter a day

Judges 3

Day 361

Mark 13:19

*For there will be greater anguish in those days than at any time since **God created the world.** And it will never be so great again.*

Like yesterday with the story of Jonah, Jesus affirms the Bible. This event, God created the earth and the universe. Stop for a second and think about the earth today. In the name of science, mankind is literally spending trillions of dollars to break down the word of God. Governments are forcing their populations to get in line with some very sketchy ideas. Telescopes have been launched into space to prove theories that would try to discredit the Bible's version of creation. But it happened, and it is just as the Bible reminds us. God did create and sustains (maintains, continues, or prolongs) this world. What is ironic is that his greatest creation is trying to rob from God his creation. Make no mistake about it, this is all about God!

Supporting Scripture:
Genesis 1

Read through the Bible a Chapter a day

Judges 4

Day 362

Philippians 4:19

*And this same God who **takes care** of me **will** supply **all** your needs from his glorious riches, which have been given to us in Christ Jesus.*

God is taking care of us and he will supply all our needs. It took me a long time to realize that is more than physical (although it is that as well). Go to God with everything, nothing is beyond his abilities! As a matter of fact, he already knows what you need and has been working that out (whatever that is) long before we ever realized we needed it.

Supporting Scripture:
Psalm 23:1
2 Corinthians 9:8
Romand 2:4

Read through the Bible a Chapter a day

Judges 5

Day 363

1 John 4:10

***This is real love**—not that we loved God, but that he loved us and sent his Son as a sacrifice to take away our sins.*

It is fitting that we would include this verse towards the end of this book. It wraps up the Gospel of Jesus. It brings us full circle on the freedom we have because of God's love. From day one (remember 1 Samuel 3:21) this is God's story, and your story and my story. As you have read the Bible, hopefully you recognize yourself in some of these men and women of the Bible. This is truly real love. God loved us first and He took the appropriate steps to adopt us as his (not just) children, but his heirs.

Supporting Scripture:
Romans 5:8

Read through the Bible a Chapter a day

Judges 6

Day 364

Numbers 23:19

God is not a man, so he does not lie.
He is not human, so he does not change his mind.
Has he ever spoken and failed to act?
Has he ever promised and not carried it through?

Look carefully at this verse. It is impossible for God to lie (Hebrews 6:18 - So God has given both his promise and his oath. These two things are unchangeable because it is impossible for God to lie.) He does not change his mind, although there are instances where he changed outcomes (2 Kings 20:1-6 - About that time Hezekiah became deathly ill, and the prophet Isaiah son of Amoz went to visit him. He gave the king this message: "This is what the LORD says: Set your affairs in order, for you are going to die. You will not recover from this illness."
When Hezekiah heard this, he turned his face to the wall and prayed to the LORD, "Remember, O LORD, how I have always been faithful to you and have served you single-mindedly, always doing what pleases you." Then he broke down and wept bitterly.
But before Isaiah had left the middle courtyard, this message came to him from the LORD: "Go back to Hezekiah, the leader of my people. Tell him, 'This is what the LORD, the God of your ancestor David, says: I have heard your prayer and seen your tears. I will heal you, and three days from now you will get out of bed and go to the Temple of the LORD. I will add fifteen years to your life, and I will rescue you and this city from the king of Assyria. I will defend this city for my own honor and for the sake of my servant David.'") Finally, God is true to his promises - every single one.

Supporting Scripture:
Hebrew 6:18
2 Kings 20:1-6

Read through the Bible a Chapter a day

Judges 7

Day 365

Revelation 22:20-21

*He who testifies to these things says, **"Yes, I am coming soon."***
Amen. Come, Lord Jesus.
The grace of the Lord Jesus be with God's people.
Amen.

These are the final words of Revelation, the final words of Jesus in the Bible. It is the **promise** of eternity for each of us. It is the Promise of God having the final say. He is completely in control, no matter what anyone says or how things progress around us.
We may well be in the season of the return of Christ. No predictions on **when** He will return here.... however there are plenty of references to the time of his return and we could to be in the middle of it. My point in writing this is that we should always be ready. He himself makes the promise - "Yes, I am coming soon." When He does, every promise will have been fulfilled! Someday we all will meet Jesus face to face. We should be preparing for that day, today!

Supporting Scripture:
Acts 1:11
Matthew 16:27

Read through the Bible a Chapter a day

Judges 8

To continue reading through the Bible a chapter a day - simply turn the page

Notes

Table 1

Judges	Galatians	1 Samuel	2 Samuel	1 Kings
9	1	26	19	21
10	2	27	20	22
11	3	28	21	Colossians
12	4	29	22	1
13	5	30	23	2
14	6	31	24	3
15	1 Samuel	Ephesians	Philippians	4
16	1	1	1	2 Kings
17	2	2	2	1
18	3	3	3	2
19	4	4	4	3
20	5	5	1 Kings	4
21	6	6	1	5
2 Corinthians	7	2 Samuel	2	6
1	8	1	3	7
2	9	2	4	8
3	10	3	5	9
4	11	4	6	10
5	12	5	7	11
6	13	6	8	12
7	14	7	9	13
8	15	8	10	14
9	16	9	11	15
10	17	10	12	16
11	18	11	13	17
12	19	12	14	18
13	20	13	15	19
Ruth	21	14	16	20
1	22	15	17	21
2	23	16	18	22
3	24	17	19	23
4	25	18	20	24
				25

1 Thessalonians	1 Chronicles	2 Chronicles	Nehemiah	Job
1	28	27	1	4
2	29	28	2	5
3	**2 Thessalonians**	29	3	6
4	1	30	4	7
5	2	31	5	8
1 Chronicles	3	32	6	9
1	**2 Chronicles**	33	7	10
2	1	34	8	11
3	2	35	9	12
4	3	36	10	13
5	4	**1 Timothy**	11	14
6	5	1	12	15
7	6	2	13	16
8	7	3	**Titus**	17
9	8	4	1	18
10	9	5	2	19
11	10	6	3	20
12	11	**Ezra**	**Esther**	21
13	12	1	1	22
14	13	2	2	23
15	14	3	3	24
16	15	4	4	25
17	16	5	5	26
18	17	6	6	27
19	18	7	7	28
20	19	8	8	29
21	20	9	9	30
22	21	10	**Philemon**	31
23	22	**2 Timothy**	1	32
24	23	1	**Job**	33
25	24	2	1	34
26	25	3	2	35
27	26	4	3	36

Job	Psalms	Psalms	Psalms	Psalms	Psalms
37	13	46	79	112	145
38	14	47	80	113	146
39	15	48	81	114	147
40	16	49	82	115	148
41	17	50	83	116	149
42	18	51	84	117	150
Hebrews	19	52	85	118	**James**
1	20	53	86	119	1
2	21	54	87	120	2
3	22	55	88	121	3
4	23	56	89	122	4
5	24	57	90	123	5
6	25	58	91	124	**Proverbs**
7	26	59	92	125	1
8	27	60	93	126	2
9	28	61	94	127	3
10	29	62	95	128	4
11	30	63	96	129	5
12	31	64	97	130	6
13	32	65	98	131	7
Psalms	33	66	99	132	8
1	34	67	100	133	9
2	35	68	101	134	10
3	36	69	102	135	11
4	37	70	103	136	12
5	38	71	104	137	13
6	39	72	105	138	14
7	40	73	106	139	15
8	41	74	107	140	16
9	42	75	108	141	17
10	43	76	109	142	18
11	44	77	110	143	19
12	45	78	111	144	20

Proverbs	Song of Songs	Isaiah	Isaiah	Jeremiah
21	1	19	52	17
22	2	20	53	18
23	3	21	54	19
24	4	22	55	20
25	5	23	56	21
26	6	24	57	22
27	7	25	58	23
28	8	26	59	24
29	**1 John**	27	60	25
30	1	28	61	26
1 Peter	2	29	62	27
1	3	30	63	28
2	4	31	64	29
3	5	32	65	30
4	**Isaiah**	33	66	31
5	1	34	**2 John**	32
Ecclesiastes	2	35	**Jeremiah**	33
1	3	36	1	34
2	4	37	2	35
3	5	38	3	36
4	6	39	4	37
5	7	40	5	38
6	8	41	6	39
7	9	42	7	40
8	10	43	8	41
9	11	44	9	42
10	12	45	10	43
11	13	46	11	44
12	14	47	12	45
2 Peter	15	48	13	46
1	16	49	14	47
2	17	50	15	48
3	18	51	16	49

Jeremiah	Ezekiel	Revelation	Hosea	Nahum
50	22	13	10	1
51	23	14	11	2
52	24	15	12	3
3 John	25	16	13	Habakkuk
Lamentation	26	17	14	1
1	27	18	Joel	2
2	28	19	1	3
3	29	20	2	Zephaniah
4	30	21	3	1
5	31	22	Amos	2
Jude	32	Daniel	1	3
Ezekiel	33	1	2	Haggai
1	34	2	3	1
2	35	3	4	2
3	36	4	5	Zechariah
4	37	5	6	1
5	38	6	7	2
6	39	7	8	3
7	40	8	9	4
8	41	9	Obadiah	5
9	42	10	Jonah	6
10	Revelation	11	1	7
11	1	12	2	8
12	2	Hosea	3	9
13	3	1	4	10
14	4	2	Micah	11
15	5	3	1	12
16	6	4	2	13
17	7	5	3	14
18	8	6	4	Malachi
19	9	7	5	1
20	10	8	6	2
21	11	9	7	3
				4

About the Author

My friend Newton OldCrow and I in
Lodge Grass, Montana

In many ways, I feel I have led a Forrest Gump styled life. In the right place at the right time. I do have the memories of a man who has traveled all 50 states and other countries, with memories of many places and times none quite like the family times and the trips to Montana to visit the Crow Indian Reservation in Lodge Grass, Montana. With three children, Two Grandkids and the best wife a fella could have, I have been blessed. Starting with parents who loved my sister and I, my childhood was good and there are little to no bad vibes there. I was introduced to Jesus Christ when I was sixteen years old. That meeting was relevant although I did not really take it serious until I was nearly fifty. God never left me even if I paid little attention to Him. It was His Book, The Bible where I began to understand, or so I thought. After spending the majority of my life working in the printing industry, the brakes were applied and I was able to hop off that train into a real challenge - Teaching! After 10 years of teaching teens Radio and TV, I have seen the world in a new pair of glasses and realize how much I did not know. It's all good and the statement is true: "If you don't like your surroundings, wait for a bit, it changes"!

One of my students asked me the question: Mr. Mathews, is there anything you have not done? Yes, there is a lot of things I have not done, I am however, thankful for all I have been able to do. As I mention in my radio show, The Classics with DJPOPS - Be sure and thank someone who has made an impact in your life. I am still working through that list, there are so many!

Jeff

www.ingramcontent.com/pod-product-compliance
Lightning Source LLC
Chambersburg PA
CBHW081201170426

43197CB00018B/2891